بسم الله الرحمن الرحيم

"The house of al-Arqam is the house of Islām"

Al-Ḥākim (d.403h) in *al-Mustadrak ʿala al-Ṣaḥiḥayn* (6185)

Secrets Within the

Order of the Qurʾān

سر ترتيب القرآن

للحافظ جلال الدين السيوطي

al-Ḥāfiẓ, al-Mufassir

Jalāl al-Dīn al-Suyūṭī

(d. 911h)

DAR AL-ARQAM

ISBN: 978-1-9164756-0-1

British Library Cataloguing in Publishing Data
A catalogue record for this book is available from the British Library

Prepared and published by Dar al-Arqam Publishing,
Birmingham, United Kingdom

Translated by:

Adnan Karim
Head of translation at Dar al-Arqam. He has translated and edited a number of works for Dar al-Arqam.

Edited by:

Ayman Khalid
He studied the Islamic sciences under scholars in his homeland of Jordan, and has translated and edited a number of works for Dar al-Arqam.

www.daral-arqam.co.uk
Email: daralarqam@hotmail.co.uk

Printed in Turkey by Mega | export@mega.com.tr

SECRETS WITHIN THE

ORDER OF THE QUR'ĀN

Jalạl al-Dīn al-Suyūṭī (d. 911H)

الفهرس

Contents

Translator's Foreword | تقديم المترجم 15

Biography of Jalāl al-Dīn al-Suyūṭī | ترجمة جلال الدين السيوطي 19

Preface | المدخل 21

Introduction | مقدمة في ترتيب السور 29

Sūrah al-Fātiḥah | سورة الفاتحة 43

Sūrah al-Baqarah | سورة البقرة 51

Sūrah Ālī 'Imrān | سورة آل عمران 70

Sūrah al-Nisā | سورة النساء 83

Sūrah al-Mā'idah | سورة المائدة 96

Sūrah al-An'ām | سورة الأنعام 104

Sūrah al-A'rāf | سورة الأعراف 115

Sūrah al-Anfāl | سورة الأنفال 120

Sūrah al-Tawbah | سورة براءة 130

Sūrah Yūnus | سورة يونس 132

Sūrah Hūd | سورة هود 135

Sūrah Yūsuf | سورة يوسف 137
Sūrah al-Raʿd | سورة الرعد 139
Sūrah Ibrāhīm | سورة إبراهيم 141
Sūrah al-Ḥijr | سورة الحِجْر 143
Sūrah al-Naḥl | سورة النحل 146
Sūrah Banī Isrāʾīl (al-Isrā) | سورة بني إسرائيل 149
Sūrah al-Kahf | سورة الكهف 152
Sūrah Maryam | سورة مريم 157
Sūrah Ṭa-ha | سورة طه 159
Sūrah al-Anbiyā | سورة الأنبياء 162
Sūrah al-Ḥajj | سورة الحج 164
Sūrah al-Muʾminūn | سورة المؤمنون 165
Sūrah al-Nūr | سورة النور 167
Sūrah al-Furqān | سورة الفرقان 169
Sūrah al-Shuʿarā | سورة الشعراء 173
Sūrah al-Naml | سورة النمل 176
Sūrah al-Qaṣaṣ | سورة القصص 178
Sūrah al-ʿAnkabūt | سورة العنكبوت 181
Sūrah al-Rūm | سورة الروم 183
Sūrah Luqmān | سورة لقمان 185

Sūrah al-Sajdah | سورة السجدة 187
Sūrah al-Aḥzāb | سورة الأحزاب 190
Sūrah Saba' | سورة سبأ 191
Sūrah Fāṭir | سورة فاطر 193
Sūrah al-Ṣāffāt | سورة الصافات 198
Sūrah Ṣād | سورة ص 199
Sūrah al-Zumar | سورة الزمر 200
Sūrah Ghāfir | سورة غافر 202
Sūrah Muḥammad | سورة القتال 207
Sūrah al-Fatḥ | سورة الفتح 209
Sūrah al-Ḥujarāt | سورة الحجرات 210
Sūrah al-Dhariyāt | سورة الذاريات 211
Sūrah al-Ṭūr | سورة الطور 212
Sūrah al-Najm | سورة النجم 213
Sūrah al-Qamar | سورة القمر 216
Sūrah al-Raḥmān | سورة الرحمن 218
Sūrah al-Wāqiʿah | سورة الواقعة 220
Sūrah al-Ḥadīd | سورة الحديد 223
Sūrah al-Mujādilah | سورة المجادلة 224
Sūrah al-Ḥashr | سورة الحشر 226

Sūrah al-Mumtaḥinah | سورة الممتحنة 228

Sūrah al-Ṣaff | سورة الصف 230

Sūrah al-Jumu'ah | سورة الجمعة 231

Sūrah al-Munāfiqūn | سورة المنافقون 234

Sūrah al-Taghābun | سورة التغابن 237

Sūrah al-Ṭalāq | سورة الطلاق 240

Sūrah al-Taḥrīm | سورة التحريم 241

Sūrah al-Tabārak | سورة تبارك 243

Sūrah Nūn | سورة ن 245

Sūrah al-Ḥāqqah | سورة الحاقة 247

Sūrah Sa'ala | سورة سأل 248

Sūrah Nūḥ | سورة نوح 249

Sūrah al-Jinn | سورة الجن 251

Sūrah al-Muzzamil | سورة المزمل 252

Sūrah al-Mudathir | سورة المدثر 253

Sūrah al-Qiyāmah | سورة القيامة 254

Sūrah al-Insān | سورة الإنسان 255

Sūrah al-Mursalāt | سورة المرسلات 258

Sūrah 'Amma | سورة عم 260

Sūrah al-Nāzi'āt | سورة النازعات 262

Sūrah ʿAbasa | سورة عبس 263
Sūrah al-Takwīr | سورة التكوير 264
Sūrah al-Infiṭār | سورة الانفطار 265
Sūrah al-Muṭaffifīn | سورة المطففين 266
Sūrah al-Inshiqāq | سورة الانشقاق 271
Sūrah al-Burūj and al-Ṭalāq | سورة البروج والطارق 272
Sūrah al-Aʿlā | سورة الأعلى 273
Sūrah al-Ghāshiyah | سورة الغاشية 275
Sūrah al-Fajr | سورة الفجر 277
Sūrah al-Balad | سورة البلد 279
Sūrah al-Shams, al-Layl and al-Ḍuḥā | سورة الشمس والليل والضحى 280
Sūrah al-Sharḥ | سورة أَلَمْ نَشْرَحْ 284
Sūrah al-Tīn | سورة التين 286
Sūrah al-ʿAlaq | سورة العلق 289
Sūrah al-Qadr | سورة القدر 290
Sūrah al-Bayyinah | سورة لم يكن 291
Sūrah al-Zalzalah | سورة الزلزلة 294
Sūrah al-ʿĀdiyāt | سورة العاديات 297
Sūrah al-Qāriʿah | سورة القارعة 298
Sūrah al-Takāthur | سورة التكاثر 299

Sūrah al-Fīl | سورة الفيل 301
Sūrah Quraysh | سورة قريش 303
Sūrah al-Māʿūn | سورة الماعون 304
Sūrah al-Kawthar | سورة الكوثر 305
Sūrah al-Kāfirūn | سورة الكافرون 307
Sūrah al-Naṣr | سورة النصر 308
Sūrah al-Masad | سورة تبت 311
Sūrah al-Ikhlāṣ | سورة الإخلاص 314
Sūrah al-Falaq and al-Nās | سورة الفلق والناس 317

تقديم المترجم

Translator's Foreword

All praises are due solely for Allah, the One who sent down this Book arranged in the best of orders, the meanings of which are clear yet carry many hidden meanings. I bear witness that there is no deity worthy of worship except Allah, the One who perfected His religion with His Words and I bear witness that Muḥammad is His slave and messenger – the final one of the Messengers that were sent, entrusted to convey the message of His final revelation.

The Qur'ān is an extremely powerful book which came to eradicate false beliefs and reform the hearts of men. So when the Jinn heard the Qur'ān recited, without any delay, their hearts were transformed:

﴿أَنَّهُ اسْتَمَعَ نَفَرٌ مِّنَ الْجِنِّ فَقَالُوا إِنَّا سَمِعْنَا قُرْآنًا عَجَبًا﴾

{A group of Jinn listened [to this Qur'ān]. They said: "Verily! We have heard a wonderful Recital."}[1]

The miracle which is the Qur'ān has been preserved by all Muslim generations. It became the legislation and lifestyle the Ummah lived by; reciting it, memorising it and studying it. One of the biggest relationships that a believer can have with the Qur'ān is to ponder upon its words and meanings. This is the command from the One who revealed it and the key to truly benefiting from it:

﴿كِتَابٌ أَنزَلْنَاهُ إِلَيْكَ مُبَارَكٌ لِّيَدَّبَّرُوا آيَاتِهِ وَلِيَتَذَكَّرَ أُولُو الْأَلْبَابِ﴾

1 Jinn: 1

{A Book which We have sent down to you, full of blessings that they may ponder over its *āyāt*, and that men of understanding may remember.}[2]

In fact, the greatest form of regret and blame is attached to those who do not fit the above description:

﴿أَفَلَا يَتَدَبَّرُونَ الْقُرْآنَ أَمْ عَلَىٰ قُلُوبٍ أَقْفَالُهَا﴾

{Don't they think deeply about the Qur'ān or are their hearts locked up (from understanding)?}[3]

This objective cannot be truly fulfilled unless the reader of the Qur'ān is aware of the deeper meanings of it, the themes and objectives of the *ṣūrahs* and the wisdoms found within them. For this reason, the scholars both past and present possessed a stimulus in understanding in a deeper manner and gave importance to documenting them within their works.

The true miracle of the Qur'ān can be excavated when one realises that its miraculous nature is combined in all of the disciplines of the Sharī'ah. The deeper meanings are intertwined within the religion as a whole. So it may appear that the meaning of a particular *āyah* or *ṣūrah* is clear to the reader, however the Qur'ān is something which cannot be reproduced by man—therefore, what may appear to be plain and simple is actually something which is refined in wisdom and unlimited in knowledge. For this reason, the earliest disbelievers in it described it as enchanting witchcraft.

Ibn 'Atiyyah said in the introduction of his *Tafsīr* (1/278):

> Allah is All-Encompassing in His Knowledge and the Qur'ān consists of His Words. If one realises this, then they will be

2 Ṣād: 29

3 Muḥammad: 24

> quick to realise that the particular wording used in the Qur'ān and the arrangement given to it cannot be matched. If someone tried to replace the vocabulary or rearrange the sentences its meaning and effects would be lost. Its fluency would be lost, its connection disjointed and man would remain in ignorance and lack any memorisation in it. Man is not all-encompassing in his knowledge, and that is why the Qur'ān set down the framework for human life to live by.

To understand the clearer and the hidden meanings found in the Qur'ān, the scholars of *tafsīr* have given the topic of theming and discussing the arrangement of the *ṣūrahs* a great deal of importance. From them, Imām Fakhr al-Dīn al-Rāzī was a pioneer in this, of which he said in his *tafsīr*, "The greatest delicacies of the Qur'ān are in understanding its order and connection with one another."

Others stated that the best way of understanding speech is to understand how it links, so that the paragraphs and chapters are not interrupted and its flow disturbed.[4]

From those that authored on this topic also is Imām Jalāl al-Dīn al-Suyūṭī in this book entitled, *Asrār Tartīb al-Qur'ān*. Unlike many of those who preceded him, this is a separately authored book and not included within a broader work of *tafsīr*. Imām Jalāl al-Dīn was someone who was well-established in *uṣūl al-tafsīr* and *tafsīr* itself, being a reference point in both disciplines. He relied on the works of many that came before him, especially from the likes of Imām Fakhr al-Dīn al-Rāzī and this book also became a basis for those who authored on this topic after him. All of this creates the conditions for this book being of utmost benefit for the English reader, enabling them to understand *tafsīr* in a manner never seen before in the English language.

The copy we have relied upon was edited by Abd al-Qādir Aḥmad 'Aṭā

---

4 See *al-Burhān fī 'Ulūm al-Qur'ān* (1/35-36).

in which he references narrations and cites quotations. He also adds further benefits which can be found in the footnotes. Therefore, the default for all the footnotes mentioned in this book is that they are cited from the editorial of Abd al-Qādir Aḥmad 'Aṭā. If anything has been added by the translator then this is preceded with the abbreviation [T].

I ask Allah to make this a beneficial book for the author, the reader and all those involved in producing it. Likewise, I ask Allah to give this Ummah a stronger connection with the Noble Qur'ān, that it becomes a guidance for their lives—being a criterion for them between right and wrong. Also, I ask Allah to give us the ability to reflect upon its deeper meanings and allow us to understand His Speech.

May the peace and blessings of Allah be upon our Prophet Muḥammad, his family, companions and all those who follow them in guidance until the Last Day.

Note: Square brackets (i.e. []) within the Arabic text denote additions from different manuscripts.

ترجمة جلال الدين السيوطي

Biography of Jalāl al-Dīn al-Suyūṭī[5]

849–911H

His level of intellect and knowledge was a rarity, unique amongst his contemporaries, and he was an *imām* amongst the scholars, an authority in giving critique, firmly established in knowledge, an icon in giving explanation, the crown that sits on top of the efforts placed by the earlier generations, the flag-bearer of eloquence and expression.

His name is Jalāl al-Dīn, Abū al-Faḍl, Abd al-Raḥmān ibn Abī Bakr ibn Muḥammad ibn Sābiq al-Dīn al-Khuḍayrī al-Suyūṭī. He was a *ḥafiẓ* and a *muḥaddith*, an *imām* in the Arabic language, *uṣūl al-fiqh* and *tafsīr*.

He was born in 849h and became an orphan at an early age. He memorised the Qur'ān in his childhood and then sought knowledge. In this he showed a high level of enthusiasm and exertion. He was very quick in making the scholars his companions and was a constant attendee in their sittings and lessons.

When he reached the age of forty years, al-Ḥafiẓ al-Suyūṭī secluded himself in Rawḍat al-Miqyās (which was in Cairo, by the Nile) and concentrated on worship and authoring, and it was at this point in his life that he began to author some of his most famous works. These include:

- *Jam' al-Jawāmi'* (in *uṣūl al-fiqh*).

---

5 See *al-Ḍaw' al-Lāmi'* (4/65) and *al-I'lām* (3/301).

- *Al-Ḥāwī* (in *fiqh*).
- *Tadrīb al-Rāwī* (in *mustalah al-ḥadīth*).
- *Ṭabaqāt al-Ḥuffāẓ* (in the science of narrators of ḥadīth).
- *Al-Jāmiʿ al-Saghīr* (a compilation of ḥadīth).
- *Al-Itqān* (in *uṣūl al-tafsīr*).
- The completion of the *tafsīr* of Jalāl al-Dīn al-Maḥallī (which was later known as *Tafsīr al-Jalalayn*).

He later died in Rawdat al-Miqyās and was buried in Cairo in 911h.

[المدخل]

[Preface]

بسم الله الرحمن الرحيم
وصلى الله على سيدنا محمد وآله وصحبه وسلم:

الحمد لله الذي أنزل كتابه المجيد على أحسن أسلوب، وبهر بحسن أساليبه وبلاغة تركيبه القلوب، نزله آيات بينات، وفصله سورًا وآيات، ورتبه بحكمته البالغة أحسن ترتيب، ونظمه أعظم نظام بأفصح لفظ وأبلغ تركيب.

All praises are due to Allah, the One who sent down the Glorious Book having the best of styles. Its eloquence and rhetoric are breath-taking, constructing the hearts of those who hear it. He sent down clear *āyāt*, correlating them with one another in chapters. He organised it through His infinite wisdom and fluency in the best of fashions. He systemised it with the best of systems, with the most articulate of words and with the richest of meanings.

صلى الله على مَن أنزل إليه لينذر به وذكرى، ونزله على قلبه الشريف، فنفى عنه الحرج وشرح له صدرًا، وعلى آله وصحبه مُهَاجِرة ونصرًا ...

وبعد:

May the blessings of Allah be upon whom this revelation was sent down to—a warner by it and a reminder. He is the One who placed it in his noble heart, negating any form of hardship from within it. The one whose heart was cast open, blessings be upon him, his family and companions, those who migrated and supported him.

To begin:

فإن الله سبحانه مَنَّ عليَّ بالنظر في مواقع نجومه، وفتح لي أبواب التطرق إلى استخراج ما أودع فيه من علومه، فلا أزال أسرِّح النظر في بساتينه من نوع إلى نوع، وأَسْتَسنح الخاطر في ميادينه فيبلغ الغرض ويرجع وهو يقول: لا روع، فتقت عن أنواع علومه ولقبتها، وأودعت ما أوعيت منها في دواوين وأعيتها، ونقبت عن معادن معانيه وأبرزتها، وأوقدت عليها نار القريحة وميزتها، وألفت في ذلك جامعًا ومفردًا، ومطنبًا ومقصدًا، ومن خلق لشيء فإلى تيسره، ومن أحب شيئًا أكثر من ذكره.

Surely, Allah, the Glorified, has favoured me and taught me to understand the stages of His revelation. He has opened the doors for me and enabled me to extract the sciences He has placed within it. [Even up until the point of authoring this book,] I still find pleasure in looking at its gardens and the different pastures it has. I was worried about entering its courtyards but my self comes back to me and says, "Do not be scared, enter." So I was able to take its fruits out of its shells and its sciences and expressions. I left the vessels as they were, but borrowed from them small samples for me to take away. I dug deep to make holes in the fields of meaning and collected them in mounds on the gardens surface. I lit fires within the boundaries, igniting them with intense heat but maintaining firm control over its blaze. On the back of this excursion, I authored comprehensive and specific works;

detailed and brief. Surely, if one is created for a purpose he should prepare it, and anyone who loves something will always mention it.

وإن مما ألفت في تعلقات القرآن كتاب (أسرار التنزيل) الباحث عن أساليبه، المبرز أعاجيبه، المبين لفصاحة ألفاظه وبلاغة تراكيبه، الكاشف عن وجه إعجازه، الداخل إلى حقيقته من مجازه، المطلع على أفانينه، المبدع في تقرير حججه وبراهينه، فإنه اشتمل على بضعة عشر نوعًا:

From what I have authored connected to understanding the Qur'ān is a book called "The Secrets of the Revelation"[6]; researching its structure, explaining its wonders, giving examples of its eloquence in wording and rhetoric of its composition, unravelling its miracles, taking its literal and metaphorical meanings, knowing of its styles and methods, refreshing its solidity of objectiveness and proofs. All of this comprises of variant aspects that exceed ten in number:

الأول: بيان مناسبات ترتيب سوره، وحكمة وضع كل سورة منها.

One. An explanation regarding the concordance of the sequential order of the *sūrahs* and the wisdom of their positions within the Qur'ān.

الثاني: بيان أن كل سورة شارحة لما أُجْمِلَ في السورة التي قبلها.

Two. An explanation that each *sūrah* explains that which is general in the *sūrah* which comes before it.

---

6 [T] This has been printed in Qatar by Wazārat al-Awqāf (1994), and the research into the manuscripts was performed by Aḥmad ibn Muḥammad al-Ḥamādī. The author reached Sūrah al-Tawbah: 92. The title is *Qaṭf al-Azhār fī Kashf al-Asrār*.

الثالث: وجه اعتلاق فاتحة الكتاب بخاتمة التي قبلها.

Three. The manner of connection between the opening of the Book and its ending, which was [revealed] before it.[7]

الرابع: مناسبة مطلع السورة للمقصد الذي سيقت له، وذلك براعة الاستهلال.

Four. The concordance of the start of the *sūrah* to its intended purpose, which manifests the marvellous manner of its introduction.

الخامس: مناسبة أوائل السور لأواخرها.

Five. The concordance between the beginning and end of each *sūrah*.

السادس: مناسبات ترتيب آياته، واعتلاق بعضها ببعض، وارتباطها وتلاحمها وتناسقها.

Six. The appropriateness of the ordering of the *āyāt*, the connection each one has with the other and the reason for their order and coordination.

السابع: بيان أساليبه في البلاغة، وتنويع خطاباته وسياقاته.

Seven. An explanation to the rhetoric found within the chapters, the manner in which people are addressed and its contexts.

الثامن: بيان ما اشتمل عليه من المحسنات البديعية على كثرتها،

7 [T] This seems to be the clearest translation, and Allah knows best.

كالاستعارة، والكناية، والتعريض، والالتفات، والتورية، والاستخدام واللف والنشر، والطباق، والمقابلة، وغير ذلك، والمجاز بأنواعه، وأنواع الإيجاز والإطناب.

Eight. An explanation to the profound intelligence of its rhetoric and an illustration into its vastness; with the use of similes, parables, connotations, use of metonymy, grammatical shifts for rhetorical purposes, structure, foreshadowing, rhetorical shifts, flash-backing, parallel narratives, epanodos, indications as well as other literary elements and techniques.

التاسع: بيان فواصل الآي، ومناسبتها للآي التي ختمت بها.

Nine. An explanation into where each *āyah* ends and the relevance of the *āyahs* ending with them.

العاشر: مناسبة أسماء السور لها.

Ten. The concordance of the *sūrah* names to them.

[الحادي عشر: الألفاظ التي ظاهرها الترادف وبينهما فرق دقيق].

Eleven. An explanation regarding words that appear as synonyms but have subtle differences.

الثاني عشر: بيان وجه اختيار مرادفاته ولِمَ عُبِّرَ به دون سائر المرادفات.

Twelve. An explanation as to why some vocabulary is chosen over others and the reason why they are selected to be part of the expressions they are in.

الثالث عشر: بيان القراءات المختلفة، مشهورها، وشاذها، وما تضمنته من المعاني والعلوم، فإن ذلك من جملة وجوه إعجازه.

Thirteen. An explanation to the different methods of recitation; the well-known ones, the odd ones and the meanings and sciences found within them. This by itself shows the miraculous nature of the Qur'ān.

الرابع عشر: بيان وجه تفاوت الآيات المتشابهات في القصص وغيرها؛ بالزيادة والنقص، والتقديم والتأخير، وإبدال لفظة مكان أخرى، ونحو ذلك.

Fourteen. An explanation as to why the description of stories and subjects other than stories in the Qur'ān differ in their wording, vary in their length, change in their sequencing, as well as in other matters.

وقد أردت أن أفرد جزءًا لطيفًا في نوع خاص من هذه الأنواع، هو: مناسبات ترتيب السور، ليكون عجالة لمريده، وبغية لمستفيده، وأكثره من نتاج فكري، وولاد نظري، لقلة من تكلم في ذلك، أو خاض في هذه المسالك، وما كان فيه لغيري صرحت بعزوه إليه، ولا أذكر منه إلا ما استُحْسِن، ولا انتقاد عليه.

Thus I desired to single out an interesting part from the aspects found in the aforementioned work—that being the rationale of the order of the *sūrahs*—so it can help and save the time of one who is after such knowledge. Most of its contents are from my own thoughts, contemplation and insights since only a few people have touched upon this topic. I have explicitly given reference to that which I used from others, and I would only mention that which is good and would not make me subject to criticism.

وقد كنت أولًا سميته (نتائج الفكر في تناسب السور) لكونه من مستنتجات فكري كما أشرت إليه، ثم عدلت وسميته (تناسق الدرر في تناسب السور)؛ لأنه أنسب بالمسمَّى، وأزيد بالجناس.

Previously, I entitled this book as "Deductions from Reflecting Upon the Relevance of the Order of the Sūrahs" because the book is based upon deductions from my thoughts, as indicated to by the title. However, after careful consideration, I changed it to "The Harmony of the Pearls in the Concordance of the Sūrahs" because this title best describes the genre of the book and is more comprehensive as a topic.

وبالله تعالى التوفيق، وإياه أسأل حلاوة التحقيق، بِمَنِّهِ ويُمْنِهِ.

I ask Allah's assistance for myself and the reader, and that he gives us the sweetest of attainments, by His favour and blessings.

مقدمة في ترتيب السور

Introduction

اختلف العلماء في ترتيب السور، هل هو بتوقيف من النبي صلى الله عليه وسلم أو باجتهاد من الصحابة، بعد الإجماع على أن ترتيب الآيات توقيفي، والقطع بذلك.

The scholars have differed in regards to the order of the *sūrahs* in the Qur'ān; one view being that the Qur'ān was divinely arranged by the Prophet ﷺ and the other that it was analytically arranged in this order by the Companions—whilst having an absolute consensus amongst them that the order of the *āyāt* within the *sūrahs* is divinely arranged.

فذهب جماعة إلى الثاني؛ منهم: مالك، والقاضي أبو بكر في أحد قوليه، وجزم به ابن فارس.

Many of the scholars went with the latter view; and this group included Mālik, al-Qāḍī Abū Bakr (in one of the views attributed to him)[8] and was asserted heavily by Ibn Fāris.[9]

---

8 He is Abū Bakr Muḥammad ibn al-Ṭayyib al-Bāqilānī. He was a well-known jurist who wrote extensively on the genres of the Qur'ān. He died in 403h. See al-Bāqilānī's words in *al-Intiṣar al-Qur'ān* (1/168).

9 He is Abū al-Ḥusayn Aḥmad ibn Fāris ibn Zakariyyā al-Rāzī, a major scholar of linguistics in his time, who became an authority in linguistics globally. He also had expertise in *fiqh* and died in 395h. See *Talkhīs Ibn Maktūm* (3/400).

ومما استدل به لذلك: اختلاف مصاحف السلف في ترتيب السور، فمنهم من رتبها على النزول، وهو مصحف علي، كان أوله: (اقرأ) ثم البواقي على ترتيب نزول المكي، ثم المدني، ثم كان أول مصحف ابن مسعود (البقرة) ثم (النساء) ثم (آل عمران) على اختلاف شديد، وكذا مصحف أبي بن كعب وغيره، على ما بينته في الإتقان.

They based their opinion upon the fact that the Salaf (pious predecessors) all arranged the order of the *sūrahs* in their own personal *muṣḥafs* differently. Some of them arranged them in the chronological order of revelation. From them include 'Alī ibn Abī Ṭālib, so the first *sūrah* in his *muṣḥaf* was Sūrah al-'Alaq and then the remainder of the *sūrahs* that were revealed in Makkah, then the *sūrahs* revealed in al-Madīnah. As for Ibn Mas'ūd, the first *sūrah* in his *muṣḥaf* was al-Baqarah, al-Nisā and then Āli 'Imrān; completely differing from the order of 'Ali. And likewise was the case for the *muṣḥaf* of Ubayy ibn K'ab and others, and I have explained this in depth in my book *al-Itqān*.[10]

وفي المصاحف لابن أشتة بسنده عن عثمان أنه أمرهم أن يتابعوا الطُّوَل.

In the *muṣḥaf* of Ibn Ashtah[11]—which is attributed to 'Uthmān, as

---

His words can be found in *al-Masā'il al-Khams* and this was mentioned by al-Zarkashī in *al-Burhān* (1/237).

10 For further information regarding this matter, see *al-Jāmi' li Aḥkām al-Qur'ān* by al-Qurṭubī (51/1) and *al-Itqān* (216/1).

11 He is Muhammad ibn 'Abdullāh ibn Ashtah, nicknamed Ibn Ashtah. He was a scholar in Arabic and the sciences of recitation. He died in 306h. See *Ṭabaqāt al-Qurra* (2/184).

an order from him[12]—the approach was to arrange them in order of length, starting with the longest.

وذهب جماعة إلى الأول، منهم: القاضي أبو بكر في أحد قوليه، وخلائق، قال أبو بكر بن الأنباري: (أنزل الله القرآن كلَّه إلى سماء الدنيا، ثم فرقه في بضع وعشرين سنة، فكانت السورة تنزل لأمر ينزل، والآية جوابًا لمستخبر، ويوقف جبريلُ النبيَّ صلى الله عليه وسلم على موضع الآية والسورة، فاتساق السور كاتساق الآيات والحروف كله عن النبي صلى الله عليه وسلم فمن قدم سورة أو أخرها فقد أفسد نظم القرآن).

Others from the scholars went with the former opinion. They include al-Qāḍī Abū Bakr (in one view) and a host of others. Abū Bakr ibn al-Anbārī[13] said, "Allah sent down the complete Qur'ān to the skies of the earth in one dispatchment, then it was revealed to the Prophet gradually throughout his twenty-three years as a Messenger. Each *sūrah* was revealed due to particular events and *āyāt* were revealed to explain rulings. [Towards the end of his life,] Jibrīl confirmed the arrangement of the Qur'ān with the Prophet ﷺ—in terms of its *āyāt* and *sūrahs*. So the arrangement of them was formed by him, as was the arrangement of the *āyāt* and all of its letters. So whoever brings forward a *sūrah* or delays it has corrupted the Qur'ān."[14]

---

12 See *al-Itqān* (1/216), from the route of Ismā'īl ibn 'Īyāsh to Abī Muḥammad al-Qurashī. As for Ismā'īl, scholars criticised his credibility in narration (See *al-Ḍu'afā*, the section of narrators with the name of Ismā'īl).

13 He is Muḥammad ibn al-Qāsim ibn Muḥammad, Imām Abū Bakr al-Anbārī, the grammarian and linguist. He was a distinguished figure amongst Ahl al-Sunnah, passing away in the year 304h. See *al-Ṭabaqāt al-Naḥwiyyīn wa al-Lughawīn* (171) and *Siyar* (15/274).

14 See *al-Jāmi' li Aḥkām al-Qur'ān* by al-Qurṭubī (1/60) and *al-Itqān* (1/217).

وقال الكرماني في البرهان: (ترتيب السور هكذا هو عند الله تعالى في اللوح المحفوظ على هذا الترتيب، وكان يعرض النبي -صلى الله عليه وسلم- على جبريل ما اجتمع لديه منه، وعرضه -صلى الله عليه وسلم- في السنة التي توفي فيها مرتين)، وكذلك قال الطيبي.

Al-Kirmānī[15] wrote in *al-Burhān*, "The sequential order of the Qur'ān is divinely ordered from Allah ﷻ in the same order it appears in al-Lawḥ al-Maḥfūẓ. The Prophet ﷺ used to recite what he possessed from the Qur'ān to Jibrīl, but in his final year, the Prophet ﷺ recited the Qur'ān to Jibrīl twice." A similar statement was also stated by al-Ṭībī.[16]

وقال ابن الحصار: [ترتيب السور]، ووضع الآيات موضعها إنما كان بالوحي.

Ibn al-Ḥiṣṣār[17] said, "The locational order of the *āyāt* and *sūrahs* is part of the revelation and they are divinely placed."

وقال البيهقي في المدخل: كان القرآن على عهد النبي صلى الله عليه وسلم مرتبًا سوره وآياته على هذا الترتيب، إلا الأنفال وبراءة للحديث الآتي

15 He is Burhān al-Dīn Maḥmūd ibn Ḥamza ibn Naṣr. His book *al-Burhān* was published under the name *Asrār al-Takrār fī al-Qur'ān* (p. 23).

16 He is al-Ḥasan ibn Muḥammad ibn 'Abdullāh. He was a notable scholar and famed for extracting subtleties from the Qur'ān and Sunnah. See *Baghiyyah al-Wiā'h* (1/522-523).

17 He is 'Alī ibn Muḥammad ibn Ibrāhīm al-Khazrajī al-Ishbīlī. He authored a number of works, including *Uṣūl al-Fiqh* and *al-Nāsikh wa al-Mansūkh*. He passed away during the year 611h.

فيها.

Al-Bayhaqī wrote in *al-Madkhal*, "At the time of the Prophet ﷺ, the Qur'ān was arranged in a particular order in its *āyāt* and *sūrahs*, except for al-Anfāl and Sūrah al-Tawbah due to the ḥadīth regarding this."[18]

ومال ابن عطية إلى أن كثيرًا من السور كان قد علم ترتيبها في حياته صلى الله عليه وسلم كالسبع الطوال، والحواميم، والمفصل، وأن ما سوى ذلك يمكن أن يكون قد فَوَّضَ الأمر فيه إلى الأمة بعده.

Ibn 'Atiyah[19] was of the opinion that many of the *sūrahs* were organised in a particular order during the life of the Prophet ﷺ, such as the first seven long ones and then the *sūrahs* which begin with *ḥā-mīm* and then the *sūrahs* of *al-mufaṣṣal*.[20] Besides these, it is possible that the ordering of the *sūrahs* in the Qur'ān was left up to the Ummah after him to decide.[21]

وقال أبو جعفر بن الزبير: الآثار تشهد بأكثر مما نص عليه ابن عطية، ويبقى منها القليل يمكن أن يجرى فيه الخلاف، لقوله صلى الله عليه وسلم: ((اقرأوا الزهراوين: البقرة وآل عمران))، رواه مسلم، وكحديث سعيد بن خالد أنه صلى الله عليه وسلم ((صلَّى بالسبع الطوال في ركعة،

18 See *al-Itqān* (1/83).

19 He is Imām 'Abd al-Ḥaqq ibn Ghālib, better known as Ibn 'Aṭiyah. He was well-known for his *tafsīr* work *al-Muḥarar al-Wajīz*. He died in Madīnah during the year 546h.

20 [T] These are the *sūrahs* from Sūrah Qāf to Sūrah al-Nās.

21 See *al-Muḥarar al-Wajīz fī Tafsīr al-Kitāb al-'Azīz* by Ibn 'Aṭiyah (1/53-54).

وأنه كان يجمع المفصل في ركعة)) أخرجه ابن أبي شيبة. وأنه صلى الله عليه وسلم ((كان إذا أوى إلى فراشه قرأ قل هو الله أحد، والمعوذتين)) أخرجه البخاري. وفيه عن ابن مسعود -رضي الله عنه- أنه قال في بني إسرائيل والكهف ومريم وطه والأنبياء: (إنهن من العِتَاق الأُوَل، وهنَّ من تِلَادِي).

Abū Ja'far ibn al-Zubayr stated, "Narrations verify most of what Ibn 'Aṭiyah stated, but the narrations give evidence that much more than what Ibn 'Atiyah stated was established in its order, as there are only a few *sūrahs* which can be subject to dispute and this is based on the statement of the Prophet ﷺ, 'Recite the two great ones; al-Baqarah and Ālī 'Imrān.'[22] Likewise there is the ḥadīth of Sa'īd ibn Khālid that the Prophet ﷺ recited the seven long ones in one *rak'ah* and recited the *mufaṣṣal* in one *rak'ah*. This was reported by Ibn Abī Shaybah.[23] It is also reported that the Prophet ﷺ used to recite Sūrah al-Ikhlās, al-Falaq and al-Nās (keeping them in this order) when he retired to his bed. This was narrated by al-Bukhāri.[24] It is also reported that Ibn Mas'ūd ؓ said regarding Banī Isrā'īl, al-Kahf, Maryam, Ṭa-ha and al-Anbiyā, "They were amongst the early *sūrahs* and my early possessions."[25]

---

22 Muslim (2/913) in the Chapter: Virtues of the Qur'ān, on the authority of Abū Umamah al-Bahilī.

23 The ḥadīth of "the seven long ones" was also reported by al-Haythamī in *Majma' al-Zawā'id* (7/162) and it is supported by al-Bazzār and Aḥmad with the wording, "Whoever recites the seven longs ones has done well." The ḥadīth of "*mufaṣṣal*" was narrated in a lengthier form by Muslim (2/204) and al-Bukhārī (6/240).

24 Al-Bukhārī (6/223) in the Chapter of *Tafsir*, on the authority of 'Āishah.

25 Al-Bukhārī (6/189) in the Chapter of *Tafsir*.

وقال أبو جعفر النحاس: المختار أن تأليف السور على هذا الترتيب من سول الله صلى الله عليه وسلم لحديث: ((أعطيت مكان التوراة السبع الطوال، وأعطيت مكان الإنجيل المثاني، وفُضِّلت بالمفصَّل))، أخرجه أحمد وغيره. قال: فهذا الحديث يدل على أن تأليف القرآن مأخوذ عن النبي صلى الله عليه وسلم، وأنه من هذا الوقت هكذا.

Abū Ja'far al-Nuḥās[26] said, "The correct opinion is that the *sūrahs* in the Qur'ān were set in order by the Messenger of Allah ﷺ. This is based upon the ḥadith, 'I have been given the seven long ones in exchange for the Torah and the *mathānī*[27] in exchange for the Injīl, but I have been given a special virtue over the others by the *mufaṣṣal*.'[28] This ḥadīth is proof that the Qur'ān's arrangement was set by the Prophet ﷺ and the *muṣḥaf* we have now is according to the same order."

وقال الحافظ ابن حجر: ترتيب معظم السور توقيفي، لحديث أحمد وأبي داود عن أوس الثقفي قال: كنت في وفد ثقيف، فقال [لنا] رسول الله صلى الله عليه وسلم: ((طرأ عليَّ حزبي من القرآن، فأردت ألا أخرج حتى أقضيه)). قال أوس: فسألنا أصحاب رسول الله صلى الله عليه وسلم قلنا: كيف تحزبون القرآن؟ قالوا: نحزبه ثلاث سور، وخمس سور،

26 He is Imām Abū Ja'far Aḥmad ibn Ismā'īl al-Miṣrī, a renowned grammarian and exegete who was well-known as al-Nuḥās. He died in 338h.

27 [T] This refers to the *sūrahs* which contain one hundred *āyāt* or less. The author displays this below when he discusses the four categories of the *sūrahs* of the Qur'ān in terms of their respective sizes.

28 Aḥmad in *al-Musnad* (3/124), on the authority of Wāthilah ibn al-Asqa' and al-Tirmidhī in his *Sunan* (2878) who classed it as *ḥasan*.

وسبع سور، وتسع سور، وإحدى عشرة سورة، وثلاث عشرة سورة، وحزب المفصل، من (ق) حتى نختم.

Al-Ḥāfiẓ ibn Ḥajar said, "The order of most of the *sūrahs* in the Qur'ān is divinely instructed, based on the ḥadīth reported by Aḥmad and Abū Dāwūd on the authority of Aws al-Thaqafī who said, 'I was part of the delegation of Thaqīf and the Messenger of Allah ﷺ informed us [why he arrived late,] 'I could not recite my fixed part of the Qur'ān and I did not want to leave until I had completed it.' So we asked the Companions of the Messenger of Allah ﷺ, 'How do you divide the Qur'ān?' They replied, 'We split it into three, five, seven, nine, eleven, thirteen and the *mufaṣṣal*; from Qāf until the end of the Qur'ān.'"[29]

قال: فهذا يدل على أن ترتيب السور على ما هو عليه في المصحف الآن كان على عهد النبي صلى الله عليه وسلم.

He said, "In this ḥadith there is proof that the manner in which the *muṣḥaf* is organised in its order of *sūrahs* today is the same manner in which it was done during the time of the Prophet ﷺ."[30]

وقال بعضهم: لترتيب وضع السور في المصحف أسباب تطلع على أنه توقيفي صادر من حكيم:

Some of the scholars[31] argued that the order of the *sūrahs* in the manner we have today proves that they have been divinely preserved by al-Ḥakīm (i.e. Allah), [and this is due to the following]:

29 Abū Dāwūd (1/140) and Aḥmad in *al-Musnad* (5/43).

30 See *Fatḥ al-Bārī* (No. 4710).

31 Referring to al-Zarkashī in *al-Burhān* (1/260).

الأول: بحسب الحروف، كما في الحواميم، وذوات ﴿الر﴾.

Firstly: Some of the *sūrahs* were arranged with one another because of them beginning with similar letters, such as the *ḥā-mīm* or *alif-lām-rā sūrahs* appearing together.

الثاني: لموافقة آخر السورة لأول ما بعدها كآخر الحمد في المعنى، وأول البقرة.

Secondly: Due to the end of a *sūrah* being connected to the beginning of the next one, such as the ending of al-Fātiḥah being connected in meaning to the beginning of al-Baqarah.

الثالث: الوزن في اللفظة كآخر ﴿تَبَّتْ﴾ وأول (الإخلاص).

Thirdly: Due to similarity in wording, such as the end of Sūrah al-Masad with the beginning of al-Ikhlāṣ.

الرابع: لمشابهة جملة السورة لجملة الأخرى، كالضحى وأَلَمْ نَشْرَحْ.

Fourthly: Due to a concordance in the overall meaning of one *sūrah* with that of the other, such as the concordance of al-Ḍuḥā with al-Sharḥ.[32]

وقال بعضهم: إذا اعتبرت افتتاح كل سورة وجدت في غاية المناسبة لما ختمت به السورة التى قبلها، ثم [هو] يخفى تارة، ويظهر أخرى.

Other scholars stated: If the opening of each *sūrah* is reflected upon, one would see the appropriateness of it being appended to the closing of the previous *sūrah*. This, however, is sometimes apparent and at

32 See *al-Burhān* (1/260).

other times not.

وأخرج ابن أشتة عن ربيعة أنه سئل: لِمَ قدمت البقرة وآل عمران وقد نزل قبلهما بضع وثمانون سورة بمكة، وإنما نزلتا بالمدينة؟ فقال: قدمتا، وأُلِّفَ القرآن على علم ممن ألفه [به ومن كان معه فيه واجتماعهم] على علمهم بذلك، فهذا مما ينتهى إليه، ولا يُسأل عنه.

Ibn Ashtah reported that Rabī'ah was asked, "Why does the *muṣḥaf* begin with al-Baqarah and Āli 'Imrān—two *sūrahs* revealed in al-Madīnah—when there were more than eighty *sūrahs* revealed in Makkah before the both of them?" He replied, "They have been placed there intentionally. The one who organised the Qur'ān knew how to organise it, and so did his Companions after him. They had full knowledge of it and yet accepted it. So this is a subject that should not be questioned or investigated."[33]

فإن قلت: فما عندك في ذلك؟ قلت:

If someone was to ask me about my opinion, I would say:

الذي عندي أولًا: تحديد محل الخلاف، وأنه خاص بترتيب سور الأقسام الأربعة، وأما نفس الأقسام الأربعة، من تقديم الطوال، ثم المئين، ثم المثاني، ثم المفصل، فهذا ينبغي أن يقطع بأنه توقيفي، وأن يدَّعى فيه الإجماع، وإن لم أرَ من سبقني إلى ذلك؛ وإنما دعاني إلى هذا أمران:

Firstly, one must define and locate where the difference of opinion actually lies. The scholars differed as to the order of *sūrahs* from the

33 See *Tafsīr al-Qurṭubī* (1/52).

four categories of *sūrahs* in the Qur'ān. As for the four categories, they commence with: the long *sūrahs*, the *sūrahs* that exceed a hundred *āyāt*, the *sūrahs* which are one hundred or less *āyāt*, and then the *mufaṣṣal*. These four appear in the *muṣḥaf* in this exact order. So we can conclude that the order of these categories of *sūrahs* is divinely ordained, and it can be argued that there is scholarly consensus upon this point. And I have not seen anyone precede me in stating this. [As for the proof for this categorisation,] then I bring the two following points:

أحدهما: ما تقدم من الأحاديث قريبًا، وحديث ابن عباس رضي الله عنهما الآتي في الأنفال.

Firstly, all of the narrations and reports that have been quoted above, and the narration that is yet to be quoted of Ibn 'Abbās ﷺ about Sūrah al-Anfāl, is proof that the Qur'ān has been ordered in this divine manner.

والثاني: أن المصاحف التي وقع فيها الاختلاف في الترتيب اتفقت على ذلك؛ فإن مصحف أبي بن كعب وابن مسعود كلاهما قدم فيه الطوال، ثم المثاني، ثم المفصل؛ كمصحف عثمان؛ وإنما اختلفا في ترتيب سور كل قسم كما بينت [ذلك] في الإتقان.

Secondly, despite the differences in the *muṣḥafs* that belonged to some of the Companions, they all agreed in the above categorisation. So the *muṣḥaf* of Ubayy ibn Ka'b and Ibn Mas'ūd had the long *sūrahs* in the beginning, then the *mathānī* and then the *mufaṣṣal*, and this is the same in the *muṣḥaf* of 'Uthmān. The differing found in them is in regards to the order of the *sūrahs* within each category, and I have explained this in further detail in *al-Itqān*.[34]

[وهذا دليل قوي في دعوى القطع بأن ذلك توقيفي].

These two points act as clear proofs that the order of categorisation is divinely instructed.

فإذا تحرر ذلك، ونظرنا إلى محل الخلاف، فالمختار عندي في ذلك: ما قاله البيهقي؛ وهو: أن ترتيب كل السور توقيفي، سوى الأنفال وبراءة.

Based on this, we come to the point where the scholars differed. My opinion is that which was stated by al-Bayhaqī, which is, "The order of each *sūrah* is divinely instructed except for *al-Anfāl* and *al-Tawbah*."

ومما يدل على ذلك ويؤيده: توالي الحواميم، وذوات ﴿الر﴾ والفصل بين المسبحات، وتقديم ﴿طس﴾ على القصص، مفصولًا بها بين النظيرتين [طسم الشعراء، وطسم القصص] في المطلع والطول، وكذلك الفصل بين الانفطار والانشقاق بالمطففين، وهما نظيرتان في المطلع والمقصد، وهما أطول منها، فلولا أنه توقيفي لحكمة لتوالت المسبحات، وأخرت (طس) عن القصص، وأخرت ﴿المطففين﴾ أو قدمت، ولم يفصل بين ﴿الر﴾ و﴿الر﴾.

From the evidence proving and aiding this is the succession of the *ḥā-mīm sūrahs* and the *alif-lām-ra sūrahs*, the gap between the *sūrahs* of *tasbīḥ*, and the preceding of the *ṭā-sīn sūrah* (al-Naml) over al-Qaṣaṣ; which is placed to separate between Sūrah al-Shuʿarā and al-Qa-

34 See *al-Itqān* (1/222-224).

ṣaṣ, which are both similar in length. Likewise, Sūrah al-Infiṭar and al-Inshiqāq are separated from al-Muṭaffifīn despite their beginnings and message being similar, and both being greater in length than al-Muṭaffifīn. If the order of the *sūrahs* was not ordained for a divine wisdom then the *sūrahs* beginning with *sabbaḥa* would have been placed together, and *Ṭā-sīn* would be after al-Qaṣaṣ, and al-Muṭaffifīn would come before or after and there would be no separation between the *alif-lām-ra sūrahs*.

وليس هنا شيء أعارض به سوى اختلاف مصحف أبي وابن مسعود رضي الله عنهما، ولو كان توقيفيًّا لم يقع فيهما اختلاف، كما لم يقع في [ترتيب] الآيات.

There is nothing to suggest any contradiction to this view except for the difference in the *muṣḥafs* of Ubayy and Ibn Mas'ūd ﷺ. So [it could be stated that] had they not differed then it would be understood that the order of the *sūrahs* is divinely ordained just as the ordering of the *āyāt* are divine and cannot be rearranged.

وقد مَنَّ الله عليَّ بجواب لذلك نفيس، وهو: أن القرآن وقع فيه النسخ كثيرًا للرسم، حتى لسور كاملة، وآيات كثيرة، فلا بدع أن يكون الترتيب العثماني هو الذي استقر في العرضة الأخيرة؛ كالقراءات التي في مصحفه، ولم يبلغ ذلك أبيًّا وابن مسعود رضي الله عنهما، كما لم يبلغهما نسخ ما وضعاه في مصاحفهما من القراءات التي تخالف المصحف العثماني، ولذلك كتب أبي في مصحفه سورة الحفد، والخلع، وهما منسوختان.

After understanding this, I say: Allah has favoured me with an answer to this problem. My answer is: The Qur'ān has abrogation of written script aplenty (i.e. the way words are written) to the extent that full *sūrahs* were subject to this and many *āyāt*. It is not a surprising thing that the arrangement of *sūrahs* in the *'Uthmānī muṣḥaf* was the final version— such as the recitations in it—and that may not have reached Ubayy or Ibn Mas'ūd, similar to how they did not know about the abrogation of some of the parts in their copies of the *muṣḥaf* which differed with the *'Uthmānī* script. For example, the *muṣḥaf* of Ubayy had *sūrahs* called Sūrah al-Ḥafd and al-Khul' written in it, which were both abrogated.[35]

فالحاصل أني أقول: ترتيب كل [من] المصاحف بتوقيف، واستقر التوقيف في العرضة الأخيرة على [الترتيب العثماني، كما أن جميع القراءات والمنسوخات] المثبتة في مصاحفهم بتوقيف، واستقر التوقيف في العرضة الأخيرة على القراءات [العثمانية، ورتب أولئك ما كان عندهم] ولم يبلغهم النسخ.

To conclude, I say: The different order of *sūrahs* found in the various *muṣḥafs*—including the different Qur'ān recitations and abrogations in the *muṣḥafs* of the Companions—are all *tawqīfī* (i.e. set by divine ordainment). The final divine ordainment was formed upon that which we find in the *'Uthmānī muṣḥaf*, which is based on the final presentations (i.e. the last time the Prophet recited it in the presence of people), and so those other Companions also arranged the *sūrahs* in their *muṣḥafs* according to the divine ordainment which reached them, but they were not aware of the abrogations that took place.

---

35 This refers to the two *sūrahs* of *al-qunūt* that are supplicated in the *witr* prayers, which were abrogated from the Qur'ān but were not lifted from the hearts. See *al-Itqān* (1/223-226).

سورة الفاتحة

Sūrah al-Fātiḥah

افتتح سبحانه كتابه بهذه السورة، لأنها جمعت مقاصد القرآن، ولذلك كان من أسمائها: أم القرآن، وأم الكتاب، والأساس، فصارت كالعنوان وبراعة الاستهلال.

Allah, the Glorified, began His Book with this *sūrah*. It is a short *sūrah* which combines all of the themes and objectives of the Qur'ān. For this reason, it has been given such names as Umm al-Qur'ān, Umm al-Kitāb, al-Asās. Therefore, Sūrah al-Fātiḥah acts as a heading and apt introduction of the Book.

قال الحسن البصري: إن الله أودع علوم الكتاب السابقة في القرآن، ثم أودع علوم القرآن في المفصل، ثم أودع علوم المفصل في الفاتحة، فمن علم تفسيرها كان كمن علم تفسير جميع الكتب المنزلة (أخرجه البيهقي في شعب الإيمان).

Al-Ḥasan al-Baṣrī[36] said, "Surely, Allah has placed the sciences and the disciplines of the previously revealed books in the Qur'ān. Then He placed the sciences and the disciplines of the Qur'ān in the *mu-*

36 He is al-Ḥasan ibn Abī al-Ḥasan al-Baṣrī, from the major scholars of the Tābi'īn. He died in 110h.

faṣṣal sūrahs. Then He placed the sciences and disciplines of the *mufaṣṣal sūrahs* in Sūrah al-Fātiḥah. So whoever understands the *tafsīr* of Sūrah al-Fātiḥah well, it is as if he understands the *tafsīr* of all of the revealed books." This was reported by al-Bayhaqī in Shu'ab al-Īmān.[37]

وبيان اشتمالها على علوم القرآن قرره الزمخشري باشتمالها على الثناء على الله بما هو أهله، وعلى التعبد، والأمر والنهي، وعلى الوعد والوعيد، وآيات القرآن لا تخلوه عن هذه الأمور.

Al-Zamakhsharī[38] also agreed with the idea that Sūrah al-Fātiḥah encompasses all of the sciences of the Qur'ān within it, including praise of Allah and singling Him in this, singling Allah in worship, the existence of commands and prohibitions and promise and threat. [39] And the *āyāt* in the Qur'ān are not free from any of these topics.[40]

---

37 Al-Bayhaqī in *Shu'ab al-Īmān* (87).

38 He is Maḥmūd ibn 'Umar al-Zamakhsharī. He has a well-known *tafsīr* called *al-Kashāf* which is filled with benefits in *tafsīr*, language, grammar and literature. He was an *imām* of the Mu'tazilah. He died in 538h.

39 [T] Even though there is nothing obscure in this quotation, it is noteworthy to aware the reader of the categorisation of the five *usūl* of the Mu'tazilah. In *Majmū' al-Fatāwā* (13/386-387), Ibn Taymiyyah said the following about al-Zamakhsharī, "His *tafsīr* is corrupted with innovations, with beliefs upon the way of the Mu'tazilah who rejected attributes for Allah... They have five core principles: (i) *tawhīd*, which is to negate Attributes for Allah, (ii) *'adl*, which is to deny divine pre-decree and that man creates his own destiny, (iii) *al-manzil bayna manzilatayn*, that major sinners are not Muslim but not Kuffār either, (iv) *al-wa'd wa al-wa'īd* or a promise and a threat, that major sinners will be in the Hellfire for eternity and (v) *al-amr bi al-ma'rūf wa al-nahī 'an al-munkar* or commanding good and forbidding evil, which refers to revolting against oppressive rulers."

40 See *al-Kashāf* (1/4).

[و] قال الإمام فخر الدين: المقصود من القرآن كله تقرير أمور أربعة: الإلهيات، والمعاد، والنبوات، وإثبات القضاء والقدر، فقوله: ﴿الْحَمْدُ لِلَّهِ رَبِّ الْعَالَمِينَ﴾ يدل على الإلهيات، وقوله: ﴿مَالِكِ يَوْمِ الدِّينِ﴾ يدل على نفي الجبر، وعلى إثبات أن الكل بقضاء الله وقدره، وقوله: ﴿اهْدِنَا الصِّرَاطَ الْمُسْتَقِيمَ﴾ إلى آخر السورة يدل على إثبات قضاء الله، وعلى النبوات، فقد اشتملت هذه السورة على المطالب الأربعة، التي هي المقصد الأعظم من القرآن.

Imām Fakhr al-Dīn[41] said, "The purpose of the Qur'ān as a whole is to assert four genres: divinity [of Allah], resurrection, prophethood and the affirmation of divine pre-decree. The statement, {**All the praises and thanks be to Allah, the Lord of all creation**} gives the message of lordship. And the statement, {**The Owner of the Day of Recompense**} negates the idea of *al-jabr* (lack of free-will for humans in the *dunyā*)[42] and affirms the message of resurrection and divine pre-decree. And the statement, {**Guide us to the straight path**} to the end of the *sūrah* affirms the message of divine pre-decree again but also of prophethood. This shows that all four categories of genre found in the entire

41 He is Fakhr al-Dīn Muḥammad ibn 'Umar al-Rāzī. He has a well-known *tafsīr* called *al-Musammā*. He died in 606h. See: *Wafayāt al-A'yān* (1/474).

42 [T] The Jabriyya sect believe in the idea of *jabr*, where people are compelled and do not possess any free-will. The point behind this *āyah* is that the Day of Judgement is the point in time where free-will to gain a reward stops. Shaykh Muḥammad ibn al-'Uthaymīn said, "The belief of the Jabriyya is completely false. It is nullified by the Book, the Sunnah, intellect, senses and the consensus of the Salaf. No one who believes truly in Allah would suggest such a thing, and no one who realises that all wisdom and mercy belongs to Him would ever propose it." See *Majmū' Fatāwā wa Rasā'il* 10/290).

Qur'ān are all present in Sūrah al-Fātiḥah, and these categories are the primary objective of the message of the Qur'ān."

وقال البيضاوي: هي مشتملة على الحِكَم النظرية، والأحكام العملية، التي هي سلوك الصراط المستقيم، والاطلاع على مراتب السعداء، ومنازل الأشقياء.

Al-Bayḍāwī[43] said, "This *sūrah* includes matters [that are relevant to the practical aspects of creed] which are intended to be contemplated upon, as well as matters that are relevant to the acts of worship—[both of] which direct to the straight path, and acquaint one with the ranks of the blessed (i.e. believers) and the end of the wretched (disbelievers)."[44]

وقال الطيبي: هي مشتملة على أربعة أنواع من العلوم التي هي مناط الدين:

Al-Ṭībī said, "This *sūrah* has four types sciences within it which serve as the symbols of the whole religion:

أحدها: علم الأصول، ومعاقده معرفة الله عز وجل وصفاته، وإليها الإشارة بقوله: ﴿رَبِّ الْعَالَمِينَ ۝ الرَّحْمَٰنِ الرَّحِيمِ﴾ ومعرفة المعاد، وهو المومأ إليه بقوله: ﴿مَالِكِ يَوْمِ الدِّينِ﴾.

One. The knowledge of *'aqīdah*, which relates to knowing Allah ﷻ

---

43 He is 'Abdullāh ibn 'Umar al-Bayḍāwī. Known as the supreme judge, who was considered to be an *imām* and an *'allāmah* in *fiqh*, *tafsīr* and *uṣūl*. See *Baghiyyat al-Wia'āh* (2/50-51).

44 See *Tafsīr al-Bayḍāwī* (1/35).

and His Attributes, and this is eluded to in His statement: **{Lord of all creation. The Most Beneficent, the Most Merciful.}** *'Aqīdah* also includes knowledge of the resurrection, and this is referred to in the statement: **{The Owner of the Day of Recompense.}**

وثانيها: علم الفروع، وأسّه العبادات، وهو المراد بقوله: ﴿إِيَّاكَ نَعْبُدُ﴾.

Two. The knowledge of actions, and the foundation of this is *al-'ibādāt* (acts of worship), and this is intended by His statement: **{You [Alone] we worship.}**

وثالثها: علم ما يحصل به الكمال، وهو علم الأخلاق، وأجله الوصول إلى الحضرة الصمدانية، والالتجاء إلى جناب الفردانية، والسلوك لطريقة الاستقامة فيها، وإليه الإشارة بقوله: [﴿وَإِيَّاكَ نَسْتَعِينُ۝اهْدِنَا الصِّرَاطَ الْمُسْتَقِيمَ﴾.

Three. The knowledge which brings about perfection, meaning the knowledge of ethics and mannerisms. The ultimate fruit of this knowledge is being constantly conscious of Allah's presence, resorting to Him [in all affairs], knowing He is the one and only God, and embarking upon the straight path. This is alluded to in His statement: **{And You [Alone] we ask for help. Guide us to the Straight Path.}**

ورابعها: علم القصص والإخبار عن الأمم السالفة والقرون الخالية، السعداء منهم والأشقياء، وما يتصل بها من وعد محسنهم ووعيده مسيئهم، وهو المراد بقوله:] ﴿أَنْعَمْتَ عَلَيْهِمْ غَيْرِ الْمَغْضُوبِ عَلَيْهِمْ وَلَا الضَّالِّينَ﴾.

Four. The knowledge of those who came before: Stories of previous nations and generations which have passed. Those who were successful from them and those who were wretched, and the respective recompense given to each one of those parties. This is the purport of the statement of the Most High: {**The Way of those on whom You have bestowed Your Grace, not of those who earned Your Anger, nor of those who went astray.**}"

قال: وجميع القرآن تفصيل لما أجملته الفاتحة، فإنها بُنيت على إجمال ما يحويه القرآن مفصلًا، فإنها واقعة في مطلع التنزيل، والبلاغة فيه: أن تتضمن ما سيق الكلام لأجله، ولهذا لا ينبغي أن يقيد شيء من كلماتها ما أمكن الحمل على الإطلاق.

He continued to say, "The whole of the Qur'ān is a detailed account of that which is summarised in Sūrah al-Fātiḥah. It is structured to represent the overall messages that are detailed in the entire Qur'ān, and so it is placed in the beginning. The rhetorical aspect of it is that it includes the purpose for which the words were intended. For this reason, the meaning of the words of al-Fātiḥah should not be restricted so long as it is possible to understand them without restriction."[45]

وقال الغزالي في (خواص القرآن): مقاصد القرآن ستة: ثلاثة مهمة، وثلاثة تتمة:

Al-Ghazālī[46] wrote in *Khawaṣ al-Qur'ān*, "The objectives of the Qur'ān are six; three of them are essential with the other three causing perfection:

45 See *Sharḥ al-Kashāf* by al-Ṭībī (1/29).

46 He is the famous *imām*, a sea of knowledge and promoter of Islām; Zayn al-Dīn Abū Ḥāmid Muḥammad al-Ghazālī. He is well-known for a range of efforts in various disciplines. He died in 505h.

الأول: تعريف المدعو إليه، كما أشير إليه بصدرها.

One. A definition of the deity which is supplicated to and worshipped. This is found in the very beginning of Sūrah al-Fātiḥah.

وتعريف الصراط المستقيم، وقد صرح به فيها.

Two. A definition as to what the correct path is, and this is explained explicitly in Sūrah al-Fātiḥah.

وتعريف الحال عند الرجوع إليه تعالى، وهو الآخرة، كما أشير إليه بقوله: ﴿مَالِكِ يَوْمِ الدِّينِ﴾.

Three. A description of the state of return to Him, the Most High—i.e. the Hereafter. This is explicitly referred to in His statement: **{The Owner of the Day of Recompense.}**

والأخرى: تعريف أحوال المطيعين، كما أشار إليه بقوله: ﴿الَّذِينَ أَنْعَمْتَ عَلَيْهِمْ﴾.

The other three:

One. A description given to the obedient, as He referred to them in the statement: **{The Way of those upon whom You have bestowed Your Grace.}**

[حكاية أقوال الجاحدين، وقد أشير إليها بـ﴿الْمَغْضُوبِ عَلَيْهِمْ﴾ و﴿الضَّالِّينَ﴾].

Two. A description given to the stubbornly disobedient, as He referred to them in the statement: **{Not the way of those who earned**

Your Anger, nor of those who went astray.}

وتعريف منازل الطريق، كما أشير إليه بقوله: ﴿إِيَّاكَ نَعْبُدُ وَإِيَّاكَ نَسْتَعِينُ﴾.

A description given to the path towards Allah, He referred to this in the statement: **{You [alone] we worship, and You [alone] we ask for help}**."

سورة البقرة

Sūrah al-Baqarah

قال بعض الأئمة: تضمنت سورة الفاتحة: الإقرار بالربوبية، والالتجاء إليها في دين الإسلام، والصيانة عن دين اليهود والنصارى.

Some scholars[47] surmised that Sūrah al-Fātiḥah is a *sūrah* which affirms Allah's Lordship—resorting to it in the religion of Islam, and safeguarding one's self from the deviation of the Jews and Christians.

وسورة البقرة تضمنت قواعد الدين، وآل عمران مكملة لمقصودها.

They also suggested that Sūrah al-Baqarah contains the foundations of the religion and its purpose continues to be contemplated over in Āli 'Imrān.

فالبقرة بمنزلة إقامة الدليل على الحكم، وآل عمران بمنزلة الجواب عن شبهات الخصوم، ولهذا ورد فيها كثير من المتشابه لما تمسك به النصارى.

Al-Baqarah therefore, is a *sūrah* which establishes the evidence for a ruling and Āli 'Imrān is themed at responding to doubts and fallacies which are proposed by those who contend. For this reason, Āli 'Imrān has within it many doubtful ideas which the Christians have adopted,

---

47 See *al-Burhān* of al-Zarkashī (1/260-262).

[alongside responses to them.]

فأوجب الحج في آل عمران، وأما في البقرة فذكر أنه مشروع وأمر بإتمامه بعد الشروع فيه، وكان خطاب النصارى في آل عمران، كما أن خطاب اليهود في البقرة أكثر، لأن التوراة أصل، والإنجيل فرع لها، والنبي صلى الله عليه وسلم لما هاجر إلى المدينة دعا اليهود وجاهدهم، وكان جهاده للنصارى في آخر الأمر، كما كان دعاؤه لأهل الشرك قبل أهل الكتاب، ولهذا كانت السور المكية فيها الدين الذي اتفق عليه الأنبياء، فخُوطب به جميع الناس، والسور المدنية فيها خطاب من أقرَّ بالأنبياء من أهل الكتاب والمؤمنين، فخُوطبوا بيا أهل الكتاب، يا بني إسرائيل، يأيها الذين آمنوا.

For this reason, Hajj is obligated in Āli 'Imrān, whereas al-Baqarah explains its rulings and the manner of completing ones rituals. And Āli 'Imrān is a *sūrah* which is targeted at the Christians whereas al-Baqarah is more so targeted at the Jews. This is because the Torah is the basis and the foundation, whereas the Injīl is an extension of it. Another reason is because when the Prophet ﷺ migrated to al-Madīnah he primarily was engaging with the Jews and their contentions, and he only really engaged with Christians towards the end of his life, [thus al-Baqarah preceded Ālī 'Imrān also in this fashion.] Similar to this is the fact that the call of the Prophet ﷺ was initially targeted at the Mushriks of Quraysh and then the People of the Book. So the Makkan *sūrahs* established within themselves messages which all the Prophets had already come with, therefore these Makkan *sūrahs* are generally addressed to all mankind. As for the Madanī *sūrahs*, they address those who believed in the Prophets from amongst the People of the

Book and other believers. For this reason, the Madanī *surahs* address their listeners as, "O People of the Book", "O Children of Israel" or "O faithful."

وأما سورة النساء فتضمنت أحكام الأسباب التي بين الناس، وهي نوعان: مخلوقة لله، ومقدورة لهم، كالنسب والصهر، ولهذا افتتحت بقوله: ﴿يَا أَيُّهَا النَّاسُ اتَّقُوا رَبَّكُمُ الَّذِي خَلَقَكُمْ مِنْ نَفْسٍ وَاحِدَةٍ وَخَلَقَ مِنْهَا زَوْجَهَا﴾ [ثم] قال: ﴿وَاتَّقُوا اللَّهَ الَّذِي تَسَاءَلُونَ بِهِ وَالْأَرْحَامَ﴾.

As for Sūrah al-Nisā, [it is more generally themed.] It has rulings which all people are dependent upon. This is of two types: That which is created for Allah and that which is predestined to them such as lineage and marriage. This is why al-Nisā begins with the statement: **{O mankind! Be dutiful to your Lord, Who created you from a single person, and from him He created his wife.}**[48] And His statement [in the same *āyah*]: **{And fear Allah through whom you demand your mutual rights, and do not cut the relations of the kinship.}**

فانظر إلى هذه المناسبة العجيبة، والافتتاح، وبراعة الاستهلال، حيث تضمنت الآية المفتتح بها مافي أكثر السورة من أحكام: من نكاح النساء ومحرماته، والمواريث المتعلقة بالأرحام وأن ابتداء هذا الأمر بخلق آدم، ثم خلق زوجته منه، ثم بث منهما رجالًا كثيرًا ونساء في غاية الكثرة.

It brings amazement marvelling at this concordance and the appropriateness of this beginning, it sets the theme for what is going to be explained in the rulings connected to marriage, close family ties, inheritance laws, all of which are connected to the ties of kinship which

48 Al-Nisā: 1

all stem from the creation of their father, Ādam and then the creation of his wife Ḥawā. After this, the *āyah* mentions that from the parents of mankind there was a huge diffusion of progeny.

[و] أما المائدة فسورة العقود، [و] تضمنت بيان تمام الشرائع، ومكملات الدين، والوفاء بعهود الرسل، وما أخذ على الأمة، وبها تَمَّ الدين، فهي سورة التكميل، لأن فيها تحريم الصيد على الْمُحْرِمِ، الذي هو من تمام الإحرام، وتحريم الخمر الذي هو من تمام حفظ العقل والدين، وعقوبة المعتدين من السُّرَّاق والمحاربين، الذي هو من تمام حفظ الدماء والأموال، وإحلال الطيبات، الذي هو من تمام عبادة الله؛ ولهذا ذكر فيها ما يختص بشريعة محمد صلى الله عليه وسلم كالوضوء والتيمم، والحكم بالقرآن على كل ذي دين.

As for al-Mā'idah [which comes after al-Nisā,] it is a *sūrah* of covenants. It also represents within it rulings of the entire Sharīʿah and the Sharīʿah of the Prophets before us. It describes the fulfilment of the covenants of the Messengers and what this Ummah has been ordained with. It is the *sūrah* that identifies the perfection of religious acts; it includes that hunting is made prohibited for the pilgrim whilst in *iḥrām*, and this is from the perfectors of the state of *ihrām*, liquor is made prohibited, and this is from the perfectors of the sanctity of the intellect and religion. Al-Māʿidah also gives description to the punishment faced by those who are waging war against society and thieves, which represents the utmost level of protecting the sanctity of blood and wealth. Furthermore, it permits what is good and wholesome, which is needed for the creation to understand in order to worship Allah, so for this reason this *sūrah* gives description to that which is specific to the legislation of Islam such as the *wuḍū* and *tayammum*.

Sūrah al-Mā'idah also gives rulings connected to debts.

ولهذا كثر فيها لفظ الإكمال والإتمام، وذكر فيها: أن من ارتد عوض الله بخير منه، ولا يزال هذا الدين كاملًا، ولهذا ورد أنها آخر ما نزل لما فيها من إرشادات الختم والتمام. وهذا الترتيب بين هذه السور الأربع المدنيات من أحسن الترتيب. انتهى.

Therefore, within Sūrah al-Mā'idah there is extensive use of the words "completed" and "perfected". It also mentions that when a person apostatises Allah will replace him with someone who is better than him. Sūrah al-Mā'idah is a divine declaration that the religion of Allah has been completed and it will remain as such. For this reason, it is from the very last *sūrahs* that the Prophet received,[49] because it includes the completion of the religion and the finishing of revelation. This is the order of the first four *sūrahs* [after al-Fātiḥah] that were all revealed in al-Madīnah. All of which have been placed in the best of sequences. This is the end of [al-Zarkashī's] quote.

وقال بعضهم: افتتحت البقرة بقوله: ﴿الم ذَلِكَ الْكِتَابُ لا رَيْبَ فِيهِ﴾ فإنه إشارة إلى الصراط المستقيم في قوله: ﴿اهْدِنَا الصِّرَاطَ الْمُسْتَقِيمَ﴾ كأنهم لما سألوا الهداية إلى الصراط المستقيم، قيل لهم: ذلك الصراط الذي سألتم الهداية إليه، كما أخرج ابن جرير وغيره من حديث علي رضي الله عنه مرفوعًا: ((الصراط المستقيم كتاب الله)) وأخرجه الحاكم في المستدرك

49 Reported by al-Ḥākim in *al-Mustadrak* (2/311) from the ḥadīth of 'Āishah, who classed it as *ṣaḥīḥ* on the conditions of al-Bukhārī and Muslim, though they did not report it.

عن ابن مسعود موقوفًا.

Other scholars described the beginning of Sūrah al-Baqarah {***Alif-Lam-Mim.*** **This is the Book, whereof there is no doubt**} as a direct address regarding the straight path mentioned in His statement: {**Guide us to the straight path**}. So it is as if the person supplicates to be shown the straight path and shortly after is given the answer: This is the straight path about which you inquire [i.e. the straight path and guidance is in following the Book.] This is similar to that which Ibn Jarīr and others reported from 'Alī ﵁ (which is raised to the Prophet ﷺ), 'The straight path is the Book of Allah.'[50] And this was reported by al-Ḥākim in *al-Mustadrak* upon the authority of Ibn Mas'ūd, which is a *mawqūf* report (attributed to a Companion).

وهذا معنى حسن يظهر فيه سر ارتباط البقرة بالفاتحة.

This interpretation is befitting, as it displays a reason for the relationship between al-Fātiḥah and al-Baqarah.[51]

وقال الخويي: أوائل هذه السورة مناسبة لأواخر سورة الفاتحة، لأن الله تعالى لما ذكر أن الحامدين طلبوا الهدى، قال: قد أعطيتكم ما طلبتم: هذا الكتاب هدى لكم فاتبعوه، وقد اهتديتم إلى الصراط المستقيم المطلوب المسئول.

Al-Khuway[52] said, "The beginning of Sūrah al-Baqarah is directly

---

50 *Tafsīr al-Ṭabarī* (1/173) and al-Ḥākim in *al-Mustadrak* (4/83) from Ibn Mas'ūd.

51 See *al-Burhān fī 'Ulūm al-Qur'ān* (1/38).

52 He is Aḥmad ibn Khalīl al-Khuway, a scholar of *tafsīr* who passed away in 627h.

connected to the ending of Sūrah al-Fātiḥah because Allah, the Most High, describes those who praise Him as the people who ask Him for guidance. In response, He states, 'I have given you what you have requested—a Book of guidance, so follow it, and I have guided you to the straight path which is sought.'

ثم إنه ذكر في أوائل هذه السورة الطوائف الثلاث الذين ذكرهم في الفاتحة، فذكر الذين على هدى من ربهم، وهم المنعَم عليهم، والذين اشتروا الضلالة بالهدى، وهم الضالون، والذين باءوا بغضب من الله، وهم المغضوب عليهم. انتهى.

After this, Allah continues, in the beginning of Sūrah al-Baqarah, to describe the three groups of people whom were mentioned in Sūrah al-Fātiḥah: (i) a group that is guided by their Lord by His Favour upon them, (ii) a group who are astray by selling guidance for misguidance, and (iii) a group of people who have the anger of Allah upon them."[53] End quote.

[و] أقول: قد ظهر لي بحمد الله وجوهًا من هذه المناسبات:

I have been blessed by Allah with some insights regarding this matter:

أحدها: أن القاعدة التي استقرأتها القرآن: أن كل سورة تفصيل لإجمال ما قبلها، وشرح له، وإطناب لإيجازه، وقد استمر معي ذلك في غالب سور القرآن، طويلها وقصيرها، وسورة البقرة قد اشتملت على تفصيل جميع مجملات الفاتحة.

53 See *al-Itqān* (2/7-12).

The first of them is a principle that I noticed after my indeterminate analysis of the Qur'ān, and it is that every *sūrah* brings further details of what was generally mentioned by the *sūrah* that preceded it, explaining the previous one and elaborating upon that which is concise. I noticed this in most of the *sūrahs* of the Qur'ān, the lengthy ones and the brief. And Sūrah al-Baqarah explains in detail all of the general themes of al-Fātiḥah.

فقوله: ﴿الْحَمْدُ لِلَّهِ﴾ تفصيله: ما وقع فيها من الأمر بالذكر في عدة آيات ومن الدعاء في قوله: ﴿أُجِيبُ دَعْوَةَ الدَّاعِ إِذَا دَعَانِ﴾ (١٨٦) الآية، وفي قوله: ﴿رَبَّنَا لا تُؤَاخِذْنَا إِنْ نَسِينَا أَوْ أَخْطَأْنَا رَبَّنَا وَلا تَحْمِلْ عَلَيْنَا إِصْرًا كَمَا حَمَلْتَهُ عَلَى الَّذِينَ مِنْ قَبْلِنَا رَبَّنَا وَلا تُحَمِّلْنَا مَا لا طَاقَةَ لَنَا بِهِ وَاعْفُ عَنَّا وَاغْفِرْ لَنَا وَارْحَمْنَا أَنْتَ مَوْلانَا فَانْصُرْنَا عَلَى الْقَوْمِ الْكَافِرِينَ﴾ (٢٨٦)، وبالشكر في قوله: ﴿فَاذْكُرُونِي أَذْكُرْكُمْ وَاشْكُرُوا لِي وَلا تَكْفُرُونِ﴾ (١٥٢).

His statement {**All praise be to Allah**} is delved into in a deeper manner in the numerous *āyāt* [within al-Baqarah] where *dhikr* (remembrance) has been ordered and as *du'ā* in His statement: {**I respond to the invocations of the supplicant when he calls on Me.**}[54] And His statement: {**Our Lord! Do not punish us if we forget or make a mistake. Our Lord! Do not put hardships upon us like You did on those before us. Our Lord! Do not give us any tests that we do not have the strength to bear. Pardon us and grant us forgiveness. Have mercy on us. You are our protector and so give us victory over the disbelieving people.**}[55] And about giving thanks, He said: {**Remember Me. I will remember you. Be grateful to Me and never be ungrateful.**}[56]

54 Al-Baqarah: 186

55 Al-Baqarah: 287

56 Al-Baqarah: 152

وقوله: ﴿رَبِّ الْعَالَمِينَ﴾ تفصيله قوله: ﴿اعْبُدُوا رَبَّكُمُ الَّذِي خَلَقَكُمْ وَالَّذِينَ مِنْ قَبْلِكُمْ لَعَلَّكُمْ تَتَّقُونَ۝الَّذِي جَعَلَ لَكُمُ الْأَرْضَ فِرَاشًا وَالسَّمَاءَ بِنَاءً وَأَنْزَلَ مِنَ السَّمَاءِ مَاءً فَأَخْرَجَ بِهِ مِنَ الثَّمَرَاتِ رِزْقًا لَكُمْ فَلَا تَجْعَلُوا لِلَّهِ أَنْدَادًا وَأَنْتُمْ تَعْلَمُونَ﴾ (٢١، ٢٢)، وقوله: ﴿هُوَ الَّذِي خَلَقَ لَكُمْ مَا فِي الْأَرْضِ جَمِيعًا ثُمَّ اسْتَوَى إِلَى السَّمَاءِ فَسَوَّاهُنَّ سَبْعَ سَمَاوَاتٍ وَهُوَ بِكُلِّ شَيْءٍ عَلِيمٌ﴾ (٢٩)، ولذلك افتتحها بقصة خلق آدم الذي هو مبدأ البشر، وهو أشرف الأنواع من العالمين، وذلك شرح إجمال ﴿رَبِّ الْعَالَمِينَ﴾ .

His statement {**The Lord of all creation**} is explained further in His statement: {**O mankind! Worship your Lord, Who created you and those who were before you so that you may become pious. He Who has made the earth a resting place for you, and the sky as a shelter, and sent down rain from the sky and gave you fruits by it, as a provision for you. Then do not set up rivals unto Allah [in worship] while you know [that He alone has the right to be worshipped.]**}[57] And His statement: {**He is the One Who created everything on earth for you. Then He *istawā* (rose over) towards the heaven and made them seven heavens and He is the All-Knower of everything.**}[58] For this reason, [the story of the creation of Ādam and the creation of mankind comes directly after mentioning the Lordship of Allah and His Attribute of creating; He created all that exists and from the best of His creation is the creation of man.] Therefore, the story of the creation of Ādam—who was the first man—comes at the beginning of al-Baqarah, and his kind are the noblest of all creatures, giving a detailed explanation of His broader statement {**The Lord of all creation**}.

57 Al-Baqarah: 21-22

58 Al-Baqarah: 29

وقوله: ﴿الرَّحْمَنِ الرَّحِيمِ﴾ قد أومأ إليه بقوله في قصة [توبة] آدم: ﴿فَتَابَ عَلَيْكُمْ إِنَّهُ هُوَ التَّوَّابُ الرَّحِيمُ﴾ (٥٤)، وفي قصة إبراهيم لما سأل الرزق للمؤمنين خاصة [بقوله: ﴿وَارْزُقْ أَهْلَهُ مِنَ الثَّمَرَاتِ مَنْ آمَنَ﴾ (١٢٦)]، فقال: ﴿وَمَنْ كَفَرَ فَأُمَتِّعُهُ قَلِيلًا﴾ (١٢٦).

His statement {**The Most Beneficent, the Most Merciful**} is indicated to in al-Baqarah through the story of the repentance of Ādam: {**And his Lord pardoned him. Verily, He is the One Who forgives, the Most Merciful.**}[59] And when Ibrāhīm supplicated for the sustenance of the faithful specifically: {**And provide its people with fruits, for whomever of them who believes.**}[60] He said: {**As for him who disbelieves, I shall leave him in contentment for a while.**}[61]

وذلك لكونه رحمانًا. وما وقع في قصة بني إسرائيل: ﴿ثُمَّ عَفَوْنَا عَنْكُمْ﴾ (٥٢)، إلى أن أعاد الآية بجملتها في قوله: ﴿لا إِلَهَ إِلَّا هُوَ الرَّحْمَنُ الرَّحِيمُ﴾ (١٦٣). وذكر آية الدَّيْنِ إرشادًا للطالبين من العباد، ورحمة بهم، ووضع عنهم الخطأ والنسيان والإصر، وما لا طاقة لهم به، وختم بقوله: ﴿وَاعْفُ عَنَّا وَاغْفِرْ لَنَا وَارْحَمْنَا﴾ (٢٨٦)، وذلك شرح قوله: ﴿الرَّحْمَنِ الرَّحِيمِ﴾.

And this exemplifies His beneficence and mercy. Likewise, in the story of Banī Isrā'īl: {**Then after that We forgave you so that you might be grateful.**}[62] And also it is as if the *āyah* [in al-Fātiḥah] repeats itself in al-Baqarah in a slightly different form: {**And your God is**

59 Al-Baqarah: 54
60 Al-Baqarah: 126
61 Al-Baqarah: 126
62 Al-Baqarah: 52

One God, there is none who has the right to be worshipped except Him, the Most Beneficent, the Most Merciful.}[63] Even in the *āyah* in al-Baqarah which talks about debts; it instructs the seekers [who take or give loans] from His slaves and He pardoned them for their mistakes, forgetfulness and burdens which they may not be able to carry. As a mercy towards them this instruction is made clear and then concluded with: **{Pardon us and grant us Forgiveness. Have mercy on us.}**[64] This [completes] the explanation of **{The Most Beneficent, the Most Merciful.}**

وقوله: ﴿مَالِكِ يَوْمِ الدِّينِ﴾ (الفاتحة: ٤) تفصيله: ما وقع من ذكر يوم القيامة في عدة مواضع، ومنها قوله: ﴿وَإِنْ تُبْدُوا مَا فِي أَنْفُسِكُمْ أَوْ تُخْفُوهُ يُحَاسِبْكُمْ بِهِ اللَّهُ﴾ (٢٨٤). والدين [في الفاتحة] : الحساب [في البقرة].

His statement **{The Owner of the Day of Recompense}** is detailed in the many places within al-Baqarah which detail the Day of Judgement. From them is His statement: **{Whether you disclose what is within yourselves or conceal it, Allah will call you to account for it.}** The word *al-dīn* (religion) in Sūrah al-Fātiḥah is a synonym for *ḥisāb* (account) in al-Baqarah, [which explains the correlation between the wording in the two *sūrahs*.]

وقوله: ﴿إِيَّاكَ نَعْبُدُ﴾ مجمل شامل لجميع أنواع الشريعة الفروعية، وقد فصلت في البقرة أبلغ تفصيل، فذكر فيها: الطهارة، والحيض، والصلاة، والاستقبال، وطهارة المكان، والجماعة، وصلاة الخوف، وصلاة الجمع، والعيد، والزكاة بأنواعها، كالنبات، والمعادن، والاعتكاف، والصوم، وأنواع

63 Al-Baqarah: 163

64 Al-Baqarah: 286

الصدقات، والبر، والحج، والعمرة، والبيع، والإجارة، والميراث، والوصية، والوديعة، والنكاح، والصداق، والطلاق، والخُلع، والرجعة، والإيلاء، والعِدَّة، والرضاع، والنفقات، والقصاص، والديات، وقتال البُغاة، والردة، والأشربة، والجهاد، والأطعمة والذبائح، والأَيْمَان، والنذور، والقضاء، والشهادات، والعتق.

His statement {**You [alone] we worship**} is a general statement which includes the Sharī'ah as a whole,[65] and al-Baqarah gives details to many aspects of the Sharī'ah, ranging from purification, menses, the prayer, facing the Qiblah, purity of places, congregation, the prayer of fear, the Friday prayer, 'Eid, *zakāt* and its types—such as *zakāt* of agriculture and metals, *i'tikāf*, fasting, types of charity, piety, Hajj, 'Umrah, trade, renting, inheritance, bequeathment, deposits, marriage, dowries, divorce, forfeiture of assets divorce, reconciliation, vows of abstinence from one's wife, waiting periods, breastfeeding, maintenance, capital punishment, blood money, fighting renegades, warfare, apostasy, food and drink, slaughtering, vows and oaths, judiciary, witnessing and freeing of slaves.

فهذه أبواب الشريعة كلها مذكورة في هذه السورة.

All of these aspects of the Sharī'ah are mentioned in this *sūrah*.

وقوله: ﴿وَإِيَّاكَ نَسْتَعِينُ﴾ شامل لعلم الأخلاق. وقد ذكر منها في هذه

65 [T] This *āyah* in al-Fātiḥah has been explained by many scholars of *tafsīr* as "An abandonment from *shirk* in internal and external forms worship." Al-Qatādah said it means, "To free yourself from worshipping other than Allah and affirming *ikhlāṣ* in Him alone." See *Tafsīr Ibn Kathīr* (1/135) and *Tafsīr al-Ṭabarī* (1/160-161) for further details.

السورة الجم الغفير، من التوبة، والصبر، والشكر، والرضى، والتفويض، والذكر، والمراقبة، والخوف، وإِلَانَة القول.

His statement {**You [alone] we ask for help**} encompasses goodly-manners,[66] and there are a whole host of them mentioned in al-Baqarah; repentance, patience, thanksgiving, love, reliance, *dhikr*, god-consciousness, fear and being sound in speech.

وقوله: ﴿اهْدِنَا الصِّرَاطَ الْمُسْتَقِيمَ﴾ إلى آخره. تفصيله: ما وقع في السورة من ذكر طريق الأنبياء، ومَن حاد عنهم من النصارى، ولهذا ذكر في الكعبة أنها قبلة إبراهيم، فهي من صراط الذين أنعم عليهم، وقد حاد عنها اليهود والنصارى معًا، ولذلك قال في قصتها: ﴿يَهْدِي مَنْ يَشَاءُ إِلَى صِرَاطٍ مُسْتَقِيمٍ﴾ (١٤٢)، تنبيهًا على أنها الصراط الذي سألوا الهداية إليه.

His statement {**Guide us to the Straight Path**} until the end of the *sūrah*: Its details are noted in that which is in this *sūrah* regarding the traditions of the Prophets and the manner of those who opposed them from the Christians. This is why, when mentioning the Kaʿbah, it is referred to as the Qiblah of Ibrāhīm; for it is the straight path of which the Jews and Christians opposed. Subsequently, it is for this reason He says in its story: {**He guides whom He wills to the straight path**}[67] to display that it is the straight path upon which guidance to-

66 [T] Al-Ṭabarī said about the meaning of {**Your assistance**}, "Meaning You alone we seek to aid us in our worship and obedience of You, and in all our affairs, we have none but You. If there are those who deny seeking Your assistance and wish to seek it by worshipping something besides You, then we are the opposite—we worship You and seek Your assistance in all our affairs through You, making the religion and sincerity solely for You." See *Tafsīr al-Ṭabarī* (1/161).
67 Al-Baqarah: 142

wards it was asked for.

ثم ذكر: ﴿وَلَئِنْ أَتَيْتَ الَّذِينَ أُوتُوا الْكِتَابَ بِكُلِّ آيَةٍ مَا تَبِعُوا قِبْلَتَكَ﴾ (١٤٥)، وهم المغضوب عليهم والضالون الذين حادوا عن طريقهم. ثم أخبر بهداية الذين آمنوا إلى طريقهم. ثم قال: ﴿وَاللَّهُ يَهْدِي مَنْ يَشَاءُ إِلَى صِرَاطٍ مُسْتَقِيمٍ﴾ (٢١٣). فكانت هاتان الآيتان تفصيل إجمال: ﴿اهْدِنَا الصِّرَاطَ الْمُسْتَقِيمَ﴾ إلى آخر السورة.

Then He said: **{And even if you were to bring to the people of the Scripture proofs, they would not follow your *Qiblah*.}**[68] They are the ones who deviated either by having divine anger upon them or by being allowed to be led astray. He then said about those who remained firm on the straight path and were guided because of their belief in it: **{And Allah guides whom He wills to the straight path.}**[69] Both of these *āyāt* in al-Baqarah give detail to the manner of the straight path mentioned in al-Fātiḥah, i.e. **{Guide us to the straight path}** to the end of the *sūrah*.

وأيضًا قوله أول السورة: ﴿هُدىً لِلْمُتَّقِينَ﴾ (٢) إلى آخره في وصف الكتاب، إخبار بأن الصراط الذي سألوا الهداية إليه هو: ما تضمنه الكتاب وإنما يكون هداية لمن اتصف بما ذكر [من صفات المتقين] . ثم ذكر أحوال الكفرة، ثم أحوال المنافقين، وهم من اليهود، وذلك [أيضًا] تفصيل لمن حاد عن الصراط المستقيم، ولم يهتدِ بالكتاب.

---

68 Al-Baqarah: 145

69 Al-Baqarah: 213

And His statement at the beginning of the *sūrah* {**A guidance to those who are pious**} and all the other descriptions that come shortly after in explaining "the Book", describe that the straight path is actually the guidance that they were asking for. Therefore, the straight path comprises of the Book—which is guidance for the pious. After this, Allah describes the state of those who disbelieve and the hypocrites, and both of these traits are found within the sect of the Jews. This also gives further description as to those who were misguided from the straight path and were not guided by the Book.

وكذلك قوله هنا: ﴿قُولُوا آمَنَّا بِاللَّهِ وَمَا أُنْزِلَ إِلَيْنَا وَمَا أُنْزِلَ إِلَى إِبْرَاهِيمَ وَإِسْمَاعِيلَ وَإِسْحَاقَ وَيَعْقُوبَ وَالْأَسْبَاطِ﴾ (١٣٦) الآية. فيه تفصيل النبيين المنعَم عليهم. وقال في آخرها: ﴿لَا نُفَرِّقُ بَيْنَ أَحَدٍ مِنْهُمْ﴾ (١٣٦) تعريفًا بالمغضوب عليهم والضالين الذين فرقوا بين الأنبياء. ولذلك عقبها بقوله: ﴿فَإِنْ آمَنُوا بِمِثْلِ مَا آمَنْتُمْ بِهِ فَقَدِ اهْتَدَوْا﴾ (١٣٧) أي: إلى الصراط المستقيم، صراط المنعَم عليهم كما اهتديتم.

Also His statement {**Say, "We believe in Allah and that which has been sent down to us and that which has been sent down to Ibrāhīm, Ismā'īl, Isḥāq, Ya'qūb and to al-Asbāt (the sons of Ya'qūb)"**}[70] to the end of the *āyah* gives detailed description that the Prophets were guided by His Grace [i.e. {**The Way of those on whom You have bestowed Your Grace.**}] And at the end He said: {**We make no distinction between any of them**}[71] which gives explanation as to how the ones who have anger upon them and those who have been left to go astray deviated; they made distinctions between Prophets and as a result this is followed by: {**So if they believe in the like of that which**

70 Al-Baqarah: 136

71 Al-Baqarah: 136

you believe, then they are rightly guided}[72], i.e. guided to the straight path, the path of {**those upon whom You have bestowed Your grace.**}[73]

فهذا ما ظهر لي، والله أعلم بأسرار كتابه.

This is what appears to me to be the case and Allah knows best the inner intricacies of His Book.

الوجه الثاني: أن الحديث والإجماع على تفسير ﴿الْمَغْضُوبِ عَلَيْهِمْ﴾ باليهود، والضالين بالنصارى، وقد ذكروا في سورة الفاتحة على حسب ترتيبهم في الزمان، فعقب بسورة البقرة، وجميع ما فيها [من] خطاب أهل الكتاب لليهود خاصة، وما وقع فيها من ذكر النصارى لم يقع بذكر الخطاب.

From a second angle, the ḥadīth[74] and consensus on the exegesis of {**Those who earned Your anger**} and {**Those who went astray**} is that the former refers to the Jews and the latter refers to the Christians. They were mentioned in Sūrah al-Fātiḥah in order, according to their respective positions in history. Allah followed it with Sūrah al-Baqarah, which mostly addresses the People of the Book, the Jews in particular, and anything referring to the Christians is not phrased in a way as if it addresses them.

ثم بسورة آل عمران، وأكثر ما فيها من خطاب أهل الكتاب للنصارى، فإن ثمانين آية من أولها نازلة في وفد نصارى نجران، كما ورد في سبب

72 Al-Baqarah: 137

73 See *Naẓm al-Durar fī Tanāsab al-Āyāt wa al-Sūwar* (1/12).

74 Aḥmad in *al-Musnad* (4/378) and al-Tirmidhī (8/286-288).

نزولها، وختمت بقوله: ﴿وَإِنَّ مِنْ أَهْلِ الْكِتَابِ لَمَنْ يُؤْمِنُ بِاللَّهِ﴾ (آل عمران: ١٩٩)، وهي في النجاشي وأصحابه من مؤمني النصارى، كما ورد به الحديث. وهذا وجه بديع في ترتيب السورتين، كأنه لما ذكر في الفاتحة الفريقين، قص في كل سورة مما بعدها حال كل فريق على الترتيب الواقع فيها، ولهذا كان صدر سورة النساء في ذكر اليهود، وآخرها في ذكر النصارى.

It is followed by Sūrah Āli 'Imrān which extensively addresses the Christians. The first eighty *āyāt* of the *sūrah* were revealed in relation to the Christian delegation of Najrān, and this has been reported [by the scholars.][75] Also, Āli 'Imrān as a whole is concluded with [reference to the Christians:] **{And there are, certainly, among the people of the scripture, those who believe in Allah.}**[76] There is a ḥadīth which states that this *āyah* was revealed in relation to Najāshī, the Abyssinian king and his companions—from the faithful Christians, as stated in the ḥadīth.[77] This is an amazing aspect of the order of these two *sūrahs*. As the two groups are mentioned in al-Fātiḥah, they are subsequently detailed in the same order they were mentioned therein. For this reason the next *sūrah*—al-Nisā—combines description of both parties together within it, the Jews mentioned within the start of it and the Christians towards the end.

والوجه الثالث: أن سورة البقرة أجمع سور القرآن للأحكام والأمثال، ولهذا

75 See *Tafsīr al-Qur'ān al-'Aẓīm* (2/40) and *Sīrat Ibn Hishām* (1/573 onwards).
76 Āli 'Imrān: 199
77 Al-Bukhārī (2/108), Chapter of *al-Janā'iz* and Muslim (3/54-55), Chapter of *al-Janā'iz*.

سميت في أثر: (فسطاط القرآن)، الذي هو: المدينة الجامعة، فناسب تقديمها على جميع سوره.

From a third angle, Sūrah al-Baqarah is the most comprehensive of the Qur'ān's *sūrahs* in terms of rulings and parables. For this reason it is named as "The pavilion of the Qur'ān,"[78] which is a term used to refer to an all-inclusive city. For this reason, it is befitting that it precedes all the other *sūrahs*.

الوجه الرابع: أنها أطول سورة في القرآن، وقد افتتح بالسبع الطوال، فناسب البُدَاءة بأطولها.

From a fourth angle, it is the longest *sūrah* in the Qur'ān and the Qur'ān begins with the seven long ones, so it is most suitable that the longest of them all is listed first.

الوجه الخامس: أنها أول سورة نزلت بالمدينة، فناسب الابتداء بها، فإن للأولية نوعًا من الأولوية.

From a fifth angle, it was the first *sūrah* revealed in al-Madīnah, so by this virtue it should be listed first in the *muṣḥaf* (after al-Fātiḥah), because the first to be revealed holds a degree of deservedness to be mentioned first.

الوجه السادس: أن سورة الفاتحة لما ختمت بالدعاء للمؤمنين بألا يسلك بهم طريق المغضوب عليهم ولا الضالين إجمالًا، وخُتمت سورة البقرة بالدعاء بألا يسلك بهم طريقهم في المؤاخذة بالخطأ والنسيان،

78 Al-Dārimī (2/446) from the statement of Khālid ibn Ma'dān.

وحمل الإصر، وما لا طاقة لهم به تفصيلًا، وتضمن آخرها أيضًا الإشارة إلى طريق المغضوب عليهم والضالين بقوله: ﴿لا نُفَرِّقُ بَيْنَ أَحَدٍ مِنْ رُسُلِه﴾ (٢٨٥) فتآخت السورتان وتشابهتا في المقطع، وذلك من وجوه المناسبة في التتالي والتناسق. وقد ورد في الحديث التأمين في آخر سورة البقرة كما هو مشروع في آخر الفاتحة، فهذه ستة وجوه ظهرت لي، ولله الحمد والمنة.

From a sixth angle, as Sūrah al-Fātiḥah ends with the *duā'* of the believers; asking to be saved from the path of those whom earned His anger and were allowed to be led astray—in a general manner. Likewise Sūrah al-Baqarah ends in a similar fashion; a supplication against being held to account for mistakes, forgetfulness, hardship and anything which is too difficult to bear—in a detailed manner. This supplication at the end of al-Baqarah comes after Allah describes how these two sects earned His anger and were led astray: **{We make no distinction between one another of His Messengers}**[79] Therefore there is a striking resemblance and coordination between the content and supplications mentioned at the end of both *sūrahs*. It is even reported that it is prescribed for a person to say "*āmīn*" at the end of Sūrah al-Baqarah just as one would do so at the end of al-Fātiḥah.[80]

These are the six angles which appear most relevant to me, and all praise is to Allah for His favours.

---

79 Al-Baqarah: 285

80 It is reported that Mu'ādh ibn Jabal used to say "*āmīn*" at the end of al-Baqarah. It was reported by Ibn Jarīr with the chain: Wakī'—Sufyān—Abī Isḥāq—a man (*'an rajul*)—Mu'ādh. See *Tafsīr Ibn Kathīr* (1/509).

سورة آل عمران

Sūrah Āli ʿImrān

قد تقدم ما يؤخذ منه مناسبة وضعها.

The reason for Sūrah Āli ʿImrān being located as the third *sūrah* in the Qurʾān has already been discussed.

وقال الإمام: لما كانت هذه السورة قرينة سورة البقرة، وكالمكملة لها، افتتحت بتقرير ما افتتحت به تلك، وصرح في منطوق مطلعها بما طوي في مفهوم [مطلع] تلك.

[In addition to the aforementioned,] the *imām* said, "As this *sūrah* is directly connected to Sūrah al-Baqarah, supporting its meaning and completing it. It begins in the same manner that al-Baqarah began with, and its beginning provides explicit explanation for that which was left obscure in the beginning of al-Baqarah."[81]

وأقول: قد ظهر لي بحمد الله وجوه من المناسبات:

I say: What appears to me to be the case, and all praises are for Allah,

---

81 The obscure in al-Baqarah refers to the call to belief in Allāh in {**Those who believe in the unseen**} (al-Baqarah: 3), which is explained further in Āli ʿImrān, {**There is no god worthy of worship except He, the Ever-Alive and the Ever-Lasting**} (al-Baqarah: 2). See *Mafātīḥ al-Ghayb* (1/320 onwards).

[is that there is a strong level of connection between al-Baqarah and Āli 'Imrān.] This connection is from two angles:

أحدها: مراعاة القاعدة التي قررتها، من شرح كل سورة لإجمال ما في السورة قبلها، وذلك هنا في عدة مواضع:

The first angle—which we have already established—is from the aspect of every *sūrah* explaining the general matters of the previous *sūrah*. In terms of these two *sūrahs*, there are a number of such instances:

منها: ما أشار إليه الإمام، فإن أول البقرة افتتح بوصف الكتاب بأنه لا ريب فيه. وقال في آل عمران: ﴿نَزَّلَ عَلَيْكَ الْكِتَابَ بِالْحَقِّ مُصَدِّقًا لِمَا بَيْنَ يَدَيْهِ﴾ (١٣)، وذلك بسط وإطناب، لنفي الريب عنه.

From them is that which was alluded to by the *imām* above—[both al-Baqarah and Āli 'Imrān start off in the same manner.] Al-Baqarah describes the Book as there being no doubt in it, and He commenced Āli 'Imrān with: **{It is He Who has sent down the Book to you with truth, confirming what came before it.}**[82] This serves as an extension and amplification intended to negate doubt within it.

ومنها: أنه ذكر في البقرة إنزال الكتاب مجملًا، وقسّمه هنا إلى آيات محكمات، ومتشابهات لا يعلم تأويلها إلا الله.

From them is that in al-Baqarah the Book has been described as being revealed by Allah in a general sense. However Āli 'Imrān explains that the Book has been split into *āyat* which are *muḥkam* (clear) and

82 Al-Baqarah: 3

others which are *mutashābih* (obscure), that none know the interpretation of except Allah.

ومنها: أنه قال في البقرة: ﴿وَمَا أُنْزِلَ مِنْ قَبْلِكَ﴾ (البقرة: ٤) [مجملًا]، وقال هنا: ﴿وَأَنْزَلَ التَّوْرَاةَ وَالْإِنْجِيلَ۝مِنْ قَبْلُ هُدًى لِلنَّاسِ﴾ (٣، ٤) مفصلًا. وصرح بذكر الإنجيل هنا، لأن السورة خطاب للنصارى، ولم يقع التصريح به في سورة البقرة بطولها، وإنما صرح فيها بذكر التوراة خاصة؛ لأنها خطاب لليهود.

From them is that He says in al-Baqarah {**What was revealed to those before you**},[83] which refers to revelation in a general sense. He says here: {**He revealed the Torah and the Injīl. Before, as guidance for the people**}[84], and this gives further detail to the names of the Books that were revealed before. [This again is another example of how al-Baqarah mentions a point in its general sense and then Āli 'Imrān clarifies it further.] Furthermore, the introduction of Āli 'Imrān mentions the Injīl because the rest of the *sūrah* is set to address the Christians, and it is not mentioned explicitly in al-Baqarah despite its lengthiness. Al-Baqarah primarily addresses the Jews and as a result it explicitly mentions the Torah.

ومنها: أن ذكر القتال وقع في سورة البقرة مجملًا بقوله: ﴿وَقَاتِلُوا فِي سَبِيلِ اللَّهِ﴾ (١٩٠، ٢٤٤) [وقوله] : ﴿كُتِبَ عَلَيْكُمُ الْقِتَالُ﴾ (البقرة: ٢١٦)، وفصلت هنا قصة أُحُد بكمالها.

From them is that al-Baqarah mentions the rulings connected to

83 Al-Baqarah: 4
84 Āli 'Imrān: 3-4

fighting in a general sense. He said **{And fight in the name of Allah}**[85] and **{Fighting has been legislated for you}**[86] However, Āli 'Imrān gives further details to this in the context of the Battle of Uhud being explained within it.

ومنها: أنه أوجز في البقرة ذكر المقتولين في سبيل الله بقوله: ﴿أَحْيَاءٌ وَلَكِنْ لا تَشْعُرُونَ﴾ (البقرة: ١٥٤) وزاد هنا: ﴿عِنْدَ رَبِّهِمْ يُرْزَقُونَ۞فَرِحِينَ بِمَا آتَاهُمُ اللهُ مِنْ فَضْلِهِ وَيَسْتَبْشِرُونَ بِالَّذِينَ لَمْ يَلْحَقُوا بِهِمْ مِنْ خَلْفِهِمْ﴾ (١٦٩، ١٧٠) الآيتين، وذلك إطناب عظيم.

From them is that al-Baqarah briefly explains the virtues of those who are killed in the path of Allah: **{They are alive but you cannot perceive it.}**[87] Ālī 'Imrān adds to this: **{Alive with their lord gaining their sustenance. They are in bliss with what Allah has given to them from His Favour.}**[88] This is a weighty elaboration.

ومنها: أنه قال في البقرة: ﴿وَاللهُ يُؤْتِي مُلْكَهُ مَنْ يَشَاءُ﴾ (البقرة: ٢٤٧). وقال هنا: ﴿قُلِ اللَّهُمَّ مَالِكَ الْمُلْكِ تُؤْتِي الْمُلْكَ مَنْ تَشَاءُ وَتَنْزِعُ الْمُلْكَ مِمَّنْ تَشَاءُ وَتُعِزُّ مَنْ تَشَاءُ وَتُذِلُّ مَنْ تَشَاءُ بِيَدِكَ الْخَيْرُ إِنَّكَ عَلَى كُلِّ شَيْءٍ قَدِيرٌ﴾ (٢٦)، فزاد إطنابًا وتفصيلاً.

From them is that He says in al-Baqarah: **{And Allah grants His Kingdom to whom He wills.}**[89] And in Āli 'Imrān He said: **{Say, "O Allah,**

---

85 Al-Baqarah: 190, 244
86 Al-Baqarah: 216
87 Al-Baqarah: 154
88 Āli 'Imrān: 169-170
89 Al-Baqarah: 247

Owner of sovereignty, You give sovereignty to whom You will and You take sovereignty away from whom You will. You honour whom You will and You humble whom You will. In Your hand is [all] good. Indeed, You are over all things competent."}[90] Again, additional information is provided for something which was mentioned in less detail.

ومنها: أنه حذر من الرباء في البقرة، ولم يزد على لفظ الربا إيجازًا وزاد هنا قوله: ﴿أَضْعَافًا مُضَاعَفَةً﴾ (١٣٠)، وذلك بيان وبسط.

From them is that al-Baqarah warns against usury but does not elaborate beyond the word "usury". Āli 'Imrān, however, gives a definition as to what usury is referring to: {**Do not consume interest, doubled and multiplied.**}[91] This is an example of an explanation and providing of details.

ومنها: أنه قال في البقرة: ﴿وَأَتِمُّوا الْحَجَّ﴾ (البقرة: ١٩٦)، وذلك إنما يدل على الوجوب إجمالًا، وفصله هنا بقوله: ﴿وَلِلَّهِ عَلَى النَّاسِ حِجُّ الْبَيْتِ﴾ (٩٧). وزاد: بيان شرط الوجوب بقوله: ﴿مَنِ اسْتَطَاعَ إِلَيْهِ سَبِيلًا﴾ (٩٧). ثم زاد: تكفير من جحد وجوبه بقوله: ﴿وَمَنْ كَفَرَ فَإِنَّ اللَّهَ غَنِيٌّ عَنِ الْعَالَمِينَ﴾ (٩٧).

From them is His statement in al-Baqarah {**And complete the Hajj**}[92] which gives implicit proof that the Hajj is an obligation in a general sense. Its explicit command comes in Āli 'Imrān: {**And Hajj to the House is a duty that mankind owes to Allah.**}[93] And an additional condition is stipulated here: {**For whoever is able to find thereto a**

90 Āli 'Imrān: 26
91 Āli 'Imrān: 130
92 Al-Baqarah: 196
93 Āli 'Imrān: 97

way.} And then further information is given regarding the ruling of disbelief for those who deny it: **{And whoever disbelieves, then Allah is not in need of any of the creation.}**[94]

ومنها: أنه قال في البقرة في أهل الكتاب: ﴿ثُمَّ تَوَلَّيْتُمْ إِلَّا قَلِيلًا مِنْكُمْ﴾ (البقرة: ٨٣). فأجمل القليل، وفصله هنا بقوله: ﴿لَيْسُوا سَوَاءً مِنْ أَهْلِ الْكِتَابِ أُمَّةٌ قَائِمَةٌ يَتْلُونَ آيَاتِ اللهِ آنَاءَ اللَّيْلِ وَهُمْ يَسْجُدُونَ﴾ (١١٣، ١١٤) الآيتين.

From them is His statement in al-Baqarah regarding the People of the Book **{Then you turned away, except a few of you, and you were refusing}**[95] without adding any details, but then it is detailed in two *āyat* in Āli 'Imrān: **{Not all of them are alike; a party of the people of the Scripture stand for truth, they recite the *āyāt* of Allah during the hours of the night, prostrating themselves in prayer. They believe in Allah and the Last Day; they enjoin goodness and forbid vice; and they hasten in [all] good works; and they are among the righteous.}**[96]

ومنها: أنه قال في البقرة: ﴿قُلْ أَتُحَاجُّونَنَا فِي اللهِ وَهُوَ رَبُّنَا وَرَبُّكُمْ وَلَنَا أَعْمَالُنَا وَلَكُمْ أَعْمَالُكُمْ وَنَحْنُ لَهُ مُخْلِصُونَ﴾ (البقرة: ١٣٩). فدل بها على تفضيل هذه الأمة على اليهود تعريضًا لا تصريحًا، وكذلك قوله: ﴿وَكَذَلِكَ جَعَلْنَاكُمْ أُمَّةً وَسَطًا﴾ (البقرة: ١٤٣) في تفضيل هذه الأمة على سائر الأمم بلفظ فيه يسير إبهام، وأتى في هذه [السورة] بصريح البيان فقال: ﴿كُنْتُمْ خَيْرَ أُمَّةٍ أُخْرِجَتْ لِلنَّاسِ﴾ (١١٠). فقوله: ﴿كُنْتُمْ﴾ أصرح في قدم ذلك من

94 Āli 'Imrān: 97
95 Al-Baqarah: 83
96 Āli 'Imrān: 113-114

﴿جَعَلْنَاكُمْ﴾ ثم زاد [بيان] وجه الخيرية بقوله: ﴿تَأْمُرُونَ بِالْمَعْرُوفِ وَتَنْهَوْنَ عَنِ الْمُنْكَرِ وَتُؤْمِنُونَ بِاللَّهِ﴾ (١١٠).

From them is His statement in al-Baqarah {**Say, "Do you dispute with us about Allah, while He is our Lord and your Lord? And we are to be rewarded for our deeds and you for your deeds. And we are sincere to Him**},[97] which gives an indication that this Ummah is better and more virtuous than the Ummah of the Jews, but it is not explicit. Likewise is the case for His statement {**Thus We have made you a balanced nation, that you be witnesses over mankind and the Messenger be a witness over you.**}[98] The superiority of this Ummah over the others is detailed here but there is a slight ambiguity in wording. However this superiority is detailed explicitly in Āli 'Imrān: {**You are the best Ummah ever raised up for mankind.**}[99] The wording {**You are**} is a more explicit term than {**Made you**} in al-Baqarah. This is expanded again further in relation to the reason behind the virtuousness: {**You enjoin good and forbid evil, and you believe in Allah.**}[100]

ومنها: أنه قال في البقرة: ﴿وَلَا تَأْكُلُوا أَمْوَالَكُمْ بَيْنَكُمْ بِالْبَاطِلِ وَتُدْلُوا بِهَا إِلَى الْحُكَّامِ﴾ (البقرة: ١٨٨) الآية. وبسط الوعيد هنا بقوله: ﴿إِنَّ الَّذِينَ يَشْتَرُونَ بِعَهْدِ اللَّهِ وَأَيْمَانِهِمْ ثَمَنًا قَلِيلًا أُولَئِكَ لَا خَلَاقَ لَهُمْ فِي الْآخِرَةِ﴾ (٧٧) الآية، وصدره بقوله: ﴿وَمِنْ أَهْلِ الْكِتَابِ مَنْ إِنْ تَأْمَنْهُ بِقِنْطَارٍ يُؤَدِّهِ إِلَيْكَ وَمِنْهُمْ مَنْ إِنْ تَأْمَنْهُ بِدِينَارٍ لَا يُؤَدِّهِ إِلَيْكَ إِلَّا مَا دُمْتَ عَلَيْهِ قَائِمًا ذَلِكَ بِأَنَّهُمْ قَالُوا لَيْسَ عَلَيْنَا فِي الْأُمِّيِّينَ سَبِيلٌ﴾

---

97 Al-Baqarah: 139
98 Al-Baqarah: 143
99 Āli 'Imrān: 110
100 Al-Baqarah: 110

.(٧٥)

From them is His statement in al-Baqarah: {**And do not consume one another's property unjustly nor give bribery to the rulers**}[101] This warning is explained further in His statement: {**Surely, those who purchase a small gain at the cost of Allah's covenant and their oaths, they shall have no portion in the Hereafter.**}[102] And He preceded it with: {**And among the People of the Scripture is he who, if you entrust him with a great amount [of wealth], he will return it to you. And among them is he who, if you entrust him with a [single] silver coin, he will not return it to you unless you are constantly standing over him [demanding it]. That is because they say, "There is no blame upon us concerning the unlearned."**}[103]

فهذه عدة مواضع وقعت في البقرة مجملة، وفي آل عمران تفصيلها.

So these are many of the instances where al-Baqarah mentions a matter in a general form and then Āli ʿImrān explains in further detail.

الوجه الثاني: أن بين هذه السورة وسورة البقرة اتحادًا، وتلاحمًا متأكدًا، لما تقدم من أن البقرة بمنزلة إزالة الشبهة، ولهذا تكرر هنا ما يتعلق بالمقصود الذي هو بيان حقيقة الكتاب: من إنزال الكتاب، وتصديقه للكتب قبله، والهدى إلى الصراط المستقيم. وتكررت هنا آية: ﴿قُولُوا آمَنَّا بِاللَّهِ وَمَا أُنْزِلَ﴾ (البقرة: ١٣٦) بكمالها، ولذلك أيضًا ذكر في هذه ما هو تال لما ذكر في تلك، أو لازم في تلك، أو لازم له.

101 Al-Baqarah: 188
102 Āli ʿImrān: 77
103 Āli ʿImrān: 75

The second angle is that this *sūrah* and al-Baqarah are united in complementing and reinforcing one another, because, as previously noted, al-Baqarah serves to remove the doubt. This is why it is mentioned again here regarding what is relevant to the clarification of the reality of the Book; from its revelation, affirming that which was revealed before and it being a guide to the straight path. For this reason, the *āyah* in al-Baqarah is repeated in its exact form here: **{Say, "We believe in Allah and that which has been sent down ..."}**[104] This is why He mentions here what consequently follows that which is mentioned or necessitated there.

فذكر هناك خلق الناس، وذكر هنا تصويرهم في الأرحام، وذكر هناك مبدأ خلق آدم، وذكر هنا مبدأ خلق أولاده، وألطف من ذلك: أنه افتتح البقرة بقصة آدم حيث خلقه من غير أب ولا أم، وذكر في هذه نظيره في الخلق من غير أب، وهو عيسى عليه السلام، ولذلك ضرب له المثل بآدم، واختصت البقرة بآدم لأنها أول السور، وآدم أول في الوجود وسابق، ولأنها الأصل، وهذه كالفرع والتتمة لها، فمختصة بالإعراب [والبيان] .

So after mentioning the creation of mankind in al-Baqarah, its formation in the womb is described in Āli 'Imrān. In al-Baqarah, it mentions the creation of Ādam and in Āli 'Imrān it mentions the stages of the creation of his offspring. What is more fascinating than this is that He commenced al-Baqarah with the story of the creation of Ādam—being created without a father or a mother, and He mentioned in Āli 'Imrān the story of another individual who was similarly created without a father, that being 'Īsā ﷺ. For this reason, 'Īsā was compared to Ādam in respect to creation. Al-Baqarah included the story of Ādam exclusively because it is the first *sūrah*, and Ādam is

104 Al-Baqarah: 136

the first human being who preceded all others, and so it is the origin whilst Āli 'Imrān is a branch from it and completes it; therefore, it provides more elaboration and clarification.

ولأنها خطاب لليهود الذين قالوا في مريم ما قالوا، وأنكروا وجود ولد بلا أب، ففوتحوا بقصة آدم؛ لتثبت في أذهانهم، فلا تأتي قصة عيسى إلا وقد ذكر عندهم ما يشهد لها من جنسها.

Al-Baqarah addresses the Jews who stated about Maryam what they stated, rejecting that Maryam had a child without a father. So the story of Ādam comes at an early point in al-Baqarah to establish the idea in their minds of Allah creating a human, and the story of 'Īsā does not come until there is a proof with similar circumstances provided for them.

ولأن قصة عيسى قيست على قصة آدم في قوله: ﴿كَمَثَلِ آدَمَ﴾ (٥٩) الآية، والمقيس عليه لابُدَّ وأن يكون معلومًا، لتتم الحجة بالقياس، فكانت قصة آدم والسورة التي هي فيها جديرة بالتقدم.

The comparison from the story of Ādam to the story of 'Īsā is found in His statement: {**Surely, the likeness of 'Īsā with Allah is the likeness of Ādam.**}[105] As there is a comparison, the basis of the comparison that is compared to must be known so that it can be established as a proof. Thus, the story of Ādam and the *sūrah* it is found in are appropriate to precede.

ومن وجوه تلازم السورتين: أنه قال في البقرة في صفة النار: ﴿أُعِدَّتْ

105 Āli 'Imrān: 59

لِلْكَافِرِينَ﴾ (البقرة: ٢٤)، ولم يقل في الجنة: أعدت للمتقين، مع افتتاحها بذكر المتقين والكافرين معًا، وقال ذلك في آل عمران في قوله: ﴿وَجَنَّةٍ عَرْضُهَا السَّمَاوَاتُ وَالْأَرْضُ أُعِدَّتْ لِلْمُتَّقِينَ﴾ (١٣٣)، فكأن السورتين بمنزلة سورة واحدة.

From the aspects of the two *sūrahs* being concurrent is that which is mentioned in al-Baqarah about the description of the fire: **{Prepared for the disbelievers.}**[106] However it does not specify who Jannah is prepared for, despite the believers and disbelievers being both mentioned in its opening. However this matter is mentioned in Āli 'Imrān: **{For Paradise as wide as are the heavens and the earth, prepared for the pious.}**[107] When noting this, it is as if the two *sūrahs* are actually one and conjoined.

وبذلك يعرف أن تقديم آل عمران على النساء أنسب من تقديم النساء عليها.

Following on from this, it becomes clear that Āli 'Imrān preceding al-Nisā is more appropriate than vice versa.

وأمر آخر استقرأته، وهو: أنه إذا وردت سورتان بينهما تلازم واتحاد، فإن السورة الثانية تكون خاتمتها مناسبة لفاتحة الأولى للدلالة على الاتحاد. وفي السورة المستقلة عما بعدها يكون آخر السورة نفسها مناسب لأولها، وآخر آل عمران مناسب لأول البقرة، فإنها افتتحت بذكر المتقين، وأنهم

106 Al-Baqarah: 24

107 Āli 'Imrān: 133

المفلحون، وختمت آل عمران بقوله: ﴿وَاتَّقُوا اللَّهَ لَعَلَّكُمْ تُفْلِحُونَ﴾ (٢٠٠).

Another matter that I have concluded is that when there are two *sūrahs* that are correlated and have things in common, the ending of the second *sūrah* is concordant to the beginning of the previous one to illustrate their correlation. Whereas in the case of a *sūrah* that is independent from the one it follows, the end of it corresponds and is relevant to the beginning of the following *sūrah*. The ending of Āli 'Imrān is relevant to the beginning of al-Baqarah i.e. al-Baqarah commences with mention of those who fear Allah and that they are successful, while Āli 'Imrān ends with: **{And fear Allah, so that you may be successful.}**[108]

وافتتحت البقرة بقوله: ﴿وَالَّذِينَ يُؤْمِنُونَ بِمَا أُنْزِلَ إِلَيْكَ وَمَا أُنْزِلَ مِنْ قَبْلِكَ﴾ (البقرة: ٤)، وختمت آل عمران بقوله: ﴿وَإِنَّ مِنْ أَهْلِ الْكِتَابِ لَمَنْ يُؤْمِنُ بِاللَّهِ وَمَا أُنْزِلَ إِلَيْكُمْ وَمَا أُنْزِلَ إِلَيْهِمْ﴾ (١٩٩)، فللّه الحمد على ما ألهم.

Sūrah al-Baqarah starts with His statement: **{And who believe in which has been sent down to you and in that which was sent down before you.}**[109] And Āli 'Imrān ends with: **{And there are, certainly, among the people of the scripture, those who believe in Allah and in that which has been revealed to you, and in that which has been revealed to them.}**[110] So all praise is to Allah for the perception that He gives to His slaves.

وقد ورد أنه لما نزلت: ﴿مَنْ ذَا الَّذِي يُقْرِضُ اللَّهَ قَرْضًا حَسَنًا﴾ (البقرة: ٢٤٥)، قالت اليهود: يا محمد، افتقر ربك، فسأل عباده القرض، فنزل قوله:

108 Āli 'Imrān: 200

109 Al-Baqarah: 4

110 Āli 'Imrān: 199

﴿لَقَدْ سَمِعَ اللَّهُ قَوْلَ الَّذِينَ قَالُوا إِنَّ اللَّهَ فَقِيرٌ وَنَحْنُ أَغْنِيَاءُ﴾ (١٨١)، فذلك أيضًا من تلازم السورتين.

It is also reported that when He revealed **{Who will lend Allah a goodly loan?}**[111] The Jews [at that time] said, "O Muhammad, your Lord has become poor so He has asked His slaves for a loan [!?]" So the *āyah* was revealed: **{Indeed, Allah has heard the statement of those who said, "Truly, Allah is poor and we are rich!"}**[112] [113] Again, this highlights the relationship between these two *sūrahs* in terms of their correlation and explanation.

ووقع في البقرة حكاية عن إبراهيم: ﴿رَبَّنَا وَابْعَثْ فِيهِمْ رَسُولًا مِنْهُمْ يَتْلُو عَلَيْهِمْ آيَاتِكَ﴾ (البقرة: ١٢٩) الآية، ونزل في هذه: ﴿لَقَدْ مَنَّ اللَّهُ عَلَى الْمُؤْمِنِينَ إِذْ بَعَثَ فِيهِمْ رَسُولًا مِنْ أَنْفُسِهِمْ يَتْلُو عَلَيْهِمْ﴾ (١٦٤)، وذلك أيضًا من تلازم السورتين.

Sūrah al-Baqarah also gives description to the story of Ibrāhīm: **{Our Lord! Send amongst them a Messenger of their own who shall recite unto them Your *āyāt*.}**[114] In response to this supplication, Allah said: **{Indeed Allah conferred a great favour upon the believers when He sent amongst them a Messenger from among themselves, reciting unto them His *āyāt*.}**[115] Again, this highlights the relationship between these two *sūrahs* in correlation and explanation.

---

111 Al-Baqarah: 245

112 Āli 'Imrān: 181

113 See *Tafsīr al-Ṭabarī* (7/442).

114 Al-Baqarah: 129

115 Āli 'Imrān: 164

سورة النساء

Sūrah al-Nisā

قد تقدم وجه مناسبتها.

The reason for it being the fourth *sūrah* in the Qurʿān has been discussed previously.

وأقول: هذه السورة أيضًا شارحة لبقية مجملات سورة البقرة.

[However,] I say: This *sūrah* also adds and explains the remaining generalities found in al-Baqarah:

فمنها: أنه أجمل في البقرة قوله: ﴿اعْبُدُوا رَبَّكُمُ الَّذِي خَلَقَكُمْ وَالَّذِينَ مِن قَبْلِكُمْ لَعَلَّكُمْ تَتَّقُونَ﴾ (البقرة: ٢١)، وزاد هنا: ﴿خَلَقَكُم مِّن نَّفْسٍ وَاحِدَةٍ وَخَلَقَ مِنْهَا زَوْجَهَا وَبَثَّ مِنْهُمَا رِجَالًا كَثِيرًا وَنِسَاءً﴾ (١).

From them is the generality found in His statement in al-Baqarah **{Worship your Lord, Who created you and those who were before you so that you may become pious.}**[116] It is expanded upon here: **{Who created you from a single person, and from him He created his wife, and from them both He dispersed many men and women.}**[117]

---

116 Al-Baqarah: 21

117 Al-Nisā: 1

وانظر لما كانت آية التقوى في سورة البقرة غاية، جعلها في أول هذه السورة التالية لها مبدأ.

One should reflect upon the fact that the *āyah* of al-Baqarah explains the objective of creation—which is to attain *taqwā*—and this theme continues at the start of al-Nisā with its beginning (i.e. describing the creation of the first man and attaching it to the idea of *taqwā* also).

ومنها: أنه أجمل في سورة البقرة: ﴿اسْكُنْ أَنْتَ وَزَوْجُكَ الْجَنَّةَ﴾ (البقرة: ٣٥)، وبين هنا أن زوجته خلقت منه في قوله: ﴿وَخَلَقَ مِنْهَا زَوْجَهَا﴾ (١).

From them is the generality found in His statement in Sūrah al-Baqarah {**Stay, you and your wife, in the Paradise.**}[118] Here the relationship between Ādam and his wife is explained: {**And from him He created his wife.**}[119]

ومنها: أنه أجمل في البقرة آية اليتامى، وآية الوصية، والميراث، والوارث، في قوله: ﴿وَعَلَى الْوَارِثِ مِثْلُ ذَلِكَ﴾ (البقرة: ٢٣٣)، وفصل ذلك في هذه السورة أبلغ تفصيل.

From them is the generality found in al-Baqarah when discussing orphans, bequests, inheritance and heirs in His statement: {**And on the [father's] heir is incumbent the like of that [which was incumbent on the father.]**}[120] Al-Nisā explains in further detail, all of the above (i.e. laws of inheritance).[121]

---

118 Al-Baqarah: 35

119 Al-Nisā: 1

120 Al-Baqarah: 233

121 See al-Nisā: 7, 11, 12, 33 and 176

و[منها أنه] فصل هنا من الأنكحة ما أجمله هناك.

And from them is that matters of marriage are detailed here which were general there.

ومنها: أنه قال في البقرة: ﴿وَلَأَمَةٌ مُّؤْمِنَةٌ خَيْرٌ مِّن مُّشْرِكَةٍ﴾ (البقرة: ٢٢١) فذكر نكاح الأمة إجمالًا، وفصل هنا شروطه.

From them is His statement in al-Baqarah: **{And a believing slave woman is better than a polytheist}**[122] where marriage with a slave woman is mentioned generally. This subject is detailed in this *sūrah*.[123]

ومنها: أنه ذكر الصداق في البقرة مجملًا بقوله: ﴿وَلَا يَحِلُّ لَكُمْ أَن تَأْخُذُوا مِمَّآ آتَيْتُمُوهُنَّ شَيْئًا﴾ (البقرة: ٢٩٩)، وشرحه هنا مفصلًا.

From them is that al-Baqarah generalises mention of the dowry **{And it is not lawful for you to take back any of the dowry which you have given them.}**[124] Its details are explained in al-Nisā (i.e. laws connected to the dowry).[125]

ومنها: أنه ذكر هناك الخلع، وذكر هنا أسبابه ودواعيه، من النشوز وما يترتب عليه، وبعث الحكمين.

From them is that al-Baqarah[126] mentions *khul'* and then al-Nisā mentions its reasons and causes from marital discord, what stems from it

122 Al-Baqarah: 221
123 See al-Nisā: 25
124 Al-Baqarah: 229
125 See al-Nisā: 20-21
126 See al-Baqarah: 229

and steps to reconciliation.[127]

ومنها: أنه فصل هنا من أحكام المجاهدين، وتفصيلهم درجات، والهجرة، ما وقع هناك مجملًا، أو مرموزًا.

From them is that al-Nisā details the rulings pertaining to warfare, the virtue of the warriors and their different levels. Likewise is the case for the matters related to migration which were general or hinted to in al-Baqarah.

وفيها من الاعتلاق بسورة الفاتحة: تفسير: ﴿الَّذِينَ أَنْعَمْتَ عَلَيْهِمْ﴾ في قوله: ﴿مِنَ النَّبِيِّينَ وَالصِّدِّيقِينَ وَالشُّهَدَاءِ وَالصَّالِحِينَ﴾ (٦٩).

Furthermore, there appears to be a strong connection between it and al-Fātiḥah. There is an explanation of **{Whom You have bestowed Your grace}** in His statement: **{Whom Allah has bestowed His Grace, of the Prophets, the *ṣiddiqūn*, the martyrs, and the righteous.}**[128]

وأما وجه اعتلاقها بآل عمران فمن وجوه:

As for the connection between al-Nisā and Āli 'Imrān, then this can also be explained from several angles:

منها: أن آل عمران ختمت بالأمر بالتقوى، وافتتحت هذه السورة به وذلك من آكد وجوه المناسبات في ترتيب السور، وهو نوع من [أنواع] البديع يسمى: تشابه الأطراف.

---

127 See al-Nisā: 34-35

128 Al-Nisā: 69

From them is that Āli 'Imrān ends with the command of piety[129] and al-Nisā begins directly with it.[130] This clearly shows a strong correlation between the order of these two *sūrahs*, and this is a well-known technique in Arabic rhetoric known as *tashābih al-aṭrāf*.[131]

ومنها: أن سورة آل عمران ذكر فيها قصة أحد مستوفاة وذكر في هذه السورة ذيلها، وهو قوله: ﴿فَمَا لَكُمْ فِي الْمُنَافِقِينَ فِئَتَيْنِ﴾ (٨٨)، فإنها نزلت لما اختلف الصحابة فيمن رجع من المنافقين من غزوة أُحُد، كما في الحديث.

From them is that Āli 'Imrān gives a detailed account of the story of Uhud, which is later completed in al-Nisā with His statement: {**Then what is the matter with you that you are divided into two parties about the hypocrites?**}[132] This was revealed in relation to when the Companions ﷽ differed on their attitudes towards the hypocrites after returning from the Battle of Uhud, as mentioned in the ḥadīth.[133]

ومنها: أن في آل عمران ذكرت الغزوة التي بعد أُحُد بقوله: ﴿الَّذِينَ اسْتَجَابُوا لِلَّهِ وَالرَّسُولِ مِنْ بَعْدِ مَا أَصَابَهُمُ الْقَرْحُ﴾ (آل عمران: ١٧٢)، وأشير إليها هنا بقوله: ﴿وَلَا تَهِنُوا فِي ابْتِغَاءِ الْقَوْمِ إِنْ تَكُونُوا تَأْلَمُونَ فَإِنَّهُمْ يَأْلَمُونَ كَمَا تَأْلَمُونَ﴾

129 Āli 'Imrān: 200

130 Al-Nisā: 1

131 [T] This is where the message or theme at the end of a chapter continues on to the beginning of the one that follows it. This is a point which reoccurs heavily in the book in order to establish connection between the *sūrahs*.

132 Al-Nisā: 88

133 Al-Bukhārī (6/59), Chapter of *Tafsīr*, on the authority of Zayd ibn Thābit and Muslim (8/128), Chapter of the Hypocrites.

(١٠٤) الآية.

From them is that in Āli 'Imrān the battle that took place after Uhud is also mentioned: **{Those who answered the call of Allah and the Messenger after being wounded.}**[134] This is indicated towards in the *āyah* in al-Nisā: **{And do not weaken in the pursuit of the enemy; if you are suffering then surely, they too are suffering as you are suffering.}**[135]

وبهذين الوجهين عرف أن تأخير النساء عن آل عمران أنسب من تقديمها عليها في مصحف ابن مسعود؛ لأن المذكور هنا ذيل ما في آل عمران وتابعه ولاحقه، فكانت بالتأخير أنسب.

From these viewpoints, we know that al-Nisā is rightly placed after Āli 'Imrān instead of vice versa, as it appears in the *muṣḥaf* of Ibn Mas'ūd. Al-Nisā concludes much of what Āli 'Imran opens, therefore al-Nisā following Āli 'Imrān is much more appropriate.

ومنها: أنه [لما] ذكر في آل عمران قصة خلق عيسى بلا أب، وأقيمت له الحجة بآدم، وفي ذلك تبرئة لأمه، خلافًا لما زعم اليهود، وتقريرًا لعبوديته، خلافًا لما ادعته النصارى، وذكر في هذه السورة الرد على الفريقين معًا: فرد على اليهود بقوله: ﴿وَقَوْلِهِمْ عَلَىٰ مَرْيَمَ بُهْتَانًا عَظِيمًا﴾ (١٥٦)، وعلى

134 This is in reference to the Battle of Ḥamra al-Asad which was a continuation of the Battle of Uhud. Once the Quraysh left the battle, they regretted that they did not seize al-Madīnah whilst they had the chance. This news reached the Messenger of Allah ﷺ and in a show of strength, they went out in pursuit of the Quraysh despite having injuries. See *Saḥīḥ al-Bukhārī* (5/130) and *Sīrat Ibn Hishām* (2/101).

135 Al-Nisā: 104

النصارى بقوله: ﴿لا تَغْلُوا فِي دِينِكُمْ وَلا تَقُولُوا عَلَى اللهِ إِلَّا الْحَقَّ إِنَّمَا الْمَسِيحُ عِيسَى ابْنُ مَرْيَمَ رَسُولُ اللهِ وَكَلِمَتُهُ أَلْقَاهَا إِلَى مَرْيَمَ وَرُوحٌ مِنْهُ﴾ إلى قوله: ﴿لَنْ يَسْتَنْكِفَ الْمَسِيحُ أَنْ يَكُونَ عَبْدًا لِلَّهِ﴾ (١٧١، ١٧٢).

From them is that Āli 'Imrān describes the story of 'Īsā being created without a father and draws a comparison with the creation of Ādam as proof for this, which absolves Īsā's mother from any blame; opposing what the Jews believed. At the same time it affirms his servitude to Allah, [refuting the idea of divinity for him and] opposing what the Christians believed. Al-Nisā refutes the beliefs of both aforementioned parties. In relation to what the Jews believed: {**And because of their disbelief and uttering against Maryam a grave slander.**}[136] And in relation to what the Christians believed: {**Do not exceed the limits in your religion, and do not say anything about Allah except the truth—surely the Messiah 'Īsā the son of Maryam was a messenger of Allah and His Word which He bestowed on Maryam and a spirit created by Him**} until His statement: {**Never would the Messiah disdain to be a servant of Allah.**}[137]

ومنها: أنه لما ذكر في آل عمران: ﴿إِنِّي مُتَوَفِّيكَ وَرَافِعُكَ إِلَيَّ﴾ (آل عمران: ٥٥)، ورد هنا على من زعم قتله بقوله: ﴿وَقَوْلِهِمْ إِنَّا قَتَلْنَا الْمَسِيحَ عِيسَى ابْنَ مَرْيَمَ رَسُولَ اللهِ وَمَا قَتَلُوهُ وَمَا صَلَبُوهُ وَلَكِنْ شُبِّهَ لَهُمْ وَإِنَّ الَّذِينَ اخْتَلَفُوا فِيهِ لَفِي شَكٍّ مِنْهُ مَا لَهُمْ بِهِ مِنْ عِلْمٍ إِلَّا اتِّبَاعَ الظَّنِّ وَمَا قَتَلُوهُ يَقِينًا، بَلْ رَفَعَهُ اللهُ﴾ (١٥٧، ١٥٨).

From them is due to that which is mentioned in Āli 'Imrān {**I will**

136 Al-Nisā: 156
137 Al-Nisā: 171-172

cause you to die and raise you to Myself.}[138] The doubt of him being killed is refuted and answered in al-Nisā: {**And because of their saying [in boast], "We killed the Messiah 'Īsā son of Maryam, the Messenger of Allah," but they did not kill him, nor crucify him, but it was a person who resembled him, and those who differ about this are full of doubts. They have no certain knowledge, they follow nothing but conjecture. For surely; they did not kill him, rather Allah raised him to Himself.}**[139]

ومنها: أنه لما قال في آل عمران في المتشابه: ﴿وَالرَّاسِخُونَ فِي الْعِلْمِ يَقُولُونَ آمَنَّا بِهِ كُلٌّ مِنْ عِنْدِ رَبِّنَا﴾ (آل عمران: ٧)، قال هنا: ﴿لَكِنِ الرَّاسِخُونَ فِي الْعِلْمِ مِنْهُمْ وَالْمُؤْمِنُونَ يُؤْمِنُونَ بِمَا أُنْزِلَ إِلَيْكَ﴾ (١٦٢) الآية.

From them is what Āli 'Imran includes regarding the obscure *āyāt*: {**And those who are firmly grounded in knowledge say: "We believe in it; the whole of it is from our Lord."}**[140] In al-Nisā He said: {**But those among them who are well-grounded in knowledge, and the faithful, believe in what has been sent down to you.}**[141]

ومنها: أنه لما قال في آل عمران: ﴿زُيِّنَ لِلنَّاسِ حُبُّ الشَّهَوَاتِ مِنَ النِّسَآءِ وَالْبَنِينَ وَالْقَنَاطِيرِ الْمُقَنْطَرَةِ مِنَ الذَّهَبِ وَالْفِضَّةِ وَالْخَيْلِ الْمُسَوَّمَةِ وَالْأَنْعَامِ وَالْحَرْثِ ذَلِكَ مَتَاعُ الْحَيَاةِ الدُّنْيَا﴾ (آل عمران: ١٤) الآية. فصل هذه الأشياء في السورة التي بعدها على نسق ما وقعت في الآية، ليعلم ما أحل الله من ذلك فيقتصر عليه، وما حرم فلا يتعدى إليه، لميل النفس إليه.

138 Āli 'Imrān: 55
139 Al-Nisā: 157-158
140 Āli 'Imrān: 7
141 Al-Nisā: 162

From them is that He said in Āli 'Imrān: {**Beautified for men is the love of things they desire, from women, children, amassing gold and silver, branded beautiful horses, cattle and well-tilled land. This is the pleasure of the present world's life; but Allah has the excellent return with Him.**}[142] These things are explained in greater detail throughout the following *sūrah* (al-Nisā), following the same arrangement of this *āyah* in order for the people to know what Allah has made permissible so they suffice with it, and what is made forbidden so they avoid it and do not like it.

ففصل في هذه السورة أحكام النساء ومباحاتها للابتداء بها في الآية السابقة في آل عمران، ولم يحتج إلى تفصيل البنين؛ لأن الأولاد أمر لازم [للإنسان] لا يترك منه شيء كما يترك من النساء، فليس فيهم مباح فيحتاج إلى بيانه، ومع ذلك أشير إليهم في قوله: ﴿وَلْيَخْشَ الَّذِينَ لَوْ تَرَكُوا مِنْ خَلْفِهِمْ ذُرِّيَّةً ضِعَافًا خَافُوا عَلَيْهِمْ فَلْيَتَّقُوا اللَّهَ وَلْيَقُولُوا قَوْلًا سَدِيدًا﴾ (٩).

Al-Nisā describes rulings pertaining to women; to whom marriage is permitted.[143] The desire for getting married to women was quoted in the *āyah* of Āli 'Imrān above. It does not require to elaborate upon offspring, because interaction with children is lawful and is not subject to constraints. As for women, clarification is needed to clarify who can be lawful and who cannot. Nonetheless, they were referred to in the statement of the Most High: {**And let those (guardians) have the same fear in their minds as they would have for their own, if they had left weak offspring behind. So let them fear Allah and speak right words.**}[144]

142 Āli 'Imrān: 14

143 Al-Nisā: 27-22

144 Al-Nisā: 9

ثم فصل في سورة المائدة أحكام السراق، وقطاع الطريق، لتعلقهم بالذهب والفضة الواقعين في الآية بعد النساء والبنين. ووقع في سورة النساء إشارة إلى ذلك في قسمة المواريث.

Thereafter, al-Mā'idah gives description to rulings pertaining to theft and robbery—due to them being related to the wealth of gold and silver, which were mentioned in the aforementioned *āyah* after women and offspring.[145] This is indicated to in Sūrah al-Nisā when the division of inheritance is discussed.

ثم فصل في سورة الأنعام أمر الحيوان والحرث، وهو بقية المذكور في آية آل عمران. فالنظر إلى هذه اللطيفة التي مَنَّ الله بإلهامها!

After this, there is found in Sūrah al-An'ām rulings connected to animals and agriculture. This is the remaining thing mentioned in the *āyah* of Āli 'Imrān above. So look at how delicate this sequence is, and awareness towards it is from the favour of Allah.

ثم ظهر لي أن سورة النساء فصل فيها ذكر البنين أيضًا، لأنه لما أخبر بحب الناس لهم وكان من ذلك إيثارهم على البنات في الميراث، وتخصيصهم به دونهن، تولى قسمة المواريث بنفسه، فقال: ﴿يُوصِيكُمُ اللَّهُ فِي أَوْلَادِكُمْ لِلذَّكَرِ مِثْلُ حَظِّ الْأُنْثَيَيْنِ﴾ (١١)، وقال: ﴿لِلرِّجَالِ نَصِيبٌ مِمَّا تَرَكَ الْوَالِدَانِ وَالْأَقْرَبُونَ وَلِلنِّسَاءِ نَصِيبٌ﴾ (٧). فرد على ما كانوا يصنعون من تخصيص البنين بالميراث، لحبهم إياهم، فكان ذلك تفصيلًا لما يحل

145 Al-Mā'idah: 33

ويحرم من إيثار البنين، اللازم عن الحب، وفي ضمن ذلك تفصيل لما يحل للذكر أخذه من الذهب والفضة وما يحرم.

What appears to be the case to me is that Sūrah al-Nisā also has rulings connected to sons within it. As Allah mentions that people love sons and such love made them favour sons over daughters in the matter of inheritance, giving all of the inheritance to their sons, He Himself undertook specification of the ratio of inheritance. He said: **{Allah commands you as regards your children's (inheritance); to the male, a portion equal to that of two females.}**[146] And He said: **{There is a share for men and a share for women from what is left by parents.}**[147] This rebukes the practice of those who designate their inheritance to their sons only, due to the bias in love given to them. This serves to clarify that which is permissible and that which is forbidden when it comes to favouring sons due to their love. It also clarifies what a male can and cannot have from gold and silver.

ومن الوجوه المناسبة لتقدم آل عمران على النساء: اشتراكها مع البقرة في الافتتاح بإنزال الكتاب، وفي الافتتاح بـ﴿الم﴾ وسائر السور المفتتحة بالحروف المقطعة كلها مقترنة، كيونس وتواليها، ومريم وطه، والطواسين، و﴿الم﴾ العنكبوت وتواليها، والحواميم، وفي ذلك أول دليل على اعتبار المناسبة في الترتيب بأوائل السور.

Also from the viewpoints as to why Āli 'Imrān precedes al-Nisā is that both *sūrahs*—like al-Baqarah—begin with the sending down of the revelation and with *alif-lām-mīm*. [You will find that this is a common

146 Al-Nisā: 11

147 Al-Nisā: 7

pattern in the Qur'ān,] that the *sūrahs* that commence with the same split letters are connected to each other. So the *sūrahs* that commence with *alif-lām-mīm* and other *sūrahs* which begin with letters, such as Yūnus being next to Hūd and Yūsuf, and Maryam next to Ṭa-ha, the *sūrahs* that begin with *ṭā-sīn*, the *alif-lām-mīm* of al-'Ankabūt and that which follows it, the *ḥā-mīm sūrahs* etc. all act as a primary proof that the order of the *sūrahs* in the arrangement of the Qur'ān takes into account their beginnings.

ولم يفرق بين السورتين من ذلك بما ليس مبدوءًا به سوى بين الأعراف ويونس اجتهادًا لا توقيفًا [كما سيأتي] ، والفصل بالزمر بين ﴿حم﴾ غافر و ﴿ص﴾ وسيأتي.

The exception to this, i.e. when two *sūrahs* with this type of beginning are not next to each other, is only between al-A'rāf and Yūnus, but this is due to *ijtihād* (scholarly judgement), and not because of it being from divine order. And also al-Zumar is placed between Sūrah Ghāfir—which begins with *ḥā-mīm*—and Sūrah Ṣād. Further detail regarding this will follow.

ومن الوجوه في ذلك أيضًا: اشتراكهما في التسمية بالزهراوين في حديث: ((اقرءوا الزهراوين: البقرة وآل عمران))، فكان افتتاح القرآن بهما نظير اختتامه بسورتي الفلق والناس، المشتركتين في التسمية بالمعوذتين.

Also from the reasons of the order [of al-Baqarah, Āli 'Imrān and then al-Nisā] is that al-Baqarah and Āli 'Imrān have been called al-Zahrāwayn (the two illuminating ones), as it appears in the ḥadīth, "Recite the Zahrāwayn; al-Baqarah and Āli 'Imrān."[148] [And it is noteworthy

148 Muslim (804), and it was collected by others.

to mention] that the Qur'ān commences with these two *sūrahs* and ends in a comparable manner, with al-Falaq and al-Nās being coupled together—which are named al-Mu'awidhatayn.

سورة المائدة

Sūrah al-Mā'idah

وقد تقدَّم وجه في مناسبتها.

A brief explanation of the appropriateness of the position of al-Mā'idah [being the fifth *sūrah* in the order of *sūrahs*] has somewhat preceded.

وأقول: هذه السورة أيضًا شارحة لبقية مجملات سورة البقرة، فإن آية الأطعمة والذبائح فيها أبسط منها في البقرة، وكذا ما حرمه الكفار تبعًا لآبائهم في البقرة موجز، وفي هذه السورة مطنب أبلغ إطناب في قوله: ﴿مَا جَعَلَ اللهُ مِنْ بَحِيرَةٍ وَلا سَآئِبَةٍ ...﴾ (١٠٣، ١٠٤).

I say: This *sūrah* also explains the rest of the general parts of Sūrah al-Baqarah. The *āyāt* of food and slaughtering within it (describing what is permissible from them and the laws of eating the food of non-Muslims[149]) are more detailed than that which was mentioned in al-Baqarah.[150] Likewise, al-Mā'idah addresses what the disbelievers made forbidden following the practice of their forefathers, which is a matter that was mentioned in brief in al-Baqarah. This *sūrah* addresses this topic in detail in His statement: {**Allah has not institut-**

---

149 See al-Mā'idah: 3-5

150 See al-Baqarah: 172-173

ed things like *baḥīrah* (a she-camel whose milk was spared for the idols and nobody was allowed to milk it) or a *sā'ibah* (a she-camel let loose for free pasture for their false gods, e.g. idols, etc., and nothing was allowed to be carried on it), or a *waṣīlah* (a she-camel set free for idols because it has given birth to a she-camel at its first delivery and then again gives birth to a she-camel at its second delivery) or a *ḥam* (a stallion-camel freed from work for their idols, after it had finished a number of copulations assigned for it, all these animals were liberated in honour of idols as practised by pagan Arabs in the pre-Islamic period)...}[151]

وفي البقرة ذكر القصاص في القتلى، وهنا ذكر أول من سن القتل، والسبب الذي لأجله وقع، وقال: ﴿مِنْ أَجْلِ ذَٰلِكَ كَتَبْنَا عَلَىٰ بَنِي إِسْرَائِيلَ أَنَّهُ مَن قَتَلَ نَفْسًا بِغَيْرِ نَفْسٍ أَوْ فَسَادٍ فِي الْأَرْضِ فَكَأَنَّمَا قَتَلَ النَّاسَ جَمِيعًا وَمَنْ أَحْيَاهَا فَكَأَنَّمَا أَحْيَا النَّاسَ جَمِيعًا﴾ (٣٢)، وذلك أبسط من قوله [في البقرة] : ﴿وَلَكُمْ فِي الْقِصَاصِ حَيَاةٌ﴾ (البقرة: ١٧٩).

Similarly, al-Baqarah makes reference to capital punishment for murder[152] and in al-Mā'idah it describes the first person who committed murder and the reason for why the ruling is as such: **{Because of that We ordained for the Children of Israel that if anyone killed a person not in retaliation of murder, or (and) to spread mischief in the land—it would be as if he killed all of mankind, and if anyone saved a life, it would be as if he saved the life of all mankind.}**[153] This is more detailed than that which was generally mentioned in al-Baqarah: **{And there is for you in legal retribution [saving of] life.}**[154]

151 Al-Mā'idah: 103-104

152 See al-Baqarah: 178-179

153 Al-Mā'idah: 32

154 Al-Baqarah: 179

وفي البقرة: ﴿وَإِذْ قُلْنَا ادْخُلُوا هَذِهِ الْقَرْيَةَ﴾ (البقرة: ٥٨)، وذكرت قصتها [هنا مطولة. وذكر في البقرة من ارتد مقتصرًا عليه، وقال] هنا: ﴿فَسَوْفَ يَأْتِي اللهُ بِقَوْمٍ يُحِبُّهُمْ وَيُحِبُّونَهُ﴾ (٥٤).

Also in al-Baqarah it says: {**And when We said: "Enter this town (Jerusalem)"**}[155] This incident is mentioned with full detail in al-Mā'idah, and likewise apostasy is mentioned in al-Baqarah in a concise form, whereas here He said: {**Whoever from among you turns back from his religion (Islam), Allah will bring a people whom He will love and they will love Him.**}[156]

وفي البقرة قصة الأيمان موجزة، وزاد هنا بسطًا بذكر الكفارة.

And in al-Baqarah oaths are described in brief, and in this *sūrah* they are elaborated upon through detailing the expiation for breaking them.[157]

وفي البقرة قال في الخمر والميسر: ﴿فِيهِمَآ إِثْمٌ كَبِيرٌ وَمَنَافِعُ لِلنَّاسِ وَإِثْمُهُمَآ أَكْبَرُ مِن نَّفْعِهِمَا﴾ (البقرة: ٢١٩). وزاد في هذه السورة ذمها، وصرح بتحريمها.

In al-Baqarah, laws connected to alcohol and gambling are also made clear: {**They ask you concerning alcoholic drink and gambling. Say: "In them is a great sin, and [some] benefit for men, but the sin of them is greater than their benefit."**}[158] However in al-Mā'idah there is more description and explicitness in regards to its prohibition.[159]

155 Al-Baqarah: 58
156 Al-Mā'idah: 54
157 Al-Mā'idah: 89 and al-Baqarah: 225
158 Al-Baqarah: 219
159 Al-Mā'idah: 90-91

وفيها من الاعتلاق بسورة الفاتحة: بيان المغضوب عليهم والضالين في قوله: ﴿قُلْ هَلْ أُنَبِّئُكُم بِشَرٍّ مِنْ ذَلِكَ مَثُوبَةً عِنْدَ اللَّهِ مَنْ لَعَنَهُ اللَّهُ وَغَضِبَ عَلَيْهِ﴾ (٦٠) الآية. وقوله: ﴿قَدْ ضَلُّوا مِنْ قَبْلُ وَأَضَلُّوا كَثِيرًا وَضَلُّوا عَنْ سَوَاءِ السَّبِيلِ﴾ (٧٧).

Al-Mā'idah also enjoys a connection with al-Fātiḥah as well. The path of those who have Allah's anger and the misguided is given explanation in His statement: **{Say: "Shall I inform you of something worse than that, regarding the recompense from Allah: those who incurred the curse of Allah and His wrath."}**[160] And His statement: **{People who went astray in times gone by, and who misled many, and strayed from the straight path.}**[161]

وأما اعتلاقها بسورة النساء، فقد ظهر لي فيه وجه بديع جدًّا. وذلك أن سورة النساء اشتملت على عدة عقود صريحًا وضمنًا، فالصريح: عقود الأنكحة، وعقد الصداق، وعقد الحلف، في قوله: ﴿وَالَّذِينَ عَقَدَتْ أَيْمَانُكُمْ فَآتُوهُمْ نَصِيبَهُمْ﴾ (النساء: ٣٣). وعقد الأيمان في هذه الآية، وبعد ذلك عقد المعاهدة والأمان في قوله: ﴿إِلَّا الَّذِينَ يَصِلُونَ إِلَى قَوْمٍ بَيْنَكُمْ وَبَيْنَهُمْ مِيثَاقٌ﴾ (النساء: ٩٠)، وقوله: ﴿وَإِنْ كَانَ مِنْ قَوْمٍ بَيْنَكُمْ وَبَيْنَهُمْ مِيثَاقٌ فَدِيَةٌ﴾ (النساء: ٩٢).

As for its connection to al-Nisā, then it appears to me that al-Mā'idah completed al-Nisā from [a number of] aspects. One of them is of a

160 Al-Mā'idah: 60
161 Al-Mā'idah: 77

[particularly] marvellous nature, namely that Al-Nisā includes explanations of rulings connected to contracts; both clear contracts and financial liabilities. Clear contracts include: marriage, dowries and pledges. He said about this: **{To those also with whom you have made a pledge (brotherhood), give them their due portion (which was pledged).}**[162] The pledge of oaths in this *āyah*, and then the treaty of peace and protection in His statement: **{Except those who join a group, between you and whom there is a treaty [of peace.]}**[163] And His statement: **{And if he was from a people with whom you have a treaty—then a compensation payment presented to his family.}**[164]

والضمني: عقد الوصية، والوديعة، والوكالة، والعارية، والإجارة، وغير ذلك من الداخل في عموم قوله: ﴿إِنَّ اللَّهَ يَأْمُرُكُمْ أَنْ تُؤَدُّوا الْأَمَانَاتِ إِلَى أَهْلِهَا﴾ (النساء: ٥٨)، فناسب أن يعقب بسورة مفتتحة بالأمر بالوفاء بالعقود، فكأنه قيل: ﴿يَا أَيُّهَا الَّذِينَ آمَنُوا أَوْفُوا بِالْعُقُودِ﴾ (١) التي فرغ من ذكرها في السورة التي تمت، فكان ذلك غاية في التلاحم والتناسب والارتباط.

As for financial liabilities, this refers to bequeathments, deposits for safe-keeping, agency, loans, renting and other such matters that fall under the general purport of His statement: **{Verily Allah commands that you should render back the trusts to those to whom they are due.}**[165] So it is befitting that [after such heavy reference to contracts in al-Nisā,] al-Mā'idah commences with the command to uphold oaths and contracts: **{O you who believe! Fulfil (your) obligations}**,[166] as if it is being said to fulfil that which was mentioned in the previous

162 Al-Nisā: 33
163 Al-Nisā: 90
164 Al-Nisā: 92
165 Al-Nisā: 58
166 Al-Mā'idah: 1

sūrah. So al-Mā'idah carries on from where al-Nisā finished off, and this explains how al-Mā'idah completes al-Nisā and the strong connection that they have with one another.

ووجه آخر في تقديم سورة النساء، وتأخير سورة المائدة؛ وهو: أن تلك أولها ﴿يَا أَيُّهَا النَّاس﴾ (النساء: ١)، وفيها الخطاب بذلك في مواضع، وهو أشبه بخطاب [الكفار وتنزيل] المكي، [وهذه أولها: ﴿يَا أَيُّهَا الَّذِينَ آمَنُوا﴾ (١) وفيها الخطاب بذلك في مواضع، وهو أشبه بخطاب المدني] وتقديم العام وشبه المكي أنسب.

From another perspective, al-Nisā precedes al-Mā'idah because al-Nisā begins with an address to all of mankind: {**O mankind!**} And this form of address was utilised in a number of instances within the *sūrah*. This resembles the Makkan stage where the address was for all of mankind to respond, whereas al-Mā'idah commences with: {**O you who believe!**} And this form of address was utilised in a number of instances within the *sūrah*. This resembles the Madanī period—therefore it makes chronological sense that al-Nisā comes before al-Mā'idah based on their level of address (i.e. it is more appropriate to commence with the Makkan period), and furthermore it is befitting that the general is mentioned before the specific.

ثم إن هاتين السورتين في التلازم والاتحاد نظير البقرة وآل عمران، فتلكما في تقرير الأصول، من الوحدانية، والكتاب، والنبوة، وهاتان في تقرير الفروع الحكمية.

Furthermore, these two *sūrahs* are interlinked and relevant to each other just as al-Baqarah and Āli 'Imrān are, as the latter are themed at explaining *aqīdah*; *tawḥīd*, the Book, and Prophethood while al-Nisā and al-Mā'idah are to establish rulings within the Sharī'ah.

وقد ختمت المائدة بصفة القدرة، كما افتتحت النساء بذلك.

Al-Mā'idah ends with affirmation of the attribute of All-Ability for Allah[167] and this is precisely how al-Nisā starts off.[168]

وافتتحت النساء ببدء الخلق، وختمت المائدة بالمنتهى من البعث والجزاء، فكأنهما سورة واحدة، اشتملت على الأحكام من المبتدأ إلى المنتهى.

Al-Nisā begins with description of the beginning of the creation, and al-Maidah ends with description of the resurrection and its recompense. [So from this aspect] it is as if they are one *sūrah* that encompasses all rulings from the beginning to the end.

ولما وقع في سورة النساء: ﴿إِنَّا أَنْزَلْنَا إِلَيْكَ الْكِتَابَ بِالْحَقِّ لِتَحْكُمَ بَيْنَ النَّاسِ﴾ (النساء: ١٠٥) الآيات، وكانت نازلة في قصة سارق سرق درعًا، فصل في سورة المائدة أحكام السراق والخائنين.

The connection between the two *sūrahs* can also be seen by looking at the *āyah* in al-Nisā: {**Surely, We have sent down to you the Book in truth that you might judge between people.**}[169] The context in which this *āyah* was revealed was when a person stole a shield,[170] however the rulings connected to theft and its punishment were later detailed

167 Al-Mā'idah: 120

168 Al-Nisā: 1

169 Al-Nisā: 105

170 See *Tafsīr Ibn Kathīr* (2/358-359).

in al-Mā'idah.

ولما ذكر في سورة النساء أنه أنزل إليك الكتاب لتحكم بين الناس، ذكر في سورة المائدة آيات في الحكم بما أنزل الله حتى بين الكفار، وكرر قوله: ﴿وَمَنْ لَمْ يَحْكُم بِمَا أَنْزَلَ اللَّهُ﴾ (٤٤، ٤٥، ٤٦).

Furthermore, the instance where al-Nisā explains that the Book was sent so **{That you might judge between people}**, al-Mā'idah expands upon the theme of judging with what Allah has revealed—and even detailing where the judgement is for a non-Muslim. And he repeated this statement [thrice]: **{And whosoever does not judge by what Allah has revealed.}**[171]

فانظر إلى هذه السور الأربع المدنيات، وحسن ترتيبها، وتلاحمها، وتناسقها، وتلازمها.

So contemplate upon these four Madanī *sūrahs*, their perfect order, the way they complement one another, give context to one another and complete one another.

وقد افتتحت البقرة التي هي أول ما نزل في المدينة، وختمت بالمائدة التي هي آخر ما نزل بها، كما في حديث الترمذي.

[Even more poignant] is that al-Baqarah (the opening of the four) was the first Madanī *sūrah* to be revealed and al-Mā'idah (the concluding of the four) was the last Madanī *sūrah* to be revealed, as stated in the ḥadīth of al-Tirmidhī.[172]

171 Repeated in al-Mā'idah: 44, 45 and 47

172 Al-Tirmidhī (8/436-437) on the authority of 'Abdullāh ibn 'Amr ibn al-'Āṣ.

سورة الأنعام

Sūrah al-An'ām

قال بعضهم: مناسبة هذه السورة لآخر المائدة: أنها افتتحت بالحمد، وتلك ختمت بفصل القضاء، وهما متلازمتان كما قال: ﴿وَقُضِيَ بَيْنَهُمْ بِالْحَقِّ وَقِيلَ الْحَمْدُ لِلَّهِ رَبِّ الْعَالَمِينَ﴾ (الزمر: ٧٥).

Some scholars have stated that the relationship between the beginning of al-An'ām and the end of al-Mā'idah is that al-An'ām commences with the praise of Allah and al-Mā'idah concludes whilst detailing judgement, and these two matters are often intertwined, as in His statement: {**And they will be judged with truth, and it will be said, "All praise and thanks be to Allah, the Lord of all creation."**}[173]

و[أقول] قد ظهر لي بفضل الله مع ما قدمت الإشارة إليه في آية ﴿زُيِّنَ لِلنَّاسِ﴾. أنه لما ذكر في آخر المائدة: ﴿لِلَّهِ مُلْكُ السَّمَاوَاتِ وَالْأَرْضِ وَمَا فِيهِنَّ﴾ (المائدة: ١٢٠) على سبيل الإجمال، افتتح هذه السورة بشرح ذلك وتفصيله.

I say: What appears to me to be the case—with the favour of Allah, is what I indicated towards previously in the *āyah* of Āli 'Imrān: {**Beau-**

173 Al-Zumar: 75

tified for men is the love of things they desire.}[174] This process occurs again in relation to the generalities found in the statement at the end of al-Mā'idah: **{To Allah belongs the dominion of the heavens and the earth and all that is within it.}**[175] The current *sūrah* [which we are discussing] opens with explanation of this and with further details regarding it.

فبدأ بذكر: أنه خلق السماوات والأرض، وضم إليه أنه جعل الظلمات والنور، وهو بعض ما تضمنه قوله: ﴿وَمَا فِيهِنَّ﴾ في آخر المائدة، وضمَّن قوله: ﴿الْحَمْدُ لِلَّهِ﴾ [أول الأنعام] أن له ملك جميع المحامد، وهو من بسط [جميع]: ﴿لِلَّهِ مُلْكُ السَّمَاوَاتِ وَالْأَرْضِ وَمَا فِيهِنَّ﴾ [في آخر المائدة].

So al-An'ām begins with the mention of the creation of the heavens, the earth and also light and darkness. And these are some of that which is comprised in His statement at the end of al-Mā'idah: **{And all that is within it.}** [Which then continues its theme] at the beginning of al-An'am: **{All praise be to Allah.}** Meaning that all praiseworthy things are under His dominion, expanding upon the end of al-Mā'idah: **{To Allah belongs the dominion of the heavens and the earth and all that is within it.}**

ثم ذكر: أنه خلق النوع الإنساني، وقضى له أجلًا مسمى، وجعل له أجلًا آخر للبعث، وأنه منشئ القرون قرنًا بعد قرنا، ثم قال: ﴿قُل لِّمَن مَّا فِي السَّمَاوَاتِ وَالْأَرْضِ قُل لِّلَّهِ﴾ (١٢)، فأثبت له ملك جميع المنظورات، ثم قال: ﴿وَلَهُ مَا سَكَنَ فِي اللَّيْلِ وَالنَّهَارِ﴾ (١٣)، فأثبت له ملك جميع

174 Āli 'Imrān: 12

175 Al-Mā'idah: 120

المظروفات في الزمان، ثم ذكر أنه خلق سائر الحيوان، من الدواب والطير، ثم خلق النوم واليقظة، والموت والحياة، ثم أكثر في أثناء السورة من ذكر الخلق والإنشاء لما فيهن من النيرين، والنجوم، وفلق الإصباح، وخلق الحب والنوى، وإنزال الماء، وإخراج النبات والثمار بأنواعها، وإنشاء جنات معروشات وغير معروشات، والأنعام، ومنها حمولة وفرش، وكل ذلك تفصيل لملكه ما فيهن، وهذه مناسبة جليلة.

Al-An'ām then continues to describe the creation of man and that their period within creation is limited. They will then be caused to die and then resurrected and this is evident with the passing of generations upon generations of nations having their time expired. Then He said: {**Say: "To whom belongs all that is in the heavens and the earth?" Say: "To Allah."**}[176] This affirms that all tangible objects are from the dominion that belong only to Allah, and then it says: {**And to Him belongs whatsoever exists in the night and the day.**}[177] This affirms that all intangible things also belong to Him, all time and place is within His dominion. The topic of the *sūrah* then moves on to describing the design of the rest of creation; the animals, the birds, the creation of sleep and awakening and death and life. Then praise continues to extend to Him for the creation and originating within it the sun and moon, stars, daybreak and morning, the splitting of seeds, the sending down of rain, life given to plantation and its varying types, causing gardens to grow, [both] trellised and untrellised, livestock which are also used for transportation and apparel; all of this gives explanation to whom the dominion is and what He has created within it. This is a splendid display of the appropriateness of its location.

176 Al-An'ām: 12

177 Al-An'ām: 13

ولما كان المقصود من هذه السورة بيان الخلق والملك، أكثر فيها من ذكر الرب الذي هو بمعنى المالك والخالق والمنشئ، واقتصر فيها على ما يتعلق بذلك من بدء الخلق الإنساني والملكوتي، والملكي والشيطاني، والحيواني والنباتي، وما تضمنته من الوصايا، فكلها متعلقة بالمعاش والقوام الدنيوي، ثم أشار إلى أشراط الساعة [والبعث].

As the theme of this *sūrah* is to describe the dominion of Allah and His creation; it extensively describes Allah as being the Lord, i.e. Him being the Owner, Creator and Originator. He sufficed in this *sūrah* by mentioning matters related to it such as: The beginning of the creation of humans, worlds, angels, devils, animals and plantation. All of the aforementioned are needed and connected to human life on earth. After mentioning all of this, the signs of the Hour and Resurrection are denoted.

فقد جمعت هذه السورة جميع المخلوقات بأسرها، وما يتعلق بها، وما يرجع إليها، فظهر بذلك مناسبة افتتاح السور المكية بها، وتقديمها على ما تقدم نزوله منها.

So Sūrah al-An'am describes the creation of all created beings and that which is associated to them and related to them, so it is apparent from this the appropriateness of the Makkan *sūrahs* beginning with it and likewise for it preceding those *sūrahs* which were revealed before it.

وهي في جمعها الأصول والعلوم والمصالح الدنيوية نظير سورة البقرة في جمعها [الأصول و] العلوم والمصالح الدينية، وما ذكر فيها من العبادات

المحضة، فعلى وجه الاختصار والإيماء، كنظير ما وقع في البقرة من علوم بدء الخلق ونحوه، فإنه على وجه الإيجاز والإشارة:

Al-An'ām also comprises of all fundamentals and knowledge as well as worldly interests on earth and what will create a harmonious life for them on it; just like how al-Baqarah comprises of all fundamentals and knowledge and how they can create a harmonious spiritual life. Al-Baqarah is themed at discussing worship and brief rulings connected to the materialistic world. An example of this is that al-Baqarah—like al-An'ām—also gives description to the beginning of the creation but in a short manner.

فإن قلت: فلِمَ لا أفتتح القرآن بهذه السورة مقدَّمة على سورة البقرة؛ لأن بدء الخلق سابق على الأحكام والتعبدات؟!

If it is queried: Why didn't the Qur'ān commence with al-An'ām and precede with it before al-Baqarah, considering that it is themed at describing the beginning of creation and this precedes rulings and worship?

قلت: للإشارة إلى أن مصالح الدين والآخرة مقدَّمة على مصالح المعاش والدنيا، ولأن المقصود [من الخلق] إنما هو العبادة، فقدم ما هو الأهم في نظر الشرع؛ ولأن علم بدء الخلق كالفضلة، وعلم الأحكام والتكاليف متعين على كل واحد؛ فلذلك لا ينبغي النظر في علم بدء الخلق وما جرى مجراه من التواريخ إلا بعد النظر في علم الأحكام وإتقانه.

The answer is: To give us understanding that matters of religion and the hereafter precede the worldly matters, and that worship is in fact the very reason for the creation of man. Therefore, the Qur'ān commences with that which is the most valuable according to the Sharī'ah.[178] It delays the description of the design of creation and man as this is a subsidiary knowledge, but the knowledge of the religion and its mandated rulings is binding upon everyone. So for this reason, delving into the knowledge of the beginning of creation and matters related to it such as history should not be except after delving into the rulings of religion and attaining proficiency within this.

ثم ظهر لي بحمد الله وجه آخر، أتقن مما تقدم، وهو: أنه لما ذكر في سورة المائدة: ﴿يَا أَيُّهَا الَّذِينَ آمَنُوا لا تُحَرِّمُوا طَيِّبَاتِ مَآ أَحَلَّ اللهُ لَكُمْ وَلا تَعْتَدُوا﴾ (المائدة: ٨٧) إلى آخره [ثم ذكر بعده: ﴿مَا جَعَلَ اللهُ مِنْ بَحِيرَةٍ﴾ (المائدة: ١٠٣) إلى آخره] فأخبر عن الكفار أنهم حرموا أشياء مما رزقهم الله افتراء عليه، وكان القصد بذلك تحذير المؤمنين أن يُحرِّموا شيئًا مما أحل الله، فيشابهوا بذلك الكفار في صنيعهم وكان ذكر ذلك على سبيل الإيجاز، ساق هذه السورة لبيان ما حرمه الكفار في صنيعهم، فأتى به على الوجه الأبين والنمط الأكمل، ثم جادلهم فيه، وأقام الدلائل على بطلانه، وعارضهم وناقضهم، إلى غير ذلك مما اشتملت عليه القصة، فكانت

178 An example of this is the *āyah* that comes in al-Baqarah: {**O mankind! Worship your Lord (Allah)**} [al-Baqarah: 21]. The Qur'ān does not have anything similar to this *āyah* in the same wording. Al-Kirmānī said about this *āyah*, "The command to worship here is the command to *al-tawḥīd*, it is the first matter that the Muslim is commanded with and thus it is the very first command in the Qur'ān. Then the Qur'ān describes everything which is a branch of this foundation as the whole religion is built upon it (i.e. *tawḥīd*)." See *Asrār al-Takrār fī al-Qur'ān* (p. 22).

هذه السورة شرحًا لما تضمنته المائدة من ذلك على سبيل الإجمال، وتفصيلًا وبسطًا، وإتمامًا وإطنابًا.

Also from another angle, which appears to me to be the case—which all praises are due to Allah for—is that al-Baqarah is given precedence in order over al-Anʿām because al-Anʿām continues on from al-Mā'idah where Allah said: {**O you who believe! Do not make the *ṭayyibāt* (wholesome) unlawful for yourselves, which Allah has made lawful to you, and do not transgress (in them)**}[179] until the end [of the context in describing rulings connected to what is lawful,] then He said: {**Allah has not instituted things like *baḥīrah* (a she-camel whose milk was spared for the idols and nobody was allowed to milk it)**}[180] to the end. So what is being informed about here is regarding disbelievers who declared lawful things which were provided to them by Allah to be forbidden as a lie against Him. The point in mentioning this is to explain to the believer the deviance of making unlawful what Allah had made lawful. If the believers were to do something similar, they would resemble the non-believers in this and all of this is mentioned in a concise yet comprehensive manner. However, al-Anʿām expands on the above attitude of how the non-believers changed and invented rulings in the religious code. The *sūrah* explains that this became a habit of theirs and the *sūrah* is themed at explaining this throughout, giving detailed descriptions as to how they invented and then a rebuttal of all of their accusations. It establishes the proof against them and their falsehood. It points out their fallacies and contradictions and all the other flaws found in the events this *sūrah* is aimed at explaining. As a result, this *sūrah* serves as an explanation of al-Mā'idah; the generalities that appear in al-Mā'idah are continued on in al-Anʿām but with further detail, comprehensiveness and

179 Al-Mā'idah: 87

180 Al-Mā'idah: 103

expressiveness.[181]

وافتتحت بذكر الخلق والملك؛ لأن الخالق والمالك هو الذي له التصرف في ملكه ومخلوقاته إباحة ومنعًا، وتحريمًا وتحليلًا، فيجب ألا يتعدى عليه بالتصرف في ملكه.

Al-An'ām begins with the creation and dominion of Allah,[182] as He is al-Khāliq and al-Mālik and controls and maintains His creation; creating and allowing or preventing things from occurring within it. The *sūrah* has legislation within it making things *ḥalāl* and *ḥarām*. All of this teaches us that none are able to transgress whatever He wills and creates within it.

وكانت هذه السورة بأسرها متعلقة بالفاتحة من وجه كونها شارحة لإجمال قوله: ﴿رَبِّ الْعَالَمِينَ﴾ وبالبقرة من حيث شرحها لإجمال قوله: ﴿الَّذِي خَلَقَكُمْ وَالَّذِينَ مِنْ قَبْلِكُمْ﴾ (البقرة: ٢١)، وقوله: ﴿هُوَ الَّذِي خَلَقَ لَكُم مَّا فِي الْأَرْضِ جَمِيعًا﴾ (البقرة: ٢٩)، وبآل عمران من جهة تفصيلها لقوله: ﴿وَالْأَنْعَامِ وَالْحَرْثِ﴾ (آل عمران: ١٤)، وقوله: ﴿كُلُّ نَفْسٍ ذَائِقَةُ الْمَوْتِ﴾ (آل عمران: ١٨٥) الآية.

Al-An'ām also possesses a connection with al-Fātiḥah, as it explains the generalities of His statement: **{The Lord of all creation.}** And likewise with al-Baqarah as it explains the generalities of His statement: **{Your Lord (Allah), Who created you and those who were before**

181 Al-An'ām: 139-136

182 Al-An'ām: 3-1

you.}[183] And that of His statement: **{He it is Who created for you all that is on earth.}**[184] And with Āli 'Imrān from the aspect of it explaining His statement: **{Branded beautiful horses, cattle and well-tilled land}**[185] and His statement: **{Everyone shall taste death.}**[186]

وبالنساء من جهة ما فيها من بدء الخلق، والتقبيح لما حرموه على أزواجهم، وقتل البنات بالوأد.

And likewise with al-Nisā, from the aspect of what it includes in description of the beginning of creation and also from the aspect of what it includes from censure regarding those who made the lawful forbidden with their wives, and the prohibition of the practice of burying daughters alive.[187]

وبالمائدة من حيث اشتمالها على الأطعمة بأنواعها.

And it has a connection with al-Mā'idah due to what it includes from the topic of food and its types.[188]

وفي افتتاح السور المكية بها وجهان آخران من المناسبة.

Now if we reflect upon why it is utilised as the opening of the Makkan *sūrahs*, then there are also two other perspectives that display its appropriateness:

الأول: افتتاحها بالحمد.

183 Al-Baqarah: 21
184 Al-Baqarah: 29
185 Āli 'Imrān: 14
186 Āli 'Imrān: 185
187 Al-An'ām: 140
188 Al-An'ām: 141-148

Firstly, it starts with praises for Allah alone (i.e. signalling to *tawḥīd*).

والثاني: مشابهتها للبقرة، المفتتح بها السور المدنية، من حيث أن كلًّا منهما نزل مشيعًا. ففي حديث أحمد: ((البقرة سنام القرآن وذروته، نزل مع كل آية منها ثمانون ملكًا)) ، وروى الطبراني وغيره من طرق: ((أن الأنعام شيعها سبعون ألف ملك))، وفي رواية: ((خمسمائة ملك)).

Secondly, there are parallels between it and al-Baqarah—the opening of the Madanī *sūrahs*—as both were revealed, accompanied with angels. According to the ḥadīth of Aḥmad, "Al-Baqarah is the chief of the Qur'ān and its peak. With every *āyah* of it, eighty angels descended."[189] [This is directly comparable] to the ḥadīth reported from different routes by al-Ṭabarānī and others, "Al-An'ām was accompanied with seventy thousand angels", and in another narration, "Five hundred angels."[190]

ووجه آخر، وهو: أن كل ربع من القرآن افتتح بسورة أولها الحمد. [فأول القرآن سورة ﴿الْحَمْدُ﴾] (٥)، وهذه للربع الثاني، والكهف للربع الثالث، وسبأ وفاطر للربع الرابع.

From another perspective, every fourth of the Qur'ān begins with a *sūrah* which begins with praise of Allah, and the end of al-Mā'idah signifies the completion of the first quarter of the *muṣḥaf*—which commences with {***Al-ḥamdu***}, thus the second quarter commences

189 Collected by Aḥmad in *al-Musnad* (5/26) on the authority of Ma'qal ibn Yassār, al-Dārimī in *Faḍā'il al-Qur'ān* (2/447) from Ibn Mas'ūd and al-Haythamī in *Majma' al-Zawā'id* (6/311), which was supported by al-Ṭabarānī.

190 Collected by al-Haythamī in *Majma' al-Zawā'id* (7/19-20) from Ibn 'Umar, which was supported by al-Ṭabarānī.

with al-Anʿām. The third quarter commences with al-Kahf, the fourth quarter commences with Saba and Fāṭir.

وجميع هذه الوجوه التي استنبطتها من المناسبات بالنسبة إلى أسرار القرآن كنقطة من بحر.

All of these aspects of the appropriateness of this *sūrah's* order which I have concluded are like the similitude of a drop taken from a sea compared to the actual secrets of the Qur'ān.

ولما كانت هذه السورة لبيان بدء الخلق، ذكر فيها ما وقع عند بدء الخلق، وهو قوله: ﴿كَتَبَ عَلَىٰ نَفْسِهِ الرَّحْمَةَ﴾ (١٢)، ففي الصحيح: ((لما فرغ الله من الخلق، وقضى القضية، كتب كتابًا عنده فوق العرش: إن رحمتي سبقت غضبي)).

As al-Anʿām deals with describing the beginning of creation, it mentions an event that occurred during the beginning of creation, in His statement: {**He has prescribed mercy for Himself.**}[191] The description of this event was reported in the *Ṣaḥīḥ*, "When Allah completed the creation, and decreed all its decrees; He wrote with Himself above His throne: 'My mercy superseded My anger.'"[192]

191 Al-Anʿām: 12

192 Collected by al-Bukhārī (4/129).

سورة الأعراف

Sūrah al-A'rāf

أقول: مناسبة وضع هذه السورة عقب سورة الأنعام فيما ألهمني الله سبحانه: أن سورة الأنعام لما كانت لبيان الخلق، وقال فيها: ﴿هُوَ الَّذِي خَلَقَكُمْ مِنْ طِينٍ﴾ (الأنعام: ٢)، وقال في بيان القرون: ﴿كَمْ أَهْلَكْنَا مِنْ قَبْلِهِمْ مِنْ قَرْنٍ﴾ (الأنعام: ٦)، وأشير فيها إلى ذكر المرسلين، وتعداد كثير منهم، وكانت الأمور الثلاثة على وجه الإجمال، لا التفصيل، ذُكرت هذه السورة عقبها، لأنها مشتملة على شرح الأمور الثلاثة وتفصيلها.

I say: The appropriateness of Sūrah al-A'rāf following Sūrah al-An'ām—with what Allah has inspired me with—is that al-An'am gives detail to the beginning of creation, this is found in His statement: **{He it is Who has created you from clay.}**[193] And His statement in the creation of man in a sequence of generations: **{Have they not seen how many a generation before them We have destroyed whom We had established on the earth?}**[194] There is also reference given to the sending of Messengers within this context and them being of great number. Therefore, the beginning of al-An'ām contains three general topics: [**{He it is Who has created you from clay}**, **{Have they not seen how many a generation before them We have destroyed whom We**

---

193 Al-An'ām: 2

194 Al-An'ām: 6

had established on the earth?}, and it mentioned sending the messengers and specifying many of them.] These are mentioned in a general manner and not detailed. Thus al-A'rāf concludes these matters as it contains an explanation of all three in a more detailed form.

فبسط فيها قصة خلق آدم أبلغ بسط، بحيث لم تبسط في سورة كما بسطت فيها، وذلك تفصيل إجمال قوله: ﴿خَلَقَكُمْ مِنْ طِينٍ﴾ (الأنعام: ٢)، ثم فصلت قصص المرسلين وأممهم، وكيفية إهلاكهم تفصيلًا تامًّا شافيًا مستوعبًا، لم يقع نظيره في سورة غيرها، وذلك بسط حال القرون المهلَكة ورسلهم، فكانت هذه السورة شرحًا لتلك الآيات الثلاث.

In al-A'rāf further detail to the creation of the first man is given. The story of Ādam is explained in a detailed manner which is not found in any other *sūrah*.[195] This adds explanation to the generality found in His statement: **{He it is Who has created you from clay.}**[196] Thereafter, al-A'rāf moves onto describing the stories of the Messengers, the nations they were sent to and how they were destroyed. The explanation is detailed, complete and comprehensive. This level of description in al-A'rāf is like no other in the Qur'ān[197] as al-A'rāf gives a chronological description to the sending of Messengers and the specific manner as to how each nation was destroyed. So al-A'raf serves as an explanation of those three aforementioned *āyāt*.

وأيضًا، فذلك تفصيل قوله: ﴿وَهُوَ الَّذِي جَعَلَكُمْ خَلَائِفَ الْأَرْضِ﴾ (الأنعام: ٦)، ولهذا صدَّر هذه السورة بخلق آدم الذي جعله الله في الأرض

195 Al-A'rāf: 11-25
196 Al-An'ām: 2
197 Al-A'rāf: 59-176

خليفة. وقال في قصة عاد: ﴿جَعَلَكُمْ خُلَفَآءَ مِنۢ بَعْدِ قَوْمِ نُوحٍ﴾ (٦٩) وفي قصة ثمود: ﴿جَعَلَكُمْ خُلَفَاءَ مِنۢ بَعْدِ عَادٍ﴾ (٧٤).

Also, this serves as an explanation of His statement: **{And it is He who has made you successors upon the earth.}**[198] So the beginning of al-A'rāf correlates with this by describing the creation of Ādam and how his creation marks the beginning of the generations of human creation upon earth.[199] Then it shifts to the generation of 'Ād: **{And remember that He made you successors after the people of Nūḥ.}**[200] And then the people of Thamūd: **{And remember when He made you successors after 'Ād.}**[201]

وأيضًا فقد قال في الأنعام: ﴿كَتَبَ رَبُّكُمْ عَلَىٰ نَفْسِهِ الرَّحْمَةَ﴾ (الأنعام: ٥٤) وهو موجز، وبسطه هنا بقوله: ﴿وَرَحْمَتِي وَسِعَتْ كُلَّ شَيْءٍ فَسَأَكْتُبُهَا لِلَّذِينَ يَتَّقُونَ﴾ (١٥٦) إلى آخره، فبيَّن من كتبها لهم.

It is said in al-An'ām: **{Your Lord has written mercy for Himself.}**[202] This general statement is explained with detailed wording here in al-A'rāf: **{My mercy embraces all things and I have ordained it for the pious.}**[203] This explains who has ordained the mercy for them.

وأما وجه ارتباط أول هذه السورة بآخر الأنعام فهو: أنه قد تقدم هناك: ﴿وَأَنَّ هَٰذَا صِرَاطِي مُسْتَقِيمًا فَاتَّبِعُوهُ﴾ (الأنعام: ١٥٣)، وقوله: ﴿وَهَٰذَا كِتَابٌ أَنزَلْنَاهُ

198 Al-An'ām: 165
199 Al-A'rāf: 11-25
200 Al-A'rāf: 69
201 Al-A'rāf: 74
202 Al-An'ām: 54
203 Al-A'rāf: 156

مُبَارَكٌ فَاتَّبِعُوهُ﴾ (الأنعام: ١٥٥)، فافتتح هذه السورة أيضًا [بالأمر] باتباع الكتاب في قوله: ﴿كِتَابٌ أُنْزِلَ إِلَيْكَ﴾ إلى [قوله] ﴿اتَّبِعُوا مَا أُنْزِلَ إِلَيْكُم مِن رَبِّكُمْ﴾ (٢، ٣).

As for the literal connection between the start of this *sūrah* and the end of the preceding one: Al-Anʿām ends with describing His straight path: {**And verily, this is my straight path, so follow it.**}[204] And {**And this is a blessed Book which We have sent down, so follow it.**}[205] And al-Aʿrāf begins with the same theme, i.e. with the command to follow the Book: {**A Book sent down unto you**} until His statement: {**Follow what has been sent down unto you from your Lord.**}[206]

وأيضًا لما تقدم في الأنعام: ﴿ثُمَّ يُنَبِّئُهُمْ بِمَا كَانُوا يَفْعَلُونَ﴾ (الأنعام: ١٥٩)، ﴿ثُمَّ إِلَى رَبِّكُمْ مَرْجِعُكُمْ فَيُنَبِّئُكُمْ بِمَا كُنْتُمْ فِيهِ تَخْتَلِفُونَ﴾ (الأنعام: ١٦٤)، قال في مفتتح هذه السورة: ﴿فَلَنَسْأَلَنَّ الَّذِينَ أُرْسِلَ إِلَيْهِمْ وَلَنَسْأَلَنَّ الْمُرْسَلِينَ ۝ فَلَنَقُصَّنَّ عَلَيْهِمْ بِعِلْمٍ﴾ (٦، ٧)، وذلك شرح التنبئة المذكورة.

Also, as preceded in al-Anʿām: {**Then He will inform them about what they used to do**}[207] and {**Then to your Lord is your return, and He will inform you concerning that over which you used to differ.**}[208] Then he said at the beginning of al-Aʿrāf: {**We will question those who the Book was sent to and we will ask the Messengers [about them]. Then We will surely relate [their deeds] to them with knowledge.**}[209]

204 Al-Anʿām: 153
205 Al-Anʿām: 155
206 Al-Aʿrāf: 2-3
207 Al-Anʿām: 159
208 Al-Anʿām: 164
209 Al-Aʿrāf: 6-7

So al-A'rāf explains the "informing" mentioned in al-An'ām.

وأيضًا فلما قال في الأنعام: ﴿مَنْ جَآءَ بِالْحَسَنَةِ فَلَهُ عَشْرُ أَمْثَالِهَا﴾ (الأنعام: ١٦٠) الآية، وذلك لا يظهر إلا في الميزان، افتتح هذة السورة بذكر الوزن، فقال: ﴿وَالْوَزْنُ يَوْمَئِذٍ الْحَقّ﴾ (٨). ثم ذكر من ثقلت موازينه، وهو مَن زادت حسناته على سيئاته، ثم من خفت موازينه، وهو من زادت سيئاته على حسناته، ثم ذكر بعد ذلك أصحاب الأعراف، وهم قوم استوت حسناتهم وسيئاتهم.

Another manner in how these two *sūrahs* complement one another is by looking at the statement in al-An'ām: **{Whoever brings a good deed shall have ten times the reward of it.}**[210] This multiplication of reward will only be made clear when the person is being held to account and has his deeds weighed on the *mīzān* (scale). Al-A'rāf opens with description of the *mīzān*, where He said: **{And the weighing on that Day is true.}**[211] Al-A'rāf then expands upon the types of weighing. Some will have their deeds made heavy; this is when one's good deeds outweigh the bad ones. It then describes those whose weighing of deeds will be light; this is when a person's bad deeds outweigh the good ones. After the description of the weighing, it then gives detail to the people of al-A'rāf; they are those who are equal in their level of good and bad deeds.

210 Al-An'ām: 160

211 Al-A'rāf: 8

سورة الأنفال

Sūrah al-Anfāl

اعلم أن وضع هذه السورة وبراءة ليس بتوقيف من الرسول صلى الله عليه وسلم والصحابة، كما هو الراجح في سائر السور، بل اجتهاد من عثمان رضي الله عنه.

Pay attention to the following point; the placement of this *sūrah* and al-Tawbah is not something—unlike the order of all the other *sūrahs* in the Qur'ān—instructed by the Prophet ﷺ, nor is it something that the Companions were in total agreement upon. Rather, it was the judgement of 'Uthmān ؓ to sequence them in this manner.

وقد كان يظهر في بادئ الرأي: أن المناسب إيلاء الأعراف بيونس وهود، لاشتراك كل [منهما] في اشتمالها على قصص الأنبياء، وأنها مكية النزول، خصوصًا أن الحديث ورد في فضل السبع الطوال، وعدوا السابعة يونس، وكانت تُسمى بذلك كما أخرجه البيهقي في الدلائل. ففي فصلها من الأعراف بسورتين هما الأنفال وبراءة فصل للنظير من سائر نظائره، هذا مع قصر سورة الأنفال، بالنسبة إلى الأعراف وبراءة.

What appears to me to be the case—according to my very limited knowledge—is that al-A'rāf is more appropriate to be associated with

Yūnus and Hūd as all of them are themed at describing the stories of the Prophets and the fact that all three of them were revealed in Makkah. Furthermore, "the seven long ones" have been categorised together as being the first segment of the Qur'ān, and Sūrah Yūnus was considered as being the seventh. This was reported by al-Bayhaqī in *al-Dalā'il*.[212] So to place al-Anfāl and al-Tawbah between al-A'rāf and Yūnus and interrupt the sequence of the seven long ones has some reservations; especially because al-Anfāl is shorter than al-A'rāf and al-Tawbah.

وقد استشكل ذلك قديمًا حبر الأم ابن عباس، فأخرج أحمد وأبو داود والترمذي والنسائي وابن حبان والحاكم عن ابن عباس قال: قلت لعثمان: ما حملكم على أن عمدتم إلى الأنفال وهي من المثاني، وإلى براءة وهي من المئين، فقرنتم بينهما، ولم تكتبوا بينهما سطر بسم الله الرحمن الرحيم، ووضعتموها في السبع الطوال؟ فقال عثمان: كان رسول الله صلى الله عليه وسلم ينزل عليه السور ذوات العدد، فكان إذا نزل عليه الشيء دعا بعض مَن كان يكتب، فيقول: ضعوا هؤلاء الآيات في السورة التي يذكر فيها كذا وكذا، وكانت الأنفال من أوائل ما نزل [بالمدينة]، وكانت براءة من آخر القرآن نزولًا وكانت قصتها شبيهة بقصتها، فظننت

212 Collected by al-Bayhaqī in *Dalā'il al-Nubuwwah* (7/152-153) and al-Nasā'ī (1/114) on the authority of Ibn 'Abbās that the seven long *sūrahs* are: al-Baqarah, Āli 'Imrān, al-Nisā, al-Mā'idah, al-An'ām, al-A'rāf, but the narrator said he forgot the seventh one that he heard from Ibn 'Abbās. Al-Suyūṭī reported from Ibn Abī Ḥātim and others that Sa'īd ibn Jubayr said that the seventh was Yūnus. See *al-Itqān* (1/220).

أنها منها، فقبض رسول الله صلى الله عليه وسلم ولم يبين لنا أنها منها، فمن أجل ذلك قرنت بينهما ولم أكتب بينهما سطر بسم الله الرحمن الرحيم، ووضعتها في السبع الطوال.

This has become a problematic issue for many of the scholars, even from the earliest generations, including Ibn 'Abbās. It is reported by Aḥmad, Abu Dāwūd, al-Tirmidhī, al-Nasā'ī, Ibn Ḥibbān and al-Ḥākim that Ibn 'Abbās said, "I asked 'Uthmān, 'Is there a reason for placing al-A'rāf with al-Anfāl when al-Anfāl is from those which equal or are less than a hundred *āyāt* and al-Tawbah is from those that exceed a hundred *āyāt*. By placing them in this manner [you have split up the order,] and you did not divide al-Anfāl and al-Tawbah with the *basmallah* and you placed them both together amongst the section where there are seven long ones?' So 'Uthmān replied, 'The Messenger of Allah ﷺ used to have *sūrahs* with many *āyāt* revealed to him and he would then call a scribe to write them down. He used to say to them, 'Place these *āyāt* in such-a-such *sūrah* which mentions such-and-such.' Al-Anfāl was from one of the first to be revealed (i.e. in al-Madinah) and al-Tawbah was one of the last *sūrahs* to be revealed but their theme was very similar, so I thought al-Tawbah was just an extension of al-Anfāl. The Messenger of Allah ﷺ passed away without making clear to us if al-Tawbah was part of al-Anfāl. So for this reason, I have placed them together in the *muṣḥaf* but did not separate them with the *basmallah*[213] and sequenced them to be within the seven long ones.'"[214]

---

213 Al-Bāqilānī said, "The *basmallah* is not written at the beginning of al-Tawbah by the Prophet ﷺ because it has *āyāt* which mention warfare and treaties. The *basmallah* denotes softness, mercy and care—thus it was omitted due to this." See *Nukat al-Intiṣār li Naql al-Qur'ān* (pp. 77-78).

214 Collected by Aḥmad in *al-Musnad* (1/57), Abū Dāwūd (1/208) in the Chapter of *al-Ṣalāt*, al-Tirmidhī (8/477-478) in the Chapter of *Tafsīr*, al-Ḥākim in

فانظر إلى ابن عباس رضي الله عنهما، كيف استشكل على عثمان رضي الله عنه أمرين: وضع الأنفال وهي قصيرة مع السور الطويلة، ووضعها هي وبراءة في أثناء السبع الطوال، مفصولًا بهما بين السادسة والسابعة، وانظر كيف أجاب عثمان رضي الله عنه أولًا بأنه لم يكن عنده في ذلك توقيف، فإنه استند إلى اجتهاد، وأنه قرن بين الأنفال وبراءة لكونها شبيهة بقصتها في اشتمال كل منهما على [الأمر] القتال، ونبذ العهود، وهذا وجه بيِّن المناسبة جلي، فرضي الله عن الصحابة، ما أدق أفهامهم! وأجزل آراءهم! وأعظم أحلامهم!

Look at how Ibn 'Abbas ﷺ found the decision of 'Uthmān ﷺ problematic, and this was from two perspectives: (i) The fluency of the sizes of the *sūrahs* was challenged due to al-Anfāl being placed amongst the lengthy ones. (ii) Placing both al-Anfāl and al-Tawbah between the sixth and seventh of the "seven lengthy ones". And look at how 'Uthman ﷺ responded by stating that there is no divine instruction to the order here, that he was forced to make a judgement over it and that he only placed al-Anfāl and al-Tawbah together because they resemble each other in their theme, i.e. the order to fight and the renouncement of treaties. This judgement by 'Uthmān is extremely insightful, so may Allah be pleased with all of the Companions. Look at how precise their understanding was! Look how noble and strong their opinions were! Look how great their intuition was!

---

al-Mustadrak (2/330) and others. Aḥmad Shākir declared this narration as being baseless and al-Bukhārī classed one of the narrators, Yazīd al-Fārisī, as being weak.

وأقول: يتم بيان مقصد عثمان رضي الله عنه في ذلك بأمور فتح الله بها:

I say: The intent of 'Uthmān ﷺ in sequencing the *muṣḥaf* in this fashion is due to the following reasons, which were inspired by Allah:

الأول: أنه جعل الأنفال قبل براءة مع قصرها، لكونها مشتملة على البسملة، فقدمها لتكون كقطعة منها، وتكون براءة بخلوها منها كتتمتها وبقيتها، ولهذا قال جماعة من السلف: إن الأنفال وبراءة سورة واحدة، لا سورتان.

Firstly, al-Anfāl is placed before al-Tawbah because of its small size and it having a *basmallah*. So he placed al-Anfāl before al-Tawbah and made al-Tawbah follow it as if al-Tawbah is an extension of al-Anfāl. For this reason, many scholars from the Salaf were of the view that al-Anfāl and al-Tawbah are actually one *sūrah*, and not two.[215]

الثاني: أنه وضع براءة هنا لمناسبة الطوال، فإنه ليس في القرآن بعد الأعراف أنسب ليونس طولًا منها، وذلك كافٍ في المناسبة.

Secondly, al-Tawbah is placed after al-Anfāl because of the concordance in length, as there is no other *sūrah* in the Qur'ān after al-A'rāf that is more appropriate in terms of length to Yūnus than it. This is sufficient to establish their concordance.

الثالث: أنه خلّل بالسورتين [الأنفال وبراءة] أثناء السبع الطوال المعلوم ترتيبها في العصر الأول، للإشارة إلى أن ذلك أمر صادر لا عن توقيف،

---

215 See *al-Itqān* (1/225).

وإلى أن رسول الله صلى الله عليه وسلم قُبِضَ قبل أن يبين محلهما، فوضعا [هنا] كالموضع المستعار بين السبع الطوال، بخلاف ما لو وضعتا بعد السبع الطوال، فإنه كان يوهم أن ذلك محلهما بتوقيف، وترتيب السبع الطوال يرشد إلى دفع هذا الوهم.

Thirdly, the placing of al-Anfāl and al-Tawbah within the seven long *sūrahs*—though the first generation was aware of their order—indicates that they were placed there as a personal endeavour and not based upon a divine instruction, and that the Messenger of Allah ﷺ passed away before he clarified where to place them in the *muṣḥaf*. The reason al-Anfāl and al-Tawbah were placed amongst the seven long *sūrahs*, [whose order is known] is to highlight that they are not located there due to divine instruction. However, if they were placed after the seven long *sūrahs*, it may give the impression that they are placed there according to divine instruction. That being said, knowing the order of the seven long *sūrahs* should avert such confusion.

فانظر إلى هذه الدقيقة التي فتح الله بها، ولا يغوص عليها إلا غواص.

Look at how precise their decision making was, by the facilitation of Allah, and how they took all things into consideration. It is an act that shows a high level of mastery and wisdom.

الرابع: أنه لو أخرهما وقدم يونس، وأتى بعد براءة بهود، كما في مصحف أُبي بن كعب، لمراعاة مناسبة السبع الطوال، وإيلاء بعضها بعضًا، لفات مع ما أشرنا إليه أمر آخر آكد في المناسبة، فإن الأَوْلى بسورة يونس أن تولى بالسور الخمس التي بعدها، لما اشتركت فيه من الاشتمال على

القصص، ومن الافتتاح بـ﴿الر﴾ ، وبذكر الكتاب، ومن كونها مكيات، ومن تناسب، ما عدا الحجر في المقدار، وبالتسمية باسم نبي، والرعد اسم ملك، وهو مناسب لأسماء الأنبياء.

Fourthly, if al-Anfāl and al-Tawbah were swapped with Yūnus and al-Tawbah placed before Hūd—as it was arranged in the *muṣḥaf* of Ubayy ibn Ka'b—in consideration of the concordance of the seven long ones and the connection between them, all what we have mentioned would be lost in addition to another aspect of concordance that is more established. This is because it is more correct to connect Yūnus to the five *sūrahs* that follow it because they all relate stories of the Prophets, and also because they open with the split-letters, {***Alif-Lām-Rā***} and then mention the Book. Likewise, all of them are Makkan *sūrahs*, and all of them, except al-Hijr, are named after a prophet. Al-Ra'd is a name of an angel[216] which has an element of connection to the names of Prophets.

فهذه ستة وجوه في مناسبة الاتصال بين يونس وما بعدها، وهي آكد من ذلك الوجه الواحد في تقديم يونس بعد الأعراف.

These complete the six reasons as to why Yūnus is better connected to the five that follow it and why al-Anfāl and al-Tawbah should be placed before it. And these reasons are stronger than the view we mentioned earlier regarding why Yūnus should be placed after al-A'rāf.

ولبعض هذه الأمور قدمت سورة الحجر على النحل، مع كونها أقصر

216 Collected by al-Tirmidhī (8/145) on the authority of Ibn 'Abbās. It was also the opinion of Mujāhid in his *tafsīr* of the *āyah*. See *al-Itqān* (4/79).

منها، ولو أخرت براءة عن هذه السور الست [لبعدت] المناسبة جدًّا لطولها بعد عدة سور أقصر منها بخلاف وضع سورة النحل بعد الحجر، فإنها ليست كبراءة في الطول.

In fact, it is for some of these very reasons that al-Ḥijr is placed before al-Naḥl, despite al-Ḥijr being shorter than al-Naḥl. Had al-Tawbah been placed after these six, then its appropriate place—due to its length—would have been extremely delayed. It would mean that shorter *sūrahs* would be placed before it unlike the reason for placing al-Nahl after al-Ḥijr, but it is not as long as al-Tawbah, [thus it does not affect the fluency of the Qur'ān with this arrangement.]

ويشهد لمراعاة الفواتح في مناسبة الوضع ما ذكرنا من تقديم الحجر على النحل لمناسبة ذوات ﴿الر﴾ قبلها، وما تقدم من تقديم آل عمران على النساء وإن كانت أقصر منها لمناسبة البقرة في الافتتاح بـ﴿الم﴾ وتوالي الطواسين والحواميم، وتوالي العنكبوت والروم ولقمان والسجدة، لافتتاح كل بـ﴿الم﴾، ولهذا قدمت السجدة على الأحزاب التي هي أطول منها.

Another aspect that supports the appropriateness of the start of the *sūrahs* with their placements is that which I have mentioned regarding placing al-Ḥijr before al-Naḥl. Al-Hijr commences with the split-letters *alif-lām-rā*, which is the manner of the four *sūrahs* before it, and this is one of the reasons we mentioned for Āli 'Imrān preceding al-Nisā and joining al-Baqarah, as they both begin with the split-letters *alif-lām-mīm*, despite the rule that longer *sūrahs* should come before smaller ones (i.e. al-Nisā should follow al-Baqarah based upon length). Similarly, the *ṭā-sīn* and *ḥā-mīm sūrahs* are placed together, and the *alif-lām-mīm sūrahs* of al-'Ankabūt, al-Rūm, Luqmān and al-Sajdah are together. For this reason, al-Sajdah is placed before al-Aḥzāb so that it is located with the rest of the *alif-lām-mīm sūrahs*, despite al-Aḥzāb being lengthier.

هذا ما فتح الله به.

This is what Allah has given me of understanding.

وأما ابن مسعود فقدم في مصحفه البقرة على النساء، وآل عمران، والأعراف، والأنعام، والمائدة، ويونس، فراعى [السبع] الطوال، وقدم الأطول فالأطول، ثم ثنى بالمئين، فقدم براءة، ثم النحل، ثم هود، ثم يوسف، ثم الكهف، وهكذا الأطول فالأطول، وذكر الأنفال بعد النور.

Ibn Mas'ūd in his *muṣḥaf* placed al-Nisā after al-Baqarah and made Āli 'Imrān the fourth sūrah in the Qur'ān, then al-A'rāf, al-An'ām, al-Mā'idah and then Yūnus; due to all of these being from the seven long ones and each one preceded by the other in terms of length. Then he placed the hundred or more verse *sūrahs* next to each other, ordering them according to length. He commenced with al-Tawbah before al-Naḥl, then Hūd, Yūsuf and al-Kahf—each one lengthier than the following one. Al-Anfāl was delayed and placed in his *muṣḥaf* after al-Nūr.[217]

ووجه مناسبتها لها: أن كلا منهما مدنية، ومشتملة على أحكام، وأن في النور ﴿وَعَدَ اللَّهُ الَّذِينَ آمَنُوا مِنكُمْ وَعَمِلُوا الصَّالِحَاتِ لَيَسْتَخْلِفَنَّهُمْ فِي الْأَرْضِ كَمَا اسْتَخْلَفَ الَّذِينَ مِن قَبْلِهِمْ﴾ (النور: ٥٥) الآية. وفي الأنفال: ﴿وَاذْكُرُوا إِذْ أَنتُمْ قَلِيلٌ مُّسْتَضْعَفُونَ فِي الْأَرْضِ تَخَافُونَ﴾ (٢٦) الآية. ولا يخفى ما بين الآيتين

217 See *al-Itqān* (1/224).

من المناسبة، فإن الأولى مشتملة على الوعد بما حصل، وذكَّر به في الثانية، فتأمل.

The reason why he placed them in this fashion is because they are both Madanī *sūrahs* and they are themed at explaining legislation. Furthermore al-Nūr states: {**Allah has promised those who have believed among you and done righteous deeds that He will surely grant them succession [to authority] upon the earth just as He granted it to those before them and that He will surely establish for them [therein] their religion which He has preferred for them and that He will surely substitute for them, after their fear, security, [for] they worship Me, not associating anything with Me. But whoever disbelieves after that—then those are the defiantly disobedient.**}[218] And it is said in al-Anfāl: {**And remember when you were few and oppressed in the land, fearing that people might abduct you, but He sheltered you, supported you with His victory, and provided you with good things—that you might be grateful.**}[219] So there is no doubt that both of these *āyāt* are related; the *āyah* in al-Nūr gives promise of relief whereas the one in al-Anfāl explains that the promise has been completed. So contemplate the point I have just explained.

218 Al-Nūr: 55

219 Al-Anfāl: 26

سورة براءة

Sūrah al-Tawbah

أقول: قد عرف وجه مناسبتها، ونزيد هنا أن صدرها تفصيل لإجمال قوله في الأنفال: ﴿وَإِمَّا تَخَافَنَّ مِنْ قَوْمٍ خِيَانَةً فَانْبِذْ إِلَيْهِمْ عَلَى سَوَاءٍ﴾ (الأنفال: ٥٨) الآية، وآيات الأمر بالقتال متصلة بقوله هناك: ﴿وَأَعِدُّوا لَهُمْ مَا اسْتَطَعْتُمْ مِنْ قُوَّةٍ﴾ (الأنفال: ٦٠) الآية. ولذا قال هنا في قصة المنافقين: ﴿وَلَوْ أَرَادُوا الْخُرُوجَ لَأَعَدُّوا لَهُ عُدَّةً﴾ (٤٦).

I say: We have explained above as to why al-Tawbah is located here in the *muṣḥaf*, but we can expand upon it here that al-Tawbah commences with detail[220] regarding what is mentioned concisely in al-Anfāl: {**If you fear treachery from people throwing back (their covenant), then make them aware that the covenant will be cancelled because of this action of theirs**}[221] which is followed by the command to prepare for war: {**And make ready against them all you can of power.**}[222] So for this reason, al-Tawbah makes mention of the hypocrites: {**And if they had intended to march out, certainly, they would have made some preparation for it.**}[223]

---

220 Al-Tawbah: 3-5

221 Al-Anfāl: 58

222 Al-Anfāl: 60

223 Al-Tawbah: 46

ثم بين السورتين تناسب من وجه آخر، وهو: أنه سبحانه في الأنفال تولى قسمة الغنائم، وجعل خُمسها خمسة أخماس، وفي براءة تولى قسمة الصدقات، وجعلها لثمانية أصناف.

Furthermore, between al-Anfāl and al-Tawbah there is a strong relationship [in their mention of the war booty and division of finances.] The Glorified explained in al-Anfāl that the war booty is to be split into five categories,[224] whereas al-Tawbah explains the portions of those who are eligible for *zakāt*—which has been specified into eight categories.[225]

224 Al-Anfāl: 41

225 Al-Tawbah: 60

سورة يونس

Sūrah Yūnus

أقول: قد عرف وجه مناسبتها فيما تقدم في الأنفال، ونزيد هنا: أن مطلعها شبيه بمطلع سورة الأعراف، فإنه سبحانه قال فيها: ﴿أَنْ أَنْذِرِ النَّاسَ وَبَشِّرِ الَّذِينَ آمَنُوا﴾ (٢) فقدم الإنذار وعممه، وأخَّر البشارة وخصصها، وقال تعالى في مطلع الأعراف: ﴿لِتُنْذِرَ بِهِ وَذِكْرَى لِلْمُؤْمِنِينَ﴾ (الأعراف: ٢) فخص الذكر وأخَّرها، وقدم الإنذار، وحذف مفعوله ليعم.

I say: The discussion regarding Yūnus being placed after al-Anfāl and al-Tawbah has already preceded. We expand upon this here by pointing out that the commencement of Yūnus resembles that of al-Aʿrāf. Allah, the Glorified, said in Yūnus: **{Warn mankind, and give good news to those who believe.}**[226] In this *āyah*, the warning precedes and has been generalised to mankind, whereas salvation and good tidings follow and have been specified to only a select few. And he said in the commencement of al-Aʿrāf: **{Warn thereby, and it being a reminder for the believers.}**[227] In the same fashion as the *āyah* in Yūnus, the warning is mentioned first and this is general to all mankind, but salvation and good news is delayed and given to a select few.

---

226 Yūnus: 2

227 Al-Aʿrāf: 2

وقال هنا: ﴿إِنَّ رَبَّكُمُ اللهُ الَّذِي خَلَقَ السَّمَاوَاتِ وَالْأَرْضَ فِي سِتَّةِ أَيَّامٍ ثُمَّ اسْتَوَى عَلَى الْعَرْشِ﴾ (٣)، وقال في أوائل الأعراف مثل ذلك.

He also said in this *sūrah*: {**Surely, your Lord is Allah Who created the heavens and the earth in six Days and then *istawā* (rose over) the Throne.**}[228] And He stated something similar to this in the early part of al-A'rāf: [{**Indeed your Lord is Allah, Who created the heavens and the earth in Six Days, and then He *istawā* (rose over) the Throne…**}][229]

وقال هنا: ﴿يُدَبِّرُ الْأَمْرَ﴾ (٣). وقال هناك: ﴿مُسَخَّرَاتٍ بِأَمْرِهِ أَلَا لَهُ الْخَلْقُ وَالْأَمْرُ﴾ (الأعراف: ٥٤).

He also said here: {**Disposing the affair of all things.**}[230] And in al-A'rāf He said: {**Subjected to His command. Surely, His is the Creation and Commandment.**}[231]

وأيضًا فقد ذكرت قصة فرعون وقومه في الأعراف، واختصر ذكر إغراقهم، وبسط في هذه السورة أبلغ بسط.

Furthermore, Yūnus has mention of the story of Fir'awn and likewise does al-A'rāf. His drowning is mentioned in general in al-A'rāf[232] but it is given further detail in Yūnus.[233]

فهي شارحة لما أُجمل في سورة الأعراف منه.

228 Yūnus: 3
229 Al-A'rāf: 54
230 Yūnus: 3
231 Al-A'rāf: 54
232 Al-A'rāf: 136
233 Yūnus: 90-92

So Yūnus provides detail to much of what preceded generally in al-A'rāf.

سورة هود

Sūrah Hūd

أقول: وجه وضعها بعد سورة يونس زيادة على الأوجه الستة السابقة: أن سورة يونس ذكر فيها قصة نوح مختصرة جدًّا، مجملة، فشرحت في هذه السورة وبسطت ما لم يبسطه في غيرها من السور، ولا في سورة الأعراف على طولها، ولا في سورة ﴿إِنَّا أَرْسَلْنَا نُوحًا﴾ (نوح: ١) التي أفردت لقصته.

I say: Sūrah Hūd is placed after Yūnus based upon the same six reasons which we have explained above. In addition to these six, Yūnus mentions the story of Nūḥ very briefly,[234] and it is later explained in Sūrah Hūd with extensive detail—with a level of detail not seen in any other *sūrah*.[235] This level of detail is not given in al-A'rāf despite al-A'rāf being considerably longer and it is not given in Sūrah Nūḥ itself.

فكانت هذه السورة شارحة لما أجمل في سورة يونس [توفية بالقاعدة، ثم إن مطلعها شديدا الارتباط بمقطع سورة يونس]، فإن قوله هناك: ﴿وَاتَّبِعْ مَا يُوحَى إِلَيْكَ﴾ (يونس: ١٠٩) هو عين قوله هنا: ﴿كِتَابٌ أُحْكِمَتْ آيَاتُهُ ثُمَّ فُصِّلَتْ مِنْ لَدُنْ حَكِيمٍ خَبِيرٍ﴾ (٢).

---

234 Yūnus: 71-73

235 Hūd: 25-48

So Sūrah Hūd explains what preceded it in general terms in Sūrah Yūnus, to comply with the rule, furthermore its beginning is strongly connected to the end of Sūrah Yūnus. Sūrah Yūnus concludes with the command: **{And, follow the inspiration sent unto you.}**[236] Which is that which is mentioned in Hūd: **{A Book which *āyāt* are perfected and then explained in detail from the One Who is All-Wise and Well-Acquainted.}**[237]

236 Yūnus: 109

237 Hūd: 2

سورة يوسف

Sūrah Yūsuf

أقول: وجه وضعها بعد سورة هود زيادة على الأوجه الستة السابقة: أن قوله في مطلعها: ﴿نَحْنُ نَقُصُّ عَلَيْكَ أَحْسَنَ الْقَصَصِ﴾ (٣) مناسب لقوله في مقطع تلك: ﴿وَكُلًّا نَقُصُّ عَلَيْكَ مِنْ أَنْبَاءِ الرُّسُلِ مَا نُثَبِّتُ بِهِ فُؤَادَكَ﴾ (هود: ١٢٠).

I say: Sūrah Yūsuf is placed after Hūd due to the six reasons mentioned above, and additionally because the conclusion of Hūd is expanded upon in Sūrah Yūsuf. In the beginning of Yūsuf He states: **{We relate unto you the best of stories through Our Revelations unto you.}**[238] This corresponds to His statement in Hūd: **{And all that We relate to you of the news of the Messengers is in order that We may make strong and firm your heart.}**[239]

وأيضًا فلما وقع في سورة هود: ﴿فَبَشَّرْنَاهَا بِإِسْحَاقَ وَمِنْ وَرَاءِ إِسْحَاقَ يَعْقُوبَ﴾ (هود: ٧١)، وقوله: ﴿رَحْمَتُ اللهِ وَبَرَكَاتُهُ عَلَيْكُمْ أَهْلَ الْبَيْتِ﴾ (هود: ٧٣). وذكر هنا حال يعقوب مع أولاده، وحال ولده الذي هو من أهل البيت مع إخوته، فكان كالشرح لإجمال ذلك.

Also, Sūrah Hūd contains stories of the Prophets: **{But We gave her**

238 Yūsuf: 3
239 Hūd: 120

glad tidings of Isḥaq and after him, of Ya'qūb.}[240] And it also says in Hūd: {**The Mercy of Allah and His Blessings be upon you, O people of the house.}**[241] These *āyāt* in Hūd explain the story of Ya'qūb and his children and specifically his child (Yūsuf), all of them from the family of Ibrāhīm. This is mentioned in general terms in Sūrah Hūd.

وكذلك قال هنا: ﴿وَيُتِمُّ نِعْمَتَهُ عَلَيْكَ وَعَلَىٰٓ ءَالِ يَعْقُوبَ كَمَآ أَتَمَّهَا عَلَىٰٓ أَبَوَيْكَ مِن قَبْلُ إِبْرَٰهِيمَ وَإِسْحَٰقَ﴾ (٦) فكان ذلك كالمقترن بقوله في هود: ﴿رَحْمَتُ ٱللَّهِ وَبَرَكَٰتُهُۥ عَلَيْكُمْ أَهْلَ ٱلْبَيْتِ﴾ (هود: ٧٣).

Likewise it says in Yūsuf: {**And perfect His favour on you and on the offspring of Ya'qūb, just as He perfected it on your fathers, Ibrāhīm and Isḥāq.}**[242] This seems directly linked to the *āyah* in Hūd: {**The Mercy of Allah and His Blessings be upon you, O people of the house.}**[243]

وقد روينا عن ابن عباس وجابر بن زيد في ترتيب النزول: أن يونس نزلت، ثم هود، ثم يوسف، وهذا وجه آخر من وجوه المناسبة في ترتيب هذه السور الثلاث، لترتيبها في النزول هكذا.

It is reported that Ibn 'Abbās and Jābir ibn Zayd stated about the order of revelation of these *sūrahs*, "Yūnus was revealed, then Hūd and then Yūsuf."[244] This is another aspect of the concordance of the order of these three *sūrahs*, as it corresponds to the chronological order of revelation.

240 Hūd: 71
241 Hūd: 73
242 Yūsuf: 6
243 Hūd: 73
244 See *al-Itqān* (1/97).

سورة الرعد

Sūrah al-Raʿd

أقول: وجه وضعها بعد سورة يوسف زيادة ما تقدم بعد ما فكرت فيه طائفة من الزمان: أنه سبحانه قال في آخر تلك: ﴿وَكَأَيِّنْ مِنْ آيَةٍ فِي السَّمَاوَاتِ وَالْأَرْضِ يَمُرُّونَ عَلَيْهَا وَهُمْ عَنْهَا مُعْرِضُونَ﴾ (يوسف: ١٠٥) فذكر الآيات السمائية والأرضية مجملة، ثم فصل في مطلع هذه السورة بقوله: ﴿اللَّهُ الَّذِي رَفَعَ السَّمَاوَاتِ بِغَيْرِ عَمَدٍ تَرَوْنَهَا ثُمَّ اسْتَوَى عَلَى الْعَرْشِ وَسَخَّرَ الشَّمْسَ وَالْقَمَرَ كُلٌّ يَجْرِي لِأَجَلٍ مُسَمًّى يُدَبِّرُ الْأَمْرَ يُفَصِّلُ الْآيَاتِ لَعَلَّكُمْ بِلِقَاءِ رَبِّكُمْ تُوقِنُونَ[﴾ تفصيل للآيات السمائية. وقوله: ﴿]وَهُوَ الَّذِي مَدَّ الْأَرْضَ وَجَعَلَ فِيهَا رَوَاسِيَ وَأَنْهَارًا وَمِنْ كُلِّ الثَّمَرَاتِ جَعَلَ فِيهَا زَوْجَيْنِ اثْنَيْنِ يُغْشِي اللَّيْلَ النَّهَارَ إِنَّ فِي ذَلِكَ لَآيَاتٍ لِقَوْمٍ يَتَفَكَّرُونَ ۝ وَفِي الْأَرْضِ قِطَعٌ مُتَجَاوِرَاتٌ وَجَنَّاتٌ مِنْ أَعْنَابٍ وَزَرْعٌ وَنَخِيلٌ صِنْوَانٌ وَغَيْرُ صِنْوَانٍ يُسْقَى بِمَاءٍ وَاحِدٍ وَنُفَضِّلُ بَعْضَهَا عَلَى بَعْضٍ فِي الْأُكُلِ إِنَّ فِي ذَلِكَ لَآيَاتٍ لِقَوْمٍ يَعْقِلُونَ﴾ (٢-٤) تفصيل للآيات الأرضية.

I say: After pondering about it for quite some time, I concluded that the appropriateness of al-Raʿd following Yūsuf is that Allah has said at the end of Yūsuf: {**And how many signs in the heavens and the earth**

they pass by, but they are averse from them.}[245] [This *āyah* commands contemplation upon the signs which are present for us to take notice of] in the heavens and the earth, and it does so in a general manner. Then al-R'ad continues this command during its commencement, whilst drawing to further detail: **{Allah is He Who raised the heavens without any visible pillars. Then, He *istawā* (rose above) the Throne. He has subjected the sun and the moon, each running its orbit for an appointed term, He regulates all affairs, explaining the *āyāt* in detail, that you may believe with certainty in the meeting with your Lord.}** This provides detail on the signs of the heavens. And He said: **{And it is He Who spread out the earth, and placed within it mountains and rivers and of every kind of fruits He designated pairs. He brings the night as a cover over the day. Surely, in these things, there are signs for people who reflect. And in the earth are neighbouring tracts, and gardens of vines, and green crops, and date-palms, growing out two or three from a single stem root, or otherwise (one stem root for every palm), watered with the same water, yet some of them We make more excellent than others to eat. Verily, in these things, there are signs for the people who understand.}**[246] This provides detail on the signs of the earth.

هذا مع اختتام سورة يوسف بوصف الكتاب، ووصفه بالحق، وافتتاح هذه بمثل ذلك، وهو من تشابه الأطراف.

Furthermore, Sūrah Yūsuf concludes by proclaiming the truthfulness and factualities found in the Book[247] and then Sūrah al-Ra'd begins with the same theme. This is considered back-to-back similarity where the end of a *sūrah* is similar to the beginning of a *sūrah*.[248]

---

245 Yūsuf: 105
246 Yūsuf: 2-4
247 Yūsuf: 111
248 Al-Ra'd: 1

سورة إبراهيم

Sūrah Ibrāhīm

أقول: وجه وضعها بعد سورة الرعد زيادة على ما تقدم بعد إفكاري فيه برهة: أن قوله في مطلعها: ﴿كِتَابٌ أَنزَلْنَاهُ إِلَيْكَ﴾ (١) مناسب لقوله في مقطع تلك: ﴿وَمَنْ عِندَهُ عِلْمُ الْكِتَابِ﴾ (الرعد: ٤٣) على أن المراد بـ(مَنْ) هو: الله تعالى جل جلاله.

I say: I pondered for a while to seek out a reason for Sūrah Ibrāhīm being placed after al-Raʿd besides that which was mentioned before, [and then I saw that] Sūrah Ibrāhīm commences with: **{A Book which We have revealed to you.}**[249] This bears a connection to what came before it in the very last *āyah* of al-Raʿd: **{And the One Who has Knowledge of the Book.}**[250] This is based on the fact that the one intended with the word "who" is Allah ﷻ.

وأيضًا ففي الرعد: ﴿وَلَقَدِ اسْتُهْزِئَ بِرُسُلٍ مِّن قَبْلِكَ فَأَمْلَيْتُ لِلَّذِينَ كَفَرُوا ثُمَّ أَخَذْتُهُمْ﴾ (الرعد: ٣٢)، وذلك مجمل في أربعة مواضع: الرسل، والمستهزئين، وصفة الاستهزاء، والأخذ، وقد فصلت الأربعة في قوله: ﴿أَلَمْ يَأْتِكُمْ نَبَأُ الَّذِينَ مِن قَبْلِكُمْ قَوْمِ نُوحٍ وَعَادٍ وَثَمُودَ ...﴾ (٩-١٦) الآيات.

---

249 Al-Ibrāhīm: 1

250 Al-Raʿd: 43

Also in Sūrah al-Ra'd: {**And indeed Messengers were mocked at before you, but I granted respite to those who disbelieved, and finally I punished them.**}[251] But this *āyah* is general in four aspects: It does not specify who the Messengers were, it does not mention who the mockers were, it does not mention how they were mocked and it does not mention how they were punished. All four of these points are explained in detail in Ibrāhīm: {**Has not the news reached you, of those before you, the people of Nūḥ, 'Ād, and Thamūd? And those after them? None knows them but Allah. Messengers came to them with clear proofs, but they put their hands in their mouths [biting them from anger] and said, "Surely, we disbelieve in what you have been sent with, and we are in a grave doubt to what you are calling us to."**}[252]

251 Al-Ra'd: 32

252 Ibrāhīm: 9-16 explains as to whom the Messengers that were mocked were, description of statements of their nation as to whom mocked them, description of what they said to mock and belie them and then it describes the way they were punished.

سورة الحِجْر

Sūrah al-Ḥijr

أقول: تقدمت الأوجه في اقترانها بالسورة السابقة، وإنما أُخرت عنها لقصرها بالنسبة إليها، وهذا القسم من سور القرآن للمئين، فناسب تقديم الأطول، مع مناسبة ما خُتمت به لبراعة الختام وهو قول: ﴿وَاعْبُدْ رَبَّكَ حَتَّىٰ يَأْتِيَكَ الْيَقِينُ﴾ (٩٩)، فإنه مفسر بالموت، وذلك مقطع في غاية البراعة.

I say: Some of the reasons that connect Sūrah al-Ḥijr to Sūrah Ibrāhīm have already preceded. Another reason why al-Ḥijr has been placed after Ibrāhīm is because it is shorter in length. This group of *sūrahs* are from the *ma'īn* (*sūrahs* that exceed a hundred *āyāt*). So it is appropriate that the longer *sūrahs* are placed before. Furthermore, the *sūrah* is concluded with a perfectly appropriate *āyah*, [as it talks about death]: **{And worship your Lord until there comes unto you the certainty.}**[253] "Certainty" refers to death and this conclusion shows an absolute degree of proficiency.

وقد وقع ذلك في أواخر السور المقترنة، ففي آخر آل عمران: ﴿وَاتَّقُوا اللَّهَ لَعَلَّكُمْ تُفْلِحُونَ﴾ (آل عمران: ٢٠٠)، وفي آخر الطواسين: ﴿كُلُّ شَيْءٍ هَالِكٌ إِلَّا وَجْهَهُ لَهُ الْحُكْمُ وَإِلَيْهِ تُرْجَعُونَ﴾ (القصص: ٨٨)، وفي آخر ذوات (الر):

253 Al-Ḥijr: 99

﴿وَانْتَظِرْ إِنَّهُمْ مُنْتَظِرُونَ﴾ (السجدة: ٣٠)، وفي آخر الحواميم: ﴿كَأَنَّهُمْ يَوْمَ يَرَوْنَ مَا يُوعَدُونَ لَمْ يَلْبَثُوا إِلَّا سَاعَةً مِنْ نَهَارٍ بَلَاغٌ﴾ (الأحقاف: ٣٥).

And it occurs in the connected *sūrahs* in the *muṣḥaf* that they have the same systematic conclusion [which enables the reader to draw comparisons between the *sūrahs*.] So Sūrah Āli 'Imrān[—the last *alif-lām-mīm sūrah*,] concludes with: **{And fear Allah, so that you may be successful.}**[254] At the end of al-Qaṣaṣ, the concluding *ṭā-sīn sūrah*: **{Everything will perish save His face. His is the Decision, and to Him you [all] shall be returned.}**[255] It says at the end of al-Sajdah—the conclusion of the *alif-lām-ra sūrahs*: **{And await, surely they [too] are awaiting.}**[256] And with Sūrah al-Aḥqāf, the conclusion of the *ḥā-mīm sūrahs*: **{On the Day when they will see the torment with which they are promised, as if they had not stayed more than an hour in a single day. A clear Message.}**[257]

ثم ظهر لي وجه اتصال أول هذه السورة بآخر سورة إبراهيم، فإنه تعالى لما قال هناك في وصف يوم القيامة: ﴿وَبَرَزُوا لِلَّهِ الْوَاحِدِ الْقَهَّارِ۝وَتَرَى الْمُجْرِمِينَ يَوْمَئِذٍ مُقَرَّنِينَ فِي الْأَصْفَادِ۝سَرَابِيلُهُمْ مِنْ قَطِرَانٍ وَتَغْشَى وُجُوهَهُمُ النَّارُ﴾ (إبراهيم: ٤٨-٥٠)، قال هنا: ﴿رُبَمَا يَوَدُّ الَّذِينَ كَفَرُوا لَوْ كَانُوا مُسْلِمِينَ﴾ (٢) فأخبر أن المجرمين المذكورين إذا طال مكثهم في النار، ورأوا عصاة المؤمنين الموحدين قد أُخرجوا منها تمنوا أن لو كانوا في الدنيا مسلمين، وذلك وجه حسن في الربط، مع اختتام آخر تلك بوصف الكتاب، وافتتاح هذه

254 Āli 'Imrān: 200
255 Al-Qaṣaṣ: 88
256 Al-Sajdah: 30
257 Al-Aḥqāf: 35

به، وذلك من تشابه الأطراف.

Also what appears to me to be the case is that the beginning of Sūrah al-Ḥijr connects itself with the ending of Sūrah Ibrāhīm, where Allah the Most High describes the situation of the Day of Judgement: {**And they will appear before Allah, the One, the Prevailing. And you will see the criminals that Day bound together in shackles. Their garments will be of pitch, and fire will cover their faces.**}[258] And al-Ḥijr begins with: {**Perhaps the disbelievers will wish that they were Muslims.**}[259] This explains that the aforementioned criminals—when their stay in the fire is lengthy—will see some of their companions in the fire being allowed to leave, i.e. those who had *tawḥīd* but were sinners. [This will increase the sense of punishment they feel as they will realise that there is no exit for them,] and they will regret how they were not Muslim in the *dunyā*. This shows an extremely stimulating connection between the two *sūrahs*. Sūrah Ibrāhīm[260] also gives description to the Book during its end, which is then carried on in the opening of Sūrah al-Ḥijr. This is considered as back-to-back similarity where the end of a *sūrah* is similar to the beginning of a *sūrah*.[261]

258 Ibrāhīm: 48-50

259 Al-Ḥijr: 2

260 Ibrāhīm: 52

261 Al-Ḥijr: 1

سورة النحل

Sūrah al-Naḥl

أقول: وجه وضعها بعد سورة الحجر: أن آخرها شديد الالتئام بأول هذه فإن قوله في آخر تلك: ﴿وَاعْبُدْ رَبَّكَ حَتَّى يَأْتِيَكَ الْيَقِينُ﴾ (الحجر: ٩٩) الذي هو مفسر بالموت، ظاهر المناسبة لقوله هنا: ﴿أَتَى أَمْرُ اللهِ﴾ (١)، وانظر كيف جاء في المقدَّمة بـ﴿يَأْتِيَكَ الْيَقِينُ﴾ [بلفظ المضارع]، وفي المتأخرة بلفظ الماضي، لأن المستقبل سابق على الماضي، كما تقرر في المعقول والعربية.

I say: The appropriateness of it being placed after al-Ḥijr is that al-Naḥl commences in a manner extremely correspondent to that with which al-Ḥijr concludes with. He states at the end of Al-Ḥijr: **{And worship your Lord until there comes unto you the certainty.}**[262] Certainty has been explained to mean death, which bears similitude to the beginning of al-Naḥl with His statement: **{The command of Allah has come to pass.}**[263] Look at how al-Ḥijr [commands the reader to worship Allah] using the present/future tense of the verb: **{There comes unto you the certainty.}** Whereas al-Naḥl uses the past tense of the verb: **{Has come to pass.}** This is because the future tense precedes the past tense as established in logic and Arabic language (i.e. some-

---

262 Al-Ḥijr: 99

263 Al-Naḥl: 1

thing must happen before it can be considered to have taken place).

ثم ظهر لي أن هذه السورة شديدة الاعتلاق بسورة إبراهيم، وإنما تأخرت عنها لمناسبة الحجر، في كونها من ذوات ﴿الر﴾.

Also what appears to me to be the case is that Sūrah al-Naḥl also has an extremely strong connection with Sūrah Ibrāhīm and is only delayed by al-Ḥijr due to its connection being stronger, and that Ibrāhīm is better grouped with the other *alif-lām-ra sūrahs*.

وذلك: أن سورة إبراهيم وقع فيها ذكر فتنة الميت، ومن هو مثبت وغيره، وذلك أيضًا في هذه بقوله: ﴿الَّذِينَ تَتَوَفَّاهُمُ الْمَلَائِكَةُ ظَالِمِي أَنْفُسِهِمْ﴾ (٢٨) الآيات، فذكر الفتنة، وما يحصل عندها من الثبات والإضلال، وذكر هنا ما يحصل عقب ذلك من النعيم والعذاب.

Both Sūrah Ibrāhīm and al-Naḥl give heavy detail to the tribulations of death; and those who are made steadfast and those who are not. Sūrah al-Naḥl states: **{The ones whom the angels take in death [while] wronging themselves, and [who] then offer submission, [saying], "We were not doing any evil." But, yes! Indeed, Allah is knowing of what you used to do.}**[264] This *āyah* shows that death is a test and it describes the end for those who are steadfast and those who are misguided. The following *āyāt* also give illustration to the next stage of life for these people; either wretched punishment or eternal bliss.[265]

ووقع في سورة إبراهيم: ﴿وَقَدْ مَكَرُوا مَكْرَهُمْ وَعِنْدَ اللهِ مَكْرُهُمْ وَإِنْ كَانَ مَكْرُهُمْ

264 Al-Naḥl: 28

265 Al-Naḥl: 29-31

لِتَزُولَ مِنْهُ الْجِبَالُ﴾ (إبراهيم: ٤٦)، و[قد] قيل: إنها في الجبار الذي أراد أن يصعد السماء بالنسور، ووقع هنا أيضًا في قوله: ﴿قَدْ مَكَرَ الَّذِينَ مِنْ قَبْلِهِمْ﴾ (٢٦).

Furthermore in Sūrah Ibrāhīm: **{Indeed, they planned their plot, and their plot was with Allah, though their plot was so great yet it would never be able to remove the mountains.}**[266] Some of the scholars have given this *āyah* the *tafsīr* that it refers to the tyrant who wanted to ascend to the skies using eagles, and this is referred to again later in al-Naḥl: **{Those before them indeed plotted.}**[267]

ووقع في سورة إبراهيم ذكر النعم، وقال عقبها: ﴿وَإِنْ تَعُدُّوا نِعْمَتَ اللهِ لا تُحْصُوهَآ﴾ (إبراهيم: ٣٤)، ووقع هنا ذكر ذلك معقَّبًا بمثل ذلك.

Sūrah Ibrāhīm also asks the reader to contemplate on the favours of Allah upon them, and after drawing attention to this it says: **{Never will you be able to count them.}**[268] And the command to contemplate upon his favours occurs in al-Naḥl in a similar manner.[269]

266 Ibrāhīm: 46
267 Al-Naḥl: 26
268 Ibrāhīm: 34
269 Al-Naḥl: 18

سورة بني إسرائيل

Sūrah Banī Isrā'īl (al-Isrā)

اعلم أن هذه السورة والأربع بعدها من قديم ما أنزل أخرج البخاري عن ابن مسعود أنه قال في بني إسرائيل، والكهف، ومريم، وطه، والأنبياء: ([هن] من العتاق الأول، وهن من تلادي)، وهذا وجه في ترتيبها، وهو اشتراكها في قدم النزول، وكونها مكيات، وكلها مشتملة على القصص.

Pay attention to the following point; this *sūrah* and the four after it are from the very first *sūrahs* to be revealed in Makkah. It is reported by al-Bukhārī on the authority of Ibn Mas'ūd that he described Banī Isrā'īl, al-Kahf, Maryam, Ṭa-ḥa and al-Anbiyā as follows, "They are among the best and earliest and they are among the first I received [in Makkah]."[270] This gives support to the order they have been placed in, i.e. due to them being amongst the first to be revealed, all revealed in Makkah and all of them are themed at explaining the stories of the Prophets.

وقد ظهر لي في وجه اتصالها بسورة النحل: أنه سبحانه لما قال في آخر النحل: ﴿إِنَّمَا جُعِلَ السَّبْتُ عَلَى الَّذِينَ اخْتَلَفُوا فِيهِ﴾ (النحل: ١٢٤) فسر في هذه [السورة] شريعة أهل السبت وشأنهم، فذكر فيها جميع ما شرع

270 Collected by al-Bukhārī (6/189): Chapter of *Tafsīr*.

لهم في التوراة، كما أخرج ابن جرير عن ابن عباس أنه قال: ([إن] التوراة كلها في خمس عشرة آية من سورة بني إسرائيل) ، وذكر عصيانهم وإفسادهم، وتخريب مسجدهم، ثم ذكر استفزازهم للنبي صلى الله عليه وسلم وإرادتهم إخراجه من المدينة، ثم ذكر سؤالهم إياه عن الروح، ثم ختم السورة بآيات موسى التسع، وخطابه مع فرعون، وأخبر أن [فرعون أراد أن يستفزهم من الأرض، فأُهلك، وورث بنو إسرائيل من بعده، وفي ذلك تعريض بهم، أنهم كما استفزوا النبي] صلى الله عليه وسلم ليخرجوه من المدينة هو وأصحابه كنظير ما وقع لهم مع فرعون لما استفزهم، و [قد] وقع ذلك أيضًا.

What appears to me to be the case is that from the aspects of Sūrah Banī Isrā'īl's connection to al-Naḥl is that He, the Glorified, concludes al-Naḥl with: **{The Sabbath was only prescribed for those who differed concerning it.}**[271] And Sūrah Banī Isrā'īl provides an explanation of this *āyah*; who the People of the Sabbath were, their Sharī'ah and all of the legislation in the Torah that was given to them. Ibn Jarīr reports that Ibn 'Abbās said, 'Verily the Torah is encompassed in fifteen *āyāt* which are in Sūrah Banī Isrā'īl."[272]

These fifteen are *āyāt* which mention the sins they fell into, the corruption, the spoiling of their places of worship and how they tried to instigate against the Prophet ﷺ and desired to expel him from al-Madīnah. It also makes mention of how they asked the Prophet about the soul, and ends with the story of Mūsā; the nine signs he was given

271 Al-Naḥl: 124

272 *Tafsīr al-Ṭabarī* (17/243)

and his dialogue with Fir'awn. It also explains how Fir'awn himself tried to expel a Prophet (i.e. Mūsā) and was destroyed and Banī Isrā'īl were caused to inherit the land after the removal of Fir'awn; all of which is a rebuke for how they plotted to remove the Prophet and his Companions from al-Madīnah. [This was mentioned for them to take heed that if they continued with their plots, the same punishment which afflicted Fir'awn would happen to them, i.e. their authority in the land would be removed and their wealth inherited.] And this is exactly what happened.

ولما كانت هذه السورة مصدَّرة بقصة تخريب المسجد الأقصى أُسْرِيَ بالمصطفى إليه، تشريفًا له بحلول ركابه الشريف، فلله الحمد على ما ألهم.

As Sūrah Banī Isrā'īl starts with exposing the ungodliness that took place at Masjid al-Aqṣā after the passing of Mūsā, it also explains how the Chosen One (i.e. Muhammad ﷺ) came to restore honour and peace to al-Aqṣā, and this was symbolised by his noble ascension from there [and the liberation of the *masjid* that his Ummah performed after him.] And all praises are for Allah for giving us this understanding.

سورة الكهف

Sūrah al-Kahf

قال بعضهم: مناسبة وضعها بعد سورة الإسراء: افتتاح تلك بالتسبيح، وهذه بالتحميد، وهما مقترنان في القرآن وسائر الكلام بحيث يسبق التسبيح التحميد، نحو: ﴿فَسَبِّحْ بِحَمْدِ رَبِّكَ﴾ (الحجر: ٩٨)، وسبحان الله وبحمده.

Some scholars have stated that the appropriateness of al-Kahf being placed after Sūrah al-Isrā is due to placing the *sūrahs* in accordance [to the well-known *adhkār* known as *tasbīḥ* (سبحان الله) and *tamḥīd* (الحمد لله).] As al-Isrā begins with *tasbīḥ* (سبحان الله) and al-Kahf begins with *tamḥīd* (الحمد لله); [this order is fitting.][273] These two phrases are

273 Another reason given by Ibn al-Zamlakānī is that Sūrah al-Isrā includes the event of Isrā that the disbelievers denied and because of which they accused the Prophet of being a liar, and accusing him of telling lies is like accusing Allah of the same thing. For this reason, al-Isrā starts with affirming that Allah transcends all defects and flaws (i.e. *tasbīḥ*) and dismissing the accusations made against His Prophet. Sūrah al-Kahf that follows it is themed at a response to a question that was levelled at the Prophet from the polytheists of Quraysh in asking for description of the incident that occurred at the cave, but the revelation did not descend for a period of time. So, the *sūrah* was revealed to clarify that the favours and blessings of Allah (i.e. His revelation) have not ceased from Prophet Muḥammad ﷺ and the believers. Therefore, it is appropriate that al-Kahf begins with praising Allah (*tamḥīd*). See *al-Itqān* (3/387).

connected in the Qur'ān and regular speech, and their manner is that the *tasbīḥ* precedes the *taḥmīd* e.g. in the *āyah*: **{So exalt [Allah] with praise of your Lord}**[274] and "*subḥanallah wa bi ḥamdih*."

قلت: مع اختتام ما قبلها بالتحميد أيضًا، وذلك من وجوه المناسبة بتشابه الأطراف.

I say: There is [also a more direct connection between the two]—Banī Isrā'īl ends with *tamḥīd*[275] and Sūrah al-Kaḥf begins with it. This is back-to-back similarity.

ثم ظهر لي وجه آخر أحسن في الاتصال، وذلك: أن اليهود أمروا المشركين أن يسألوا النبي صلى الله عليه وسلم عن ثلاثة أشياء: عن الروح، وعن قصة أصحاب الكهف، وعن قصة ذي القرنين، وقد ذكر جواب السؤال الأول في آخر سورة بني إسرائيل، فناسب اتصالها بالسورة التي اشتملت على جواب السؤالين الآخرين.

Furthermore, what appears to me to be the case is that there is another, but stronger, connection between the two. The Jews asked the Mushrikīn of Quraysh to approach the Prophet ﷺ and ask him three questions: what the soul is, his version of events that took place with the people of the cave and an explanation to the story of Dhu al-Qarnayn.[276] [The theme of Sūrah al-Kahf includes explanation of the latter two,] whereas the end of Sūrah Banī Isrā'īl contains the answer to the first question, so it is appropriate that it is connected in the *muṣḥaf* to the *sūrah* which possesses the answer to the rest.

---

274 Al-Ḥijr: 98

275 Sūrah Banī Isrā'īl: 111

276 See *Tafsīr Ibn Kathīr* (5/137).

فإن قلت: هلَّا جمعت الثلاثة في سورة واحدة؟

Someone may ask, "Why weren't the answers to all three given in one *sūrah*?"

قلت: لما لم يقع الجواب عن الأول بالبيان، ناسب فصله في سورة. ثم ظهر

I say in response: As the first question (i.e. about the soul) was not addressed, it was appropriate that the answers be separated.

ثم ظهر لي وجه آخر: وهو أنه لما قال فيها: ﴿وَمَآ أُوتِيتُم مِّنَ الْعِلْمِ إِلَّا قَلِيلًا﴾ (الإسراء: ٨٥)، والخطاب لليهود، واستظهر على ذلك بقصة موسى في بني إسرائيل مع الخضر، التي كان سببها ذكر العلم والأعلم، وما دلت عليه من إحاطة معلومات الله عز وجل التي لا تحصى، فكانت هذه السورة كإقامة الدليل لما ذكر من الحِكَم.

Furthermore, what appears to me to be the case—from a different viewpoint— is in explanation of the statement: **{And mankind have not been given of knowledge except a little.}**[277] This *āyah* is addressing the Jews who asked the question and a direct comparison is drawn between this point and the story of Mūsā with al-Khaḍir (which was mentioned in al-Isrā). In this incident, Mūsā mentioned knowledge and how much knowledge he was given, and it displays the all-encompassing knowledge of Allah ﷻ, which can never be limited. So al-Kahf [expands on explaining the vast knowledge and wisdom of Allah] and serves as proof for that which we cited [from the afore-

277 Al-Isrā: 85

mentioned *āyah*.]

وقد ورد في الحديث أنه لما نزل: ﴿وَمَآ أُوتِيتُم مِّنَ الْعِلْمِ إِلَّا قَلِيلًا﴾ قال اليهود: قد أوتينا التوراة، فيها علم كل شيء فنزل: ﴿قُل لَّوْ كَانَ الْبَحْرُ مِدَادًا لِّكَلِمَاتِ رَبِّي لَنَفِدَ الْبَحْرُ قَبْلَ أَن تَنفَدَ كَلِمَاتُ رَبِّي وَلَوْ جِئْنَا بِمِثْلِهِ مَدَدًا﴾ (١٠٩) في هذه السورة فهذا وجه آخر في المناسبة، وتكون السورة من هذه الجهة جوابًا عن شبهة الخصوم فيما قدر بتلك.

It is reported in a ḥadīth that when the *āyah* {**And you have only been given limited knowledge of it**} was revealed, a party of the Jews proclaimed, "We have the Torah and in it is all knowledge." So the following *āyah* was revealed in response: {**Say, "If the sea were ink for [writing] the words of my Lord, surely, the sea would be exhausted before the words of my Lord would be finished, even if we brought [another sea] like it for its aid."**}[278] This is another aspect that gives explanation as to why Banī Isrā'īl and al-Kahf are connected; making the *sūrah* from this aspect a response to the allegations made by the Jews that approached the Prophet.

وأيضًا فلما قال هناك: ﴿فَإِذَا جَآءَ وَعْدُ الْآخِرَةِ جِئْنَا بِكُمْ لَفِيفًا﴾ (الإسراء: ١٠٤) شرح ذلك هنا وبسطه بقوله: ﴿فَإِذَا جَآءَ وَعْدُ رَبِّي جَعَلَهُ دَكَّآءَ﴾ إلى ﴿وَنُفِخَ فِي الصُّورِ فَجَمَعْنَاهُمْ جَمْعًا ۝ وَعَرَضْنَا جَهَنَّمَ يَوْمَئِذٍ لِّلْكَافِرِينَ عَرْضًا﴾ (٩٨-١٠٠)، فهذه وجوه عديدة في الاتصال.

Furthermore, Sūrah Banī Isrā'īl has the statement: {**And We said after Pharaoh to the Children of Isrā'īl, "Dwell in the land, and when**

278 Al-Kahf: 109

there comes the promise of the Hereafter, We will bring you forth in [one] gathering."}[279] And this is explained further in al-Kahf: {**But when the Promise of my Lord comes, He shall level it down to the ground. And the Promise of my Lord is ever true.**} Until Allah says: {**And on that Day, We shall leave them to surge like waves on one another, and the Trumpet will be blown, and We shall collect them all together. And on that Day We shall present Hell to the disbelievers, plain to view.**}[280] So there is a firm and strong relationship between the two.

279 Al-Isrā: 104
280 Al-Kahf: 98-100

سورة مريم

Sūrah Maryam

أقول: ظهر لي في وجه مناسبتها لما قبلها: أن سورة الكهف اشتملت على عدة أعاجيب: قصة أصحاب الكهف، وطول لبثهم هذه المدة الطويلة بلا أكل ولا شرب، وقصة موسى مع الخضر، وما فيها من الخارقات، وقصة ذي القرنين، وهذه السورة فيها أعجوبتان: قصة ولادة يحيى بن زكريا، وقصة ولادة عيسى، فناسب تتاليهما.

I say: What appears to me to be the case regarding Sūrah Maryam's connection to that which precedes it is that Sūrah al-Kahf has a series of miracles; the story of the people of the cave, the length they were preserved in the cave, the miracle of living for this span of years without sustenance, the story of Mūsā with al-Khaḍir and the miracles that took place within it and the story of Dhu al-Qurnayn. Likewise, Sūrah Maryam continues in mentioning two miracles [that have occurred within the stories of the Prophets] i.e. Zakariyah being given a child named Yaḥyā [whilst old in age,] and the miraculous birth of 'Īsā ibn Maryam; so to keep this topic consecutive, it is appropriate that these two follow each other.

وأيضًا فقد قيل: إن أصحاب الكهف يُبعثون قبل قيام الساعة، ويحجون مع عيسى ابن مريم حين ينزل، ففي ذكر سورة مريم بعد [ذكر] سورة

أصحاب الكهف مع ذلك -إن ثبت- ما لا يخفى من المناسبة.

Furthermore, it has been reported by some that the people of the cave will be resurrected before the arising of the hour. It is said that they will perform the Ḥajj with 'Īsā ibn Maryam after he descends.[281] Presuming this is correct, Sūrah Maryam being mentioned after the chapter of the people of the cave displays an undeniable element of concordance.

وقد قيل أيضًا: إنهم من قوم عيسى، وإن قصتهم كانت في الفترة، فناسب توالي [سورة] قصتهم و [سورة] قصة نبيهم.

It is also reported by some that the people of the cave were from the nation of 'Īsā, and the events surrounding them occurred in the period between 'Īsā and the coming of Muḥammad ﷺ. If this is the case, then it is appropriate for the *sūrah* detailing their story to be followed by the *sūrah* detailing the story of their prophet.[282]

---

281 I have not come across any proof for this in the sources available to me.

282 Ibn Kathīr said, "What appears to be the case is that the people of the cave existed before Christianity had emerged (i.e. the event occurred before the coming of 'Īsā ibn Maryam). This is because the Jews asked the polytheists of Quraysh to ask the Prophet ﷺ to explain their story to them and this indicates that the story was known from before the time of 'Īsā ibn Maryam." See *Tafsīr Ibn Kathīr* (5/137).

سورة طه

Sūrah Ṭa-Ha

أقول: روينا عن ابن عباس وجابر بن زيد في ترتيب النزول: أن طه نزلت بعد سورة مريم، بعد ذكر سورة أصحاب الكهف، وذلك وحده كافٍ في مناسبة الوضع، مع التآخي بالافتتاح بالحروف المقطعة.

I say: It has been reported from Ibn ʿAbbās and Jābir ibn Zayd that the order of revelation was that Ṭa-ha was revealed after Sūrah Maryam, after the *sūrah* about the people of the cave. This alone is proof that this sequence of *sūrahs* is appropriate, added to the fact that Sūrah Maryam and Ṭa-ha both begin with split-letters.

وظهر لي وجه آخر، وهو: أنه لما ذكر في سورة مريم قصص عدة من الأنبياء، وهم: زكريا، ويحيى، وعيسى، الثلاثة مبسوطة وإبراهيم، وهي بين البسط والإيجاز، وموسى، وهي موجزة بجملة أشار إلى بقية النبيين في الآية الأخيرة إجمالًا. وذكر في هذه السورة شرح قصة موسى، التي أجملها هناك، فاستوعبها غاية الاستيعاب، وبسطها أبلغ بسط، ثم أشار إلى تفصيل قصة آدم، الذي وقع [في مريم] مجرد اسمه هناك، ثم أورد في سورة الأنبياء بقية قصص من لم يذكر في مريم، كنوح، ولوط، وداود،

وسليمان، وأيوب، وذي الكفل، وذي النون، وأشير إلى قصة من ذكرت قصته إشارة وجيزة، كموسى، وهارون، وإسماعيل، وزكريا، ومريم، لتكون السورتان كالمتقابلتين.

What also appears to me to be the case is that Sūrah Maryam is themed at mentioning the stories of many of the Prophets, including Zakariyah, Yahyā, 'Īsā; all three of their stories are extensively mentioned, then Ibrāhīm which is balanced in its level of description, and then the story of Mūsā[283] which is left extremely brief, and the last *āyah* points out to the rest of the Prophets in general.[284]

Sūrah Maryam only mentions the story of Mūsā in passing, but its detail is deepened in Sūrah Ṭa-ha.[285] It also only mentions the story of Ādam in passing[286] which is then later explained in Ṭa-ha in more detail.[287]

After Ṭa-ha, Sūrah al-Anbiyā gives detail to the stories of the Prophets that were not mentioned in Maryam or Ṭa-ha, such as the stories of Nūḥ, Lūṭ, Dāwūd, Sulaymān, Ayūb, Dhu al-Kifl, Dhu al-Nūn. Sūrah al-Anbiyā also makes reference to stories of those Prophets which were mentioned in the *sūrahs* before but it keeps their mention brief, including the stories of Mūsā, Hārūn, Ismā'īl, Zakariyyā and Maryam. This makes the two *sūrahs* complement each other.

وبسطت فيها قصة إبراهيم البسط التام فيما يتعلق به مع قومه، ولم تذكر

283 Maryam: 51-53
284 Maryam: 58
285 Ṭā-hā: 9-97
286 Maryam: 58
287 Ṭā-hā: 116-123

حاله مع أبيه إلا إشارة كما أنه في سورة مريم ذكر حاله مع قومه إشارة ومع أبيه مبسوطًا.

Furthermore, the story of Ibrāhīm in Sūrah al-Anbiyā is given extensive detail also, especially so in describing the struggles he faced with his people, whereas the struggles that he had with his father are only touched upon—in contrast to Sūrah Maryam,[288] which thoroughly details the troubles he faced with his father whilst only touching upon his troubles with his people.[289]

فانظر إلى عجيب هذا الأسلوب، وبديع هذا الترتيب.

So look at how the Qur'ān connects all of this in the most amazing fashion with the best of successions.

288 Maryam: 42-48

289 Al-Anbiyā: 51-73

سورة الأنبياء

Sūrah al-Anbiyā

قدمت ما فيها مستوفًى، وظهر لي في اتصالها بآخر طه: أنه سبحانه لما قال: ﴿قُلْ كُلٌّ مُتَرَبِّصٌ فَتَرَبَّصُوا﴾ (طه: ١٣٥)، وقال قبله: ﴿وَلَوْلا كَلِمَةٌ سَبَقَتْ مِنْ رَبِّكَ لَكَانَ لِزَامًا وَأَجَلٌ مُسَمًّى﴾ (طه: ١٢٩).

Sūrah al-Anbiyā has had an adequate explanation above, however it is also apparent to me that there is a connection between it and the ending of Ṭa-ha, where He stated: {**Say: "Each [one of us] is waiting, so wait you too."**}[290] Before this, He ﷻ said: {**And if not for a word that preceded from your Lord, punishment would have been an obligation [due immediately], and [if not for] a specified term [decreed].**}[291]

قال في مطلع هذه: ﴿اقْتَرَبَ لِلنَّاسِ حِسَابُهُمْ﴾ (١) إشارة إلى قرب الأجل، ودنو الأمل المنتظر.

The theme of this *sūrah* is set with the opening *āyah*: {**Draws near for mankind their reckoning.**}[292] [This continues on from Ṭa-ha,] indicating that death draws near and that the awaited end is very close.

290 Ṭa-ha: 135
291 Ṭa-ha: 129
292 Al-Anbiyā: 1

وفيه أيضًا مناسبة لقوله هناك: ﴿وَلَا تَمُدَّنَّ عَيْنَيْكَ إِلَىٰ مَا مَتَّعْنَا بِهِۦٓ أَزْوَٰجًا مِّنْهُمْ﴾ (طه: ١٣١) الآية.

Furthermore, Sūrah al-Anbiyā has relevance to the previous *sūrah* from another angle as Ṭa-ha ends with: {**And do not extend your eyes toward that by which We have given enjoyment to [some] categories of them, [it being but] the splendour of worldly life by which We test them. And the provision of your Lord is better and more enduring.**}[293]

فإن قرب الساعة يقتضي الإعراض عن هذه الحياة الدنيا، لدنوها من الزوال والفناء، ولهذا ورد في الحديث: أنها لما نزلت قيل لبعض الصحابة: هلا سألت النبي صلى الله عليه وسلم عنها؟ فقال: ((نزلت اليوم سورة أذهلتنا عن الدنيا)).

[So as Sūrah al-Anbiyā commences with a proclamation] of the hour drawing near, this dictates that the worldly life is not the objective—due to the inevitability of it passing away and perishing. This theme of the *sūrah* also explicitly appears in the ḥadīth, "When this *sūrah* was revealed some of the Companions asked, 'Shall we not ask the Prophet about it?' So he replied, 'Today, a *sūrah* has been revealed which has detached us from the pleasures of this worldly life.'"[294]

293 Ṭa-ha: 131

294 Collected by Ibn 'Asākir in *Tārīkh Dimishq* (25/327) on the authority of 'Āmir ibn Rabī'ah. See also *Tafsīr Ibn Kathīr* (3/172-173) and al-Shawkānī's *Fatḥ al-Qadīr* (3/396).

سورة الحج

Sūrah al-Ḥajj

أقول: وجه اتصالها بسورة الأنبياء: أنه ختمها بوصف الساعة في قوله: ﴿وَاقْتَرَبَ الْوَعْدُ الْحَقُّ فَإِذَا هِيَ شَاخِصَةٌ أَبْصَارُ الَّذِينَ كَفَرُوا﴾ (الأنبياء: ٩٧)، وافتتح هذه بذلك، فقال: ﴿إِنَّ زَلْزَلَةَ السَّاعَةِ شَيْءٌ عَظِيمٌ ۝ يَوْمَ تَرَوْنَهَا تَذْهَلُ كُلُّ مُرْضِعَةٍ عَمَّآ أَرْضَعَتْ وَتَضَعُ كُلُّ ذَاتِ حَمْلٍ حَمْلَهَا وَتَرَى النَّاسَ سُكَارَى وَمَا هُمْ بِسُكَارَى﴾ (١، ٢).

I say: The manner in which Sūrah al-Ḥajj is connected to Sūrah al-Anbiyā is that Sūrah al-Anbiyā concludes with the mention of the Hour: **{And the true promise (Day of Resurrection) shall draw near. Then you will see the eyes of the disbelievers fixed with a stare of horror.}**[295] And Sūrah al-Ḥajj begins immediately with it: **{O mankind, fear your Lord. Indeed, the convulsion of the [final] Hour is a terrible thing. On the Day you see it every nursing mother will be distracted from that [child] she was nursing, and every pregnant woman will abort her pregnancy, and you will see the people [appearing] intoxicated while they are not intoxicated.}**[296]

---

295 Al-Anbiyā: 97

296 Al-Ḥajj: 1-2

سورة المؤمنون

Sūrah al-Mu'minūn

أقول: وجه اتصالها بسورة الحج: أنه لما ختمها بقوله: ﴿وَافْعَلُوا الْخَيْرَ لَعَلَّكُمْ تُفْلِحُونَ﴾ (الحج: ٧٧)، وكان ذلك مجملًا، فصَّله في فاتحة هذه السورة، فذكر خصال الخير التي من فعلها فقد أفلح، فقال: ﴿قَدْ أَفْلَحَ الْمُؤْمِنُونَ۝الَّذِينَ هُمْ فِي صَلَاتِهِمْ خَاشِعُونَ﴾ (١، ٢) الآيات.

I say: The connection between Sūrah al-Mu'minūn and Sūrah al-Ḥajj [is again related to how the previous *sūrah* ends.] He stated at the end of al-Ḥajj: {**And do good deeds so that you may be successful.**}[297] And this is extremely general, whereas Sūrah al-Mu'minūn—during its commencement—defines what these good deeds are referring to, and which by doing them, one will gain the success alluded to at the end of Sūrah al-Ḥajj: {**Successful indeed are the believers. They who are during their prayer humbly submissive.**}[298]

ولما ذكر [في] أول الحج قوله: ﴿يَا أَيُّهَا النَّاسُ إِنْ كُنْتُمْ فِي رَيْبٍ مِنَ الْبَعْثِ فَإِنَّا خَلَقْنَاكُمْ مِنْ تُرَابٍ ثُمَّ مِنْ نُطْفَةٍ﴾ (الحج: ٥) الآية. زاده هنا بيانًا [وإطنابًا] في قوله: ﴿وَلَقَدْ خَلَقْنَا الْإِنْسَانَ مِنْ سُلَالَةٍ مِنْ طِينٍ۝ثُمَّ جَعَلْنَاهُ نُطْفَةً فِي قَرَارٍ مَكِينٍ﴾ (١٢، ١٣) الآيتان. فكل جملة أُوجِزَت هناك في القصة أطنب

297 Al-Ḥajj: 77

298 Al-Mu'minūn: 1-2

فيها هنا.

Just as al-Ḥajj began with His statement: {**O mankind! If you are in doubt about the Resurrection, then surely! We have created you (i.e. Ādam) from dust, then from a mixed discharge, then from a clot and then from a little lump of flesh, some formed and some unformed (miscarriage), so that We may make it clear to you.**}[299] In al-Mu'minūn there is something similar mentioned but with extra detail: {**And indeed We created man (Ādam) out of an extract of clay. Thereafter We made him (i.e. the offspring) from a mixed discharge in a safe lodging (womb of the woman).**}[300] [So the principle again, each *sūrah* that comes with a general statement is later given explanation to in a following *sūrah*]; every stage of human development mentioned in general in al-Ḥajj is then given a more detailed account in al-Mu'minūn.

299 Al-Ḥajj: 5

300 Al-Mu'minūn: 12-13

سورة النور

Sūrah al-Nūr

أقول: وجه اتصالها بسورة قَدْ أَفْلَحَ : أنه لما قال [فيها]: ﴿وَالَّذِينَ هُمْ لِفُرُوجِهِمْ حَافِظُونَ﴾ (المؤمنون: ٥)، ذكر في هذه أحكام من لم يحفظ فرجه، من الزانية والزاني، وما اتصل بذلك من شأن القذف، وقصة الإفك، والأمر بغض البصر، وأمر فيها بالنكاح حفظًا للفروج، وأمر من لم يقدر على النكاح بالاستعفاف، وحفظ فرجه، ونهى عن إكراه الفتيات على الزنا.

I say: Its connection to al-Mu'minūn is that it mentions there regarding the success given to protecting ones chastity: {**And those who guard their chastity.**}[301] Sūrah al-Nūr gives further information, providing rulings pertaining to those who do not guard their chastity. From them are fornicators (male and female),[302] there are rules connected to accusations of adultery[303] and the story of the Ifk[304] is related to this, the obligation of lowering the gaze,[305] the commandment of

301 Al-Mu'minūn: 5

302 Al-Nūr: 2-3

303 Al-Nūr: 4-10

304 Al-Nūr: 11-18

305 Al-Nūr: 30-31

marriage to preserve chastity[306] and in the event of inability to marry—to preserve one's honour and not to fall into lewdness, and it also prohibits the forcing of young women into adultery (i.e. prostitution).

ولا ارتباط أحسن من هذا الارتباط، ولا تناسق أبدع من هذا النسق.

There is no better connection that is given to these *sūrahs* than this, and this arrangement cannot be any more harmonious.

306 Al-Nūr: 32-33

سورة الفرقان

Sūrah al-Furqān

ظهر لي بفضل الله بعدما أفكرت مدة: أن نسبة هذه السورة لسورة النور، كنسبة سورة الأنعام إلى المائدة.

What appears to me to be the case, after long and careful reflection—and this knowledge is a gift from Allah—is that Sūrah al-Furqān is annexed to al-Nūr just as al-Anʿām is to al-Mā'idah.

من حيث أن النور قد ختمت بقوله: ﴿لِلَّهِ مَا فِي السَّمَاوَاتِ وَالْأَرْضِ﴾ (النور: ٦٤)، كما ختمت بقوله: ﴿لِلَّهِ مُلْكُ السَّمَاوَاتِ وَالْأَرْضِ وَمَا فِيهِنَّ﴾ (المائدة: ١٢٠).

This happens from several aspects. From them is how Sūrah al-Nūr concludes: {**To Allah belongs all that is in the heavens and the earth.**}[307] This is similar to how al-Mā'idah ends: {**To Allah belongs the dominion of the heavens and the earth and all that is within it.**}[308]

وكانت جملة النور أخصر من المائدة، ثم فصلت هذه الجملة في سورة الفرقان فافتتحت بقوله: ﴿الَّذِي لَهُ مُلْكُ السَّمَاوَاتِ﴾ إلى قوله: ﴿وَخَلَقَ كُلَّ شَيْءٍ

307 Al-Nūr: 64. Sūrah al-Furqān also has similar *āyāt* to this. See al-Furqān: 45-61.

308 Al-Mā'idah: 120

فَقَدَّرَهُ تَقْدِيرًا﴾ (٢)، كما افتتحت الأنعام بمثل ذلك. وكان قوله عقبه: ﴿وَاتَّخَذُوا مِنْ دُونِهِ آلِهَةً﴾ (٣) إلى آخره، نظير قوله هناك: ﴿ثُمَّ الَّذِينَ كَفَرُوا بِرَبِّهِمْ يَعْدِلُونَ﴾ (الأنعام: ١).

The *āyah* of al-Nūr in fact is briefer than the *āyah* in al-Mā'idah because [the next *sūrah* after it] Sūrah al-Furqān gives a direct description of it: {**To He Whom belongs the dominion of the heavens and the earth**} until He says: {**He created everything, and has measured it exactly according to its due measurements.**}[309] This is the same manner in which He opens al-An'ām: And he follows it in al-Furqān with {**Yet they have taken gods besides Him**},[310] which is similar to how He followed up in al-An'ām: {**Yet those who disbelieve hold others as equal with their Lord.**}[311]

ثم ذكر في خلال هذه السورة جملة من المخلوقات، كمد الظل، والليل، والنوم، والنهار، والرياح، والماء، والأنعام، والأناسي ومرج البحرين، والإنسان، والنسب، والصهر، وخلق السماوات والأرض في ستة أيام، والاستواء على العرش، وبروج السماء، والسراج، والقمر، إلى غير ذلك، مما هو تفصيل لجملة: ﴿لِلَّهِ مَا فِي السَّمَاوَاتِ وَالْأَرْضِ﴾ (النور: ٦٤)، كما فصل آخر المائدة في الأنعام بمثل ذلك، وكان البسط في الأنعام أكثر لطولها.

All of this sets the theme for what follows in Sūrah al-Furqān where

309 Al-Furqān: 2

310 Al-Furqān: 3

311 Al-An'ām: 1

Allah describes in greater detail the broader creation of all things: the extension of the shadows, the night, sleep, the day, the wind, water, animals, [reproduction of] men, the two seas, lineage, humans, marriage, the creation of the heavens and the earth in six days, the rising above the throne, the constellations, the sun, the moon etc. All of this acts as an explanation of what was mentioned in Sūrah al-Nūr: **{To Allah belongs all that is in the heavens and the earth.}**[312] This is the same manner in which Sūrah al-An'ām[313] explained the ending of al-Mā'idah, and the detail provided in al-An'ām was greater due to its length.

ثم أشار في هذه السورة إلى القرون المكذوبة وإهلاكهم، كما أشار في الأنعام إلى ذلك، ثم أوضح هذه الإشارة في السورة التي تليها وهي الشعراء بالبسط التام، والتفصيل البالغ، كما أوضح تلك الإشارة التي في الأنعام وفصَّلها في سورة الأعراف التي تليها.

Furthermore, Sūrah al-Furqān is parallel to al-An'ām in how it describes the astray nations and generations that came before and what led to their punishment,[314] and this explanation of what happened to the nations before us is carried forward into the next *sūrah* (al-Shu'arā) and explained in further detail there. This is exactly how Sūrah al-A'rāf extended upon concise matters from Sūrah al-An'ām in a similar fashion, and likewise they both followed each other.

فكانت هاتان السورتان في المثاني، نظير تينك السورتين [الأنعام والأعراف] في الطوال، واتصالهما بآخر النور، نظير اتصال تلك بآخر

312 Al-Nūr: 64

313 Al-An'ām: 13, 18, 59, 61, 65, 73, 95, 96, 97, 98 and 99

314 Al-An'ām: 64-189

المائدة، المشتملة على فصل القضاء.

So the two *sūrahs* are placed amongst the *mathānī sūrahs* just like al-al-A'rāf and al-An'ām are placed amongst the lengthy *surahs*, and they are connected with the end of al-Nūr, just as the aforementioned are connected to the end of al-Mā'idah, which includes judgments.

ثم ظهر لي لطيفة أخرى، وهي: أنه إذا وقعت سورة مكية بعد سورة مدنية، افتتح أولها بالثناء على الله، كالأنعام بعد المائدة، والإسراء بعد النحل، وهذه بعد النور، وسبأ بعد الأحزاب، والحديد بعد الواقعة، وتبارك بعد التحريم، لما في ذلك من الإشارة إلى نوع استقلال، وإلى الانتقال من نوع إلى نوع.

Another fine point to consider—which is apparent to me—is that if a Makkan *sūrah* follows a Madanī *sūrah*, the Makkan *sūrah* will begin with praise of Allah, similar to al-An'ām (Makkan) following al-Mā'idah (Madanī), al-Isrā following al-Naḥl, al-Furqān which follows al-Nūr, Saba' which follows al-Aḥzāb, al-Ḥadīd which follows al-Wāqi'ah and Tabārak after al-Taḥrīm; as this gives indication to the independence of each *surah*, and the shifting from one type to another.

سورة الشعراء

Sūrah al-Shu'arā

أقول: وجه اتصالها بسورة الفرقان أنه تعالى لما أشار فيها إلى قصص مجملة بقوله: ﴿وَلَقَدْ آتَيْنَا مُوسَى الْكِتَابَ وَجَعَلْنَا مَعَهُ أَخَاهُ هَارُونَ وَزِيرًا۝فَقُلْنَا اذْهَبَا إِلَى الْقَوْمِ الَّذِينَ كَذَّبُوا بِآيَاتِنَا فَدَمَّرْنَاهُمْ تَدْمِيرًا۝وَقَوْمَ نُوحٍ لَمَّا كَذَّبُوا الرُّسُلَ أَغْرَقْنَاهُمْ وَجَعَلْنَاهُمْ لِلنَّاسِ آيَةً وَأَعْتَدْنَا لِلظَّالِمِينَ عَذَابًا أَلِيمًا۝وَعَادًا وَثَمُودَا وَأَصْحَابَ الرَّسِّ وَقُرُونًا بَيْنَ ذَلِكَ كَثِيرًا﴾ (الفرقان: ٣٥-٣٨) شرح هذه القصص، وفصَّلها أبلغ تفصيل في السورة التي تليها، ولذلك رتبت على ترتيب ذكرها في الآيات المذكورة فبدئ بقصة موسى، ولو رتبت على الواقع لأخرت كما في الأعراف.

I say: Sūrah al-Furqān is connected to Sūrah al-Shu'arā from the aspect of the continued theme of Allah ﷻ explaining the stories of the Prophets. Sūrah al-Furqān mentions them in a more general fashion: {**And indeed We gave Mūsā the Scripture, and made his brother Hārūn as a helper for him; and We said: "Both of you go to the people who have denied Our *āyāt*." Then We destroyed them with utter destruction. And Nūḥ's people, when they denied the Messengers We drowned them, and We made them as a sign for mankind. And We have prepared a painful torment for the oppressors. And [also] 'Ād and Thamūd, and the dwellers of al-Rass, and many gen-**

erations in between.}[315] These stories are explained in detail in Sūrah al-Shu'arā and in the same order mentioned in al-Furqān. For this reason, the stories of the Prophets begin with the story of Mūsā in Sūrah al-Shu'arā,[316] whereas if the stories had been cited according to their chronological order, it would have been placed afterwards, as in al-A'rāf.

فانظر إلى هذا السر اللطيف الذي مَنَّ الله بإلهامه.

The reader should ponder upon this deep intricacy, [the like] of which Allah alone inspires [one to perceive.]

ولما كان في الآيات المذكورة إشارة إلى قرون بين ذلك كثيرة، زاد في الشعراء تفصيلًا لذلك قصة قوم إبراهيم، وقوم لوط، وقوم شعيب.

Furthermore, within the midst of the stories of the generations mentioned in Sūrah al-Furqān are also many others [which were not mentioned.] Sūrah al-Shu'arā thus provides detail to the stories of Ibrāhīm, Lūṭ and the people of Shu'ayb.

ولما ختم الفرقان بقوله: ﴿وَإِذَا خَاطَبَهُمُ الْجَاهِلُونَ قَالُوا سَلَامًا﴾ (الفرقان: ٦٣)، وقوله: ﴿وَإِذَا مَرُّوا بِاللَّغْوِ مَرُّوا كِرَامًا﴾ (الفرقان: ٧٢) ختم هذه السورة بذكر الشعراء الذين هم بخلاف ذلك، واستثنى منهم مَن سلك سبيل أولئك، وبيَّن ما يمدح من الشعر، و [ما] يدخل في القول (سلامًا)، وما يذم منه، ويدخل في اللغو.

315 Al-Furqān: 35-38

316 Beginning with the story of Mūsā (al-Shu'arā: 10), the story of Nūḥ (al-Shu'arā: 105) and then Ād (al-Shu'arā: 123).

As Sūrah al-Furqān concludes with His statement: {**And when the foolish address them [with bad words] they reply back with mild words of gentleness.**}[317] And His statement: {**And if they pass by evil or evil talk, they pass by it with dignity.**}[318] Al-Shu'arā also concludes in a similar manner; giving description of the poets who contradict this behaviour mentioned in al-Furqān, as well as mentioning those who have a positive description to them. These poets are included in the words "mild words of gentleness" and blame is given to those poets who contradict this with idle and foul speech.[319]

---

317 Al-Furqān: 63

318 Al-Furqān: 72

319 Al-Shu'arā: 227

سورة النمل

Sūrah al-Naml

أقول: وجه اتصالها بما قبلها: أنها كالتتمة لها، في ذكر بقية القرون، فزاد سبحانه فيها ذكر سليمان وداود، وبسط فيها قصة لوط أبسط مما هي في الشعراء.

I say: Sūrah al-Naml is connected to the *sūrah* that came before it because al-Naml completes the theme initiated by al-Shuʿarā. As mentioned before, al-Shuʿarā gives description to the generations and nations of old, but al-Naml also gives description to stories not mentioned in al-Shuʿarā. Al-Naml provides detail to the stories of Sulaymān, Dāwūd[320] and detail regarding the story of Lūṭ[321] which is more extensive than that which was mentioned in al-Shuʿarā.

وقد روينا عن ابن عباس، وجابر بن زيد، في ترتيب [نزول] السور:

---

320 Al-Naml: 15-44

321 Al-Naml: 54-58. The author mentions that al-Naml has greater detail of the story of Lūṭ than al-Shuʿarā. However, the reality proves otherwise since the account of Lūṭ is longer in al-Shuʿarā, but al-Naml clarifies the levels of immorality and irrationality that the people of Lūṭ reached; to the extent that they believed the purity of Lūṭ to be a crime that should be punished by sending him into exile from their land. The latter was not mentioned in al-Shuaʿrā, so it is possible it has greater detail with respect to meaning, not in terms of length.

أن الشعراء نزلت ثم طس، ثم القصص، وذلك كافٍ في ترتيبها في المصحف هكذا.

It is also reported that both Ibn 'Abbās and Jābir ibn Zayd placed these *sūrahs* in this very same order, as this was the order that they were revealed in. Sūrah al-Shu'arā was revealed before the *ṭā-sīn sūrahs* and then al-Qaṣaṣ was revealed. So this is sufficient for us as a precedent to place our *muṣḥaf* in the same manner.

وأيضًا فقد وقع فيها: ﴿إِذْ قَالَ مُوسَىٰ لِأَهْلِهِ إِنِّي آنَسْتُ نَارًا﴾ (٧) إلى آخره، وذلك تفصيل قوله في الشعراء: ﴿فَوَهَبَ لِي رَبِّي حُكْمًا وَجَعَلَنِي مِنَ الْمُرْسَلِينَ﴾ (الشعراء: ٢١).

Also, al-Naml contains the statement of Allah: **{When Mūsā said to his household, "Surely, I have seen a fire"}**[322] until the end of the story. This is actually giving detail to what was not given in al-Shu'arā, as a broader statement was mentioned: **{But my Lord has granted me religious knowledge, and appointed me as one of the Messengers.}**[323]

322 Al-Naml: 7

323 Al-Shu'arā: 21

سورة القصص

Sūrah al-Qaṣaṣ

أقول: ظهر لي بعد الفكرة: أنه سبحانه لما حكى في الشعراء قول فرعون لموسى: ﴿أَلَمْ نُرَبِّكَ فِينَا وَلِيدًا وَلَبِثْتَ فِينَا مِنْ عُمُرِكَ سِنِينَ ۝ وَفَعَلْتَ فَعْلَتَكَ الَّتِي فَعَلْتَ﴾ (الشعراء: ١٨، ١٩) إلى قول موسى: ﴿فَفَرَرْتُ مِنْكُمْ لَمَّا خِفْتُكُمْ فَوَهَبَ لِي رَبِّي حُكْمًا وَجَعَلَنِي مِنَ الْمُرْسَلِينَ﴾ (الشعراء: ٢١)، ثم حكى في طس النمل قول موسى لأهله: ﴿إِنِّي آنَسْتُ نَارًا﴾ (النمل: ٧) إلى آخره، الذي هو في الوقوع بعد الفرار، ولما كان [الأمران] على سبيل الإشارة والإجمال، بسط في هذه السورة ما أوجزه في السورتين، وفصل ما أجمله فيهما على حسب ترتيبهما.

I say: After placing careful thought in to this, Sūrah al-Qaṣaṣ [offers a detailed account of the story of Mūsā which was mentioned in brief in its neighbouring *sūrahs* (i.e. al-Shuʿarā and al-Naml).] He, the Glorified, explained in al-Shuʿarā the statement of Firʿawn to Mūsā: **{[Firʿawn] said [to Musa]: "Did we not bring you up when you were a child? And you lived with us for many years. And you did what you did, which you did."}**[324] Until He informed us what Mūsā said: **{So I fled from you when I feared you, but my Lord has granted me [re-**

---

324 Al-Shuʿarā: 18-19

ligious knowledge] and appointed me as one of the Messengers.}[325] And in Sūrah an-Naml—one of the *ṭā-sīn sūrahs*, where he told his family: {**Surely, I have seen a fire**}[326] until the end. This describes what happened after he fled in a brief and concise manner. Sūrah al-Qaṣaṣ gives further description to what al-Naml and al-Shu'arā had described with brevity. Sūrah al-Qaṣaṣ builds upon the two aforementioned *sūrahs* in such a manner which again gives proof that the order of the *muṣḥaf* is the most excellent and its fluency is unmatched.

فبدأ بشرح تربية فرعون له، مصدرًا بسبب ذلك: من علو فرعون، وذبح أبناء بني إسرائيل الموجب لإلقاء موسى عند ولادته في اليم خوفًا عليه من الذبح، وبسط القصة في تربيته، وما وقع فيها إلى كبره، إلى السبب الذي من أجله قتل القبطي، وهى الفعلة التي فعل، إلى الهم بذلك عليه، والموجب لفراره إلى مدين، إلى ما وقع له [فيها] مع شعيب، وتزوجه بابنته، إلى أن سار بأهله، وآنس من جانب الطور نارًا فقال لأهله: ﴿امْكُثُوا إِنِّي آنَسْتُ نَارًا﴾ (٢٩) إلى ما وقع له فيها من المناجاة لربه، وبعثه إياه رسولًا، وما استتبع ذلك، إلى آخر القصة.

Sūrah al-Qaṣaṣ also illustrates how Mūsā was brought up in the house of Fir'awn and how he looked after him during his early years. How this occurred is that Fir'awn saw himself as superior and he slaughtered the offspring of Banī Isrā'īl, and in order to save him, Mūsā's mother placed him in the river in order for him to be saved from this ordeal. This *sūrah* provides an expansion of Mūsā's story, giving detail to his early years and how he grew to adulthood, and then it provides

325 Al-Shu'arā: 21

326 Al-Naml: 7

details of the incident where he accidentally killed the Coptic man, and this is what Fir'awn was referring to in the crime that he was accused of committing.[327] This then led to him fleeing to Madyan and then al-Qaṣaṣ describes the interactions he had with Shu'ayb; marrying his daughter and to the end of his service to Shu'ayb, until he saw the fire at Mount Ṭūr: **{Wait here, I have seen a fire}**[328] until the account of his story delves into the description of his meeting with his Lord, being appointed as a messenger and all the commandments that follow on from this new found responsibility as a messenger, until the end of the story.

فكانت السورة شارحة لما أجمل في السورتين معًا على الترتيب.

As a result, Sūrah al-Qaṣaṣ explains in detail what the two *sūrahs* before had not given detail to, and thus places itself in this sequence.

وبذلك عرف وجه الحكمة في تقدم (طس) على هذه، وتأخيرها عن الشعراء، فلله الحمد على ما ألهم.

With this, we come to realise the wisdom of Sūrah al-Qaṣaṣ following al-Naml and al-Naml following al-Shu'arā. And to Allah is all thanks for giving us this understanding.

327 Al-Shu'arā: 18-19

328 Al-Qaṣaṣ: 29

سورة العنكبوت

Sūrah al-ʿAnkabūt

أقول: ظهر لي في وجه اتصالها بما قبلها: أنه تعالى لما أخبر في أول السورة السابقة عن فرعون أنه: ﴿عَلا فِي الْأَرْضِ وَجَعَلَ أَهْلَهَا شِيَعًا يَسْتَضْعِفُ طَآئِفَةً مِنْهُمْ يُذَبِّحُ أَبْنَآءَهُمْ وَيَسْتَحْيِي نِسَآءَهُمْ﴾ (القصص: ٤) افتتح هذه السورة بذكر المؤمنين الذين فتنهم الكفار وعذبوهم على الإيمان، بعذاب دون ما عذب به قوم فرعون بني إسرائيل؛ تسلية لهم، بما وقع لمن قبلهم، وحثًّا لهم على الصبر، ولذلك قال هنا: ﴿وَلَقَدْ فَتَنَّا الَّذِينَ مِنْ قَبْلِهِمْ﴾ (٣)، وهذه أيضًا من حِكَم تأخير القصص عن (طس).

I say: It appears to me that what connects al-ʿAnkabūt to al-Qaṣaṣ is the explanation given by the Most High in the beginning of al-Qaṣaṣ regarding the characteristics of Firʿawn: {**Surely, Firʿawn exalted himself in the land and made its people into factions, weakening (oppressing) a group among them, killing their sons, and letting their females live.**}[329] Sūrah al-ʿAnkabūt starts off in a similar manner [but from the opposite aspect]; explaining the characteristics of the believers, and the tests they face when being oppressed by non-believers due to their *īmān*. It also highlights that the persecution that the believers face is less than the oppression Firʿawn afflicted upon

329 Al-Qaṣaṣ: 4

the Children of Israel—and this serves as a means of empathy to oppressed believers, to remind them of the oppression that occurred to those who believed before them and inciting them to be patient. For this reason the Most High, said at the beginning of al-'Ankabūt: **{And We indeed tested those who were before them.}**[330] Not only does this describe what came before, but also gives the wisdom to this layout of al-Qaṣaṣ following al-Naml.

وأيضًا: فلما كان في خاتمة القصص الإشارة إلى هجرة النبي صلى الله عليه وسلم، وفي خاتمة هذه الإشارة إلى هجرة المؤمنين بقوله: ﴿يَا عِبَادِيَ الَّذِينَ آمَنُوا إِنَّ أَرْضِي وَاسِعَةٌ﴾ (٥٦) ناسب تتاليهما.

Furthermore, as Sūrah al-Qaṣaṣ concludes itself with indication to the *hijrah* of the Prophet ﷺ,[331] al-'Ankabūt concludes itself with an indication to the *hijrah* of the believers: **{O My slaves who believe! Certainly, My earth is spacious.}**[332] So the relationship between al-Qaṣaṣ and al-'Ankabūt is made clear with these points.

330 Al-'Ankabūt: 3

331 Al-Qaṣaṣ: 85. Ibn 'Abbās said that the meaning of this *āyah* is: You will leave Makkah and return to it, just as you were expelled from it. See *Ṣaḥīḥ al-Bukhārī* (6/142) and *Tafsīr al-Ṭabarī* (20/80).

332 Al-'Ankabūt: 56

سورة الروم

Sūrah al-Rūm

أقول: ظهر لي في اتصالها بما قبلها: أنها ختمت بقوله: ﴿وَالَّذِينَ جَاهَدُوا فِينَا لَنَهْدِيَنَّهُمْ سُبُلَنَا﴾ (العنكبوت: ٦٩)، وافتتحت هذه بوعد من غلب من أهل الكتاب بالغلبة والنصر، وفرح المؤمنين بذلك، وأن الدولة لأهل الجهاد فيه، ولا يضرهم ما وقع لهم قبل ذلك من هزيمة.

I say: It is apparent to me that Sūrah al-Rūm continues on from what al-'Ankabūt concluded with, i.e. His statement: {**As for those who strive hard in Our cause, We will surely guide them to Our paths. And verily, Allah is with good doers.**}[333] And al-Rūm begins[334] with the divine promise that the Romans—who were from the People of the Book—will prevail and defeat their [pagan] enemies, and that such a victory will cause the believers delight. Then the *sūrah* explains that power will be given to those who strive in *jihād*, and that their previous defeats will not harm them.

هذا مع تآخيها بما قبلها في المطلع، فإن كلا منهما افتتح بـ﴿الم﴾ غير معقب بذكر القرآن، وهو خلاف القاعدة الخاصة في المفتتح بالحروف المقطعة، فإنها كلها عقبت بذكر الكتاب أو وصفه، إلا هاتين السورتين

333 Al-'Ankabūt: 69

334 Al-Rūm: 1-5

وسورة القلم، لنكتة بينتها في (أسرار التنزيل).

The two *sūrahs* are also connected by the way they both begin; starting with the split-letters of *alif-lām-mīm* without being followed by the mention of the Qur'ān, and this goes against the grain of all the other *sūrahs* which begin with split-letters. This is because all of the rest are quickly followed with a statement of description of the Book or its mention, except for these two *sūrahs*—i.e. al-'Ankabūt, al-Rūm and also Sūrah al-Qalam. I have explained this point further in *Asrār al-Tanzīl*.[335]

335 See *al-Itqān* (1/281, 3/369).

سورة لقمان

Sūrah Luqmān

أقول: ظهر لي في اتصالها بما قبلها مع المؤاخاة في الافتتاح بـ﴿الم﴾: أن قوله تعالى هنا: ﴿هُدًى وَرَحْمَةً لِلْمُحْسِنِينَ ۝ الَّذِينَ يُقِيمُونَ الصَّلَاةَ وَيُؤْتُونَ الزَّكَاةَ وَهُمْ بِالْآخِرَةِ هُمْ يُوقِنُونَ﴾ (٣، ٤) متعلق بقوله في آخر سورة الروم: ﴿وَقَالَ الَّذِينَ أُوتُوا الْعِلْمَ وَالْإِيمَانَ لَقَدْ لَبِثْتُمْ فِي كِتَابِ اللَّهِ إِلَى يَوْمِ الْبَعْثِ فَهَذَا يَوْمُ الْبَعْثِ﴾ (الروم: ٥٦) الآية، فهذا عين إيقانهم بالآخرة، وهم المحسنون الموقنون بما ذكر.

I say: What appears to me to connect Luqmān and al-Rūm is how they are in unison in terms of their commencement with *alif-lām-mīm* and due to how Luqmān begins with the statement of the Most High: {**A guide and a mercy for good-doers. Those who perform the *ṣalāt* and give *zakāt* and they have certain belief in the Hereafter.**}[336] This is connected to how Sūrah al-Rūm concludes: {**And those who have been bestowed with knowledge and faith will say, "Indeed you have stayed according to the Decree of Allah, until the Day of Resurrection, so this is the Day of Resurrection."**} Both of these *āyāt* explain their certain belief in the Hereafter and that they are good doers who have faith in what He has mentioned.

---

336 Luqmān: 3-4

وأيضًا ففي كلتا السورتين جملة من الآيات وبدء الخلق.

Furthermore, both *sūrahs* al-Rūm and Luqmān give reference to description of a number of miraculous signs and touch upon the beginning of creation.[337]

وذكر في الروم: ﴿فِي رَوْضَةٍ يُحْبَرُونَ﴾ (الروم: ١٥)، وقد فسر بالسماع، وفي لقمان: ﴿وَمِنَ النَّاسِ مَنْ يَشْتَرِي لَهْوَ الْحَدِيثِ﴾ (٦) وقد فُسر بالغناء وآلات الملاهي.

He said in al-Rūm: {**They will be in a garden [of Paradise], delighted.**}[338] And this has been explained by some commentators that they will be given the enjoyment of listening to singing.[339] In Sūrah Luqmān, however, there is a rebuke: {**And of mankind are those who purchase idle talk.**}[340] Exegetes have explained this to refer to those who listen to music and musical instruments.[341]

---

337 Al-Rūm: 9-10 and 20, Luqmān: 10 and 28

338 Al-Rūm: 15

339 This was the statement of Yaḥyā ibn Abī Kathīr. See *Tafsīr Ibn Kathīr* (6/313).

340 Luqmān: 6

341 This *tafsīr* was given by Ibn Mas'ūd, Ibn 'Abbās, Jābir, 'Ikrimah, Sa'īd ibn Jubayr, Mujāhid, Makḥūl and al-Ḥasan al-Baṣrī. See *Tafsīr al-Ṭabarī* (21/39).

سورة السجدة

Sūrah al-Sajdah

أقول: وجه اتصالها بما قبلها: أنها شرحت مفاتح الغيب الخمسة التي ذكرت في خاتمة لقمان.

I say: Sūrah al-Sajdah connects itself to the previous *sūrah* by the way Luqmān ends; by mentioning the five matters of the unseen which belong only to Allah.[342]

فقوله هنا: ﴿ثُمَّ يَعْرُجُ إِلَيْهِ فِي يَوْمٍ كَانَ مِقْدَارُهُ أَلْفَ سَنَةٍ مِمَّا تَعُدُّونَ﴾ (٥)، شرح لقوله هناك: ﴿إِنَّ اللهَ عِنْدَهُ عِلْمُ السَّاعَةِ﴾ (لقمان: ٣٤) ولذلك عقب هنا بقوله: ﴿عَالِمُ الْغَيْبِ وَالشَّهَادَةِ﴾ (٦).

In al-Sajdah, He states: **{Then it will go up to Him, in one Day, the space whereof is a thousand years of your reckoning.}**[343] This is in explanation of His statement in Luqmān: **{Verily, Allah! With Him [Alone] is the knowledge of the Hour.}**[344] And this is why He described Himself in al-Sajdah: **{That is He, the All-Knower of the unseen and the seen, the All-Mighty, the Most Merciful.}**[345]

---

342 Luqmān: 34
343 Al-Sajdah: 5
344 Luqmān: 34
345 Al-Sajdah: 6

وقوله: ﴿أَوَلَمْ يَرَوْا أَنَّا نَسُوقُ الْمَاءَ إِلَى الْأَرْضِ الْجُرُزِ﴾ (٢٧)، شرح قوله: ﴿وَيُنَزِّلُ الْغَيْثَ﴾ (لقمان: ٣٤).

Likewise His statement: **{Have they not seen how We drive water (rain clouds) to the dry land without any vegetation}**[346] is an explanation of His statement: **{He sends down the rain.}**[347]

وقوله: ﴿الَّذِي أَحْسَنَ كُلَّ شَيْءٍ خَلَقَهُ﴾ (٧) الآيات، شرح لقوله: ﴿وَيَعْلَمُ مَا فِي الْأَرْحَامِ﴾ (لقمان: ٣٤).

And His statement **{Who perfected everything which He created}**[348] is an explanation of His statement: **{And knows what is in the wombs.}**[349]

وقوله: ﴿يُدَبِّرُ الْأَمْرَ مِنَ السَّمَاءِ إِلَى الْأَرْضِ﴾ (السجدة: ٥) و﴿وَلَوْ شِئْنَا لَآتَيْنَا كُلَّ نَفْسٍ هُدَاهَا﴾ (السجدة: ١٣)، شرح لقوله: ﴿وَمَا تَدْرِي نَفْسٌ مَاذَا تَكْسِبُ غَدًا﴾ (لقمان: ٣٤).

And His statement: **{He arranges every affair from the heavens to the earth}**[350] and, **{And if We had willed, surely, We would have given every person his guidance}**[351] serve as an explanation of His statement: **{No person knows what he will earn tomorrow.}**[352]

---

346 Al-Sajdah: 27
347 Luqmān: 34
348 Al-Sajdah: 7
349 Luqmān: 34
350 Al-Sajdah: 5
351 Al-Sajdah: 13
352 Luqmān: 34

وقوله: ﴿أَءِذَا ضَلَلْنَا فِي الْأَرْضِ﴾ إلى قوله: ﴿قُلْ يَتَوَفَّاكُم مَّلَكُ الْمَوْتِ الَّذِي وُكِّلَ بِكُمْ ثُمَّ إِلَىٰ رَبِّكُمْ تُرْجَعُونَ﴾ (١٠، ١١)، شرح لقوله: ﴿وَمَا تَدْرِي نَفْسٌ بِأَيِّ أَرْضٍ تَمُوتُ﴾ (لقمان: ٣٤)، فلله الحمد على ما ألهم.

His statement: {**And they say: "When we are [dead and become] lost in the earth"**} until His statement: {**Say: "The angel of death, who is set over you, will take your souls, then you shall be brought to your Lord"**}[353] explains His statement: {**And no person knows in what land he will die.**}[354] And to Allah is all thanks for teaching us.

353 Luqmān: 10-11

354 Luqmān: 34

سورة الأحزاب

Sūrah al-Aḥzab

أقول: وجه اتصالها بما قبلها: تشابه مطلع هذه ومقطع تلك، فإن تلك ختمت بأمر النبي صلى الله عليه وسلم بالإعراض عن الكافرين، وانتظار عذابهم، [ومطلع هذه الأمر بتقوى الله، وعدم طاعة الكافرين والمنافقين، فصارت كالتتمة لما ختمت به تلك، حتى كأنهما سورة واحدة].

I say: It is connected to the preceding *sūrah* due to its beginning bearing similitude to the ending of al-Sajdah. Sūrah al-Sajdah concludes with the command upon the Prophet ﷺ to distance himself from the disbelievers and to await their reckoning.[355] Al-Aḥzāb begins in a similar fashion with the command upon the Prophet ﷺ to fear Allah and not to obey the disbelievers and hypocrites. So it is as if al-Aḥzāb continues on from al-Sajdah, completing its message, as if they are conjoined *sūrahs*.

355 Al-Sajdah: 30

سورة سبأ

Sūrah Saba'

أقول: ظهر لي وجه اتصالها بما قبلها، وهو أن تلك لما ختمت بقوله: ﴿لِيُعَذِّبَ اللَّهُ الْمُنَافِقِينَ وَالْمُنَافِقَاتِ وَالْمُشْرِكِينَ وَالْمُشْرِكَاتِ وَيَتُوبَ اللَّهُ عَلَى الْمُؤْمِنِينَ وَالْمُؤْمِنَاتِ﴾ (الأحزاب: ٧٣) افتتحت هذه بأن له ما في السماوات وما في الأرض، وهذا الوصف لائق بذلك الحكم، فإن الملك العام، والقدرة التامة، يقتضيان ذلك.

I say: It is apparent to me that Saba' is connected to the previous *sūrah* due to the way al-Aḥzāb ends, with His statement: {**So that Allah will punish [in the hereafter] the hypocrites, men and women, and the men and women who are polytheists and Allah will pardon the true believers of the Islamic Monotheism, men and women.**}[356] And Saba' begins with praise for Allah[357] and stating that He has dominion of the heavens and the earth, a description that is suitable for His ownership, because His encompassing rule and all-ability over His creation necessitates such description.

وخاتمة سورة الأحزاب: ﴿وَكَانَ اللَّهُ غَفُورًا رَحِيمًا﴾ (الأحزاب: ٧٣)، وفاصلة الآية الثانية من مطلع سبأ: ﴿وَهُوَ الرَّحِيمُ الْغَفُورُ﴾ (٢).

---

356 Al-Aḥzāb: 73

357 Saba': 1

Sūrah al-Aḥzāb also ends with the statement: {**And Allah is Ever Oft-Forgiving, Most Merciful.**}[358] And Saba' opens with a similar description for Him in its second *āyah*: {**He is the Most Merciful, the Oft-Forgiving.**}[359]

358 Al-Aḥzāb: 73

359 Saba': 2

سورة فاطر

Sūrah Fāṭir

أقول: مناسبة وضعها بعد سبأ تآخيهما في الافتتاح بالحمد، مع تناسبهما في المقدار.

I say: Saba' preceding Fāṭir is appropriate because both *sūrahs* begin with praise for Allah, and due to their lengths being quite similar.

وقال بعضهم: افتتاح سورة فاطر بالحمد مناسب لختام ما قبلها، من قوله: ﴿وَحِيلَ بَيْنَهُمْ وَبَيْنَ مَا يَشْتَهُونَ كَمَا فُعِلَ بِأَشْيَاعِهِمْ مِنْ قَبْلُ﴾ (سبأ: ٥٤)، كما قال: ﴿فَقُطِعَ دَابِرُ الْقَوْمِ الَّذِينَ ظَلَمُوا وَالْحَمْدُ لِلَّهِ رَبِّ الْعَالَمِينَ﴾ (الأنعام: ٤٥)، فهو نظير اتصال أول الأنعام بفصل القضاء المختتم به المائدة.

Some opined that Sūrah Fāṭir begins with praise for Allah because Saba' ends with the statement: **{And prevention will be placed between them and what they desire, as was done with their kind before.}**[360] [So for justice over the oppressors, Sūrah Fāṭir begins with praise.] This is similar to His statement in al-An'ām: **{So the roots of the people who did wrong were cut off. And all praises and thanks are for Allah, the Lord of all creation.}**[361] This is also similar to how

360 Saba': 54

361 Al-An'ām: 45

al-An'am begins in praising Him[362], in connection to the last *āyah* of al-Mā'idah,[363] which professes His Dominion.

362 Al-An'ām: 1
363 Al-Mā'idah: 119

سورة يس

Sūrah Yā-Sīn

أقول: ظهر لي وجه اتصالها بما قبلها: أنه لما ذكر في سورة فاطر قوله: ﴿وَجَآءَكُمُ النَّذِيرُ﴾ (فاطر: ٣٧) وقوله: ﴿وَأَقْسَمُوا بِاللهِ جَهْدَ أَيْمَانِهِمْ لَئِنْ جَآءَهُمْ نَذِيرٌ لَيَكُونُنَّ أَهْدَى مِنْ إِحْدَى الْأُمَمِ فَلَمَّا جَآءَهُمْ نَذِيرٌ﴾ (فاطر: ٤٢)، والمراد به محمد صلى الله عليه وسلم وقد أعرضوا عنه وكذبوه، فافتتح هذه السورة بالإقسام على صحة رسالته، وأنه على صراط مستقيم، لينذر قومًا ما أنذر آباؤهم، وهذا وجه بيِّن.

I say: What appears to be the case is that Yā-sīn connects itself to Fāṭir by His statement: {**And the warner came to you.**}[364] And His statement: {**And they swore by Allah their most binding oath, that if a warner came to them, they would be more guided than any of the nations, yet when a warner came to them…**}[365] These *āyahs* are talking about the coming of the Prophet ﷺ,[366] [however, despite swearing their most binding oath,] they rejected him and belied his message. For this reason, this *sūrah* begins with a divine oath that the Prophet has come with a true message and that he is upon the straight path.

---

364 Fāṭir: 37

365 Fāṭir: 42

366 This was the opinion of al-Suddī and ʿAbd al-Raḥmān ibn Zayd ibn Aslam. See *Tafsīr Ibn Kathīr* (6/542).

He is a warner with the same warning their forefathers were warned of and thus it is clear [that Sūrah Yā-sīn explains the theme found in Sūrah Fāṭir.]

وفي فاطر: ﴿وَسَخَّرَ الشَّمْسَ وَالْقَمَرَ﴾ (فاطر: ١٣)، وفي يس: ﴿وَالشَّمْسُ تَجْرِي لِمُسْتَقَرٍّ لَهَا ذَلِكَ تَقْدِيرُ الْعَزِيزِ الْعَلِيمِ۝وَالْقَمَرَ قَدَّرْنَاهُ مَنَازِلَ حَتَّى عَادَ كَالْعُرْجُونِ الْقَدِيمِ﴾ (٣٨، ٣٩)، وذلك أبسط وأوضح.

Also, Allah states in Fāṭir: {**And He has subjected the sun and the moon.**}[367] And in Yā-sīn, [the same reference to the creation of the universe]: {**And the sun runs on its fixed course for a term [appointed]. That is the decree of the All-Mighty, the All-Knowing. And the moon, We have measured for it degrees until it returns like the old dried curved date stalk.**}[368] So the latter is more detailed and clearer than the former.

وفي فاطر: ﴿وَتَرَى الْفُلْكَ فِيهِ مَوَاخِرَ﴾ (فاطر: ١٢)، وفي يس: ﴿وَآيَةٌ لَهُمْ أَنَّا حَمَلْنَا ذُرِّيَّتَهُمْ فِي الْفُلْكِ الْمَشْحُونِ۝وَخَلَقْنَا لَهُمْ مِنْ مِثْلِهِ مَا يَرْكَبُونَ۝وَإِنْ نَشَأْ نُغْرِقْهُمْ فَلا صَرِيخَ لَهُمْ وَلا هُمْ يُنْقَذُونَ﴾ (يس: ٤١-٤٣) فزاد القصة بسطاً.

Also in Fāṭir: {**And you see the ships cleaving [through.]**}[369] And in Yā-sīn: {**And a sign for them is that We bore their offspring in the laden ship (of Nūḥ). And We have created for them [ships] similar to what he had so that they can ride. And if We willed, We could have drowned them, and there would be no cry of help nor would they be saved.**}[370] So Yā-sīn complements Fāṭir here by providing richer

367 Fāṭir: 13
368 Yā-sīn: 38-39
369 Fāṭir: 12
370 Yā-sīn

detail.

سورة الصافات

Sūrah al-Ṣāffāt

أقول: هذه السورة بعد (يس) كالأعراف بعد الأنعام، وكالشعراء بعد الفرقان، في تفصيل أحوال القرون المشار إلى إهلاكهم، كما أن تينك السورتين تفصيل لمثل ذلك كما تقدم.

I say: The relationship between al-Ṣāffāt and Yā-sīn resembles that of al-Aʿrāf and al-Anʿām, and that of al-Shuʿarā and al-Furqān. These *sūrahs* mention the generations and nations of old who were destroyed and these two *sūrahs* contain more detail as to how and why.[371] And we have mentioned this previously.

371 For example, see: Yā-sīn: 31 and al-Ṣāffāt: 12.

سورة ص

Sūrah Ṣād

أقول: هذه السورة بعد الصافات، كطس بعد الشعراء، وكطه والأنبياء بعد مريم، وكيوسف بعد هود، في كونها متممة لها بذكر من بقي من الأنبياء، ممن لم يذكروا فيها، فإنه سبحانه ذكر في الصافات: نوحًا، وإبراهيم، والذبيح، وموسى، وهارون، ولوطًا، وإلياس، ويونس، وذكر هنا: داود، وسليمان، وأيوب، وأشار إلي بقية من ذكر، فهي بعدها أشبه شيء بالأنبياء وطس، بعد مريم والشعراء.

I say: The reason for Ṣād being placed after al-Ṣāffāt is exactly the same reason as to why Ṭā-ṣīn follows al-Shuʿarā, why Ṭā-hā and al-Anbiyā follow Maryam, or why Yūsuf follows Hūd—all of the following *sūrahs* mentioned here complete the stories of the Prophets which appeared in the *sūrahs* that came before them, and mention stories which the preceding ones did not contain. So in al-Ṣāffāt, the Glorified and the Exalted mentioned the stories of Nūḥ, Ibrāhīm, Ismāʿīl, Mūsā, Hārūn, Lūṭ, Ilyās, Yūnus and here in Ṣād: Dāwūd, Sulaymān, Ayūb and He indicated to the rest that He mentioned. This is the most similar pattern of theming to the one used in al-Anbiyā and al-Qaṣaṣ, after Maryam and al-Shuʿarā.

سورة الزمر

Sūrah al-Zumar

[أقول]: لا يخفى وجه اتصال أولها بآخر (ص)، حيث قال في (ص): ﴿إِنْ هُوَ إِلَّا ذِكْرٌ لِلْعَالَمِينَ﴾ (ص: ٨٧)، ثم قال هنا: ﴿تَنْزِيلُ الْكِتَابِ مِنَ اللَّهِ﴾ (١)، فكأنه قيل: هذا الذكر تنزيل، وهذا تلاؤم شديد، بحيث إنه لو أسقطت البسملة لالتأمت الآيتان كالآية الواحدة.

I say: It is clear for one to see that the last *āyah* of Ṣād and the beginning of al-Zumar are directly related. Sād ends with His statement: **{It is only a reminder to the worlds.}**[372] Al-Zumar begins with: **{The revelation of this Book is from Allah.}**[373] It is as if the *āyahs* state together that this reminder is the revelation, and the resemblance is so striking that had the *basmallah* been removed before them it could have been conjoined into one longer *āyah*.

وقد ذكر الله تعالى في آخر (ص) قصة خلق آدم، وذكر في صدر هذه قصة خلق زوجه [منه]، وخلق الناس كلهم منه، وذكر خلقهم في بطون أمهاتهم خلقًا من بعد خلق، ثم ذكر أنهم ميتون، ثم ذكر وفاة النوم والموت، ثم ذكر القيامة، والحساب، والجزاء، والنار، والجنة، وقال:

372 Ṣād: 87
373 Al-Zumar: 1

﴿وَقُضِيَ بَيْنَهُمْ بِالْحَقِّ وَقِيلَ الْحَمْدُ لِلَّهِ رَبِّ الْعَالَمِينَ﴾ (٧٥).

Also at the end of Ṣād, Allah ﷻ gives description to the creation of Ādam[374] and at the start of al-Zumar this message continues with greater detail mentioning the creation of his wife,[375] the creation of his progeny—all of them created in stages in the womb, death being prescribed for all of them,[376] the resemblance of sleep to death,[377] description of the Last Day, the account, the recompense, the Fire and Jannah.[378] In concluding al-Zumar, He stated: {**And they will be judged with truth, and it will be said, "All praises and thanks are for Allah, the Lord of all creation."**}[379]

فذكر أحوال الخلق، من المبدأ إلى المعاد، متصلًا بخلق آدم المذكور في السورة التي قبلها.

So al-Zumar is themed at describing the creation; its beginning stages to death, resurrection and recompense. All of this is connected to the message taken from the story of Ādam which was mentioned in the previous *sūrah*.

374 Ṣād: 71-85
375 Al-Zumar: 6
376 Al-Zumar: 30
377 Al-Zumar: 42
378 Al-Zumar: 71
379 Al-Zumar: 75

سورة غافر

Sūrah Ghāfir

أقول: وجه إيلاء الحواميم السبع سورة الزمر: تآخي المطالع في الافتتاح بتنزيل الكتاب، وفي مصحف أُبي بن كعب أول الزمر ﴿حم﴾، وذلك مناسبة جليلة.

I say: This is the beginning of the seven *ḥā-mīm sūrahs*[380] and it is connected to al-Zumar as they all (i.e. al-Zumar and the *ḥā-mīm sūrahs*) begin in mentioning the sending down of divine revelation. It was due to this that Ubayy ibn Ka'b had al-Zumar commencing with *ḥā-mīm* in his *muṣḥaf*, and this is a sublime correlation.[381]

ثم إن الحواميم ترتبت لاشتراكها في الافتتاح بـ﴿حم﴾، وبذكر الكتاب بعد حم، وأنها مكية، بل ورد في الحديث أنها نزلت جملة [واحدة].

---

380 Ghāfir, Fuṣṣilat, al-Shūra, al-Zukhruf, al-Dukhān, al-Jāthiyyah and al-Aḥqāf.

381 See *al-Itqān* (1/222) where the author quoted it from the book of *al-Maṣāḥif* of Ibi Ashtah. In the main manuscript, it states that the beginning of al-Zumar is *ḥā-mīm* according to the *muṣḥaf* of Ibn Mas'ūd, but I have accepted that which is mentioned in *al-Itqān* and *al-Burhān* of al-Zarkashī (1/130).

I could not find a trace of the narration to Ubayy in *al-Itqān*, *al-Burhān* or any *ḥadīth* corpus within which I searched.

Furthermore, the *ḥā-mīm sūrahs* all begin with these split-letters and then move on to the praise and description of the Book. All of them are Makkan *sūrahs*, and in fact it has been narrated in a ḥadīth that all seven were revealed in one go.

وفيها شبه من ترتيب ذوات ﴿الر﴾ الست.

The *ḥā-mīm sūrahs* also resemble the six *alif-lām-rā sūrahs*.[382]

فانظر ثانية الحواميم وهي فصلت، كيف شابهت ثانية ذوات ﴿الر﴾ هود في تغيير الأسلوب في وصف الكتاب، وأن في هود: ﴿كِتَابٌ أُحْكِمَتْ آيَاتُهُ ثُمَّ فُصِّلَتْ﴾ (هود: ١)، وفي فصلت: ﴿كِتَابٌ فُصِّلَتْ آيَاتُهُ﴾ (فصلت: ٣)، وفي سائر ذوات ﴿الر﴾ ﴿تِلْكَ آيَاتُ الْكِتَابِ﴾ (الحجر: ١)، وفي سائر الحواميم: ﴿تَنْزِيلُ الْكِتَابِ﴾ (غافر: ٢) أو ﴿وَالْكِتَابِ﴾ (الدخان: ٢).

When one analyses the second *ḥā-mīm sūrah*, Fuṣṣilat, one would see its resemblance to the second *alif-lām-rā sūrah*, Hūd, in the way they alter the style of describing the book in the beginning. Sūrah Hūd begins with His statement: {**[This is] a Book whose verses are perfected and then presented in detail.**}[383] And Fuṣṣilat in a similar manner: {**A Book whose *āyāt* have been detailed.**}[384] Also, the rest of the *alif-lām-rā sūrahs* begin [with mentioning the word Book,] so in al-Ḥijr: {**The *āyāt* of the Book.**}[385] And the same is the case for the *ḥā-mīm sūrahs*, so here in Ghāfir: {**The revelation of the Book**}[386] and in al-Dhukhān:

382 Yūnus, Hūd, Yūsuf, al-Ra'd, Ibrāhīm and al-Ḥijr.

383 Hūd: 1

384 Fuṣṣilat: 3

385 Al-Ḥijr 1

386 Ghāfir: 2

{By the manifest Book.}[387]

ورويناعن جابر بن زيد، وابن عباس في ترتيب نزول السور: أن الحواميم نزلت عقب الزمر، وأنها نزلت متتاليات كترتيبها في المصحف: المؤمن، ثم السجدة، ثم الشورى، ثم الزخرف، ثم الدخان، ثم الجاثية، ثم الأحقاف، ولم يتخللها نزول غيرها، وذلك مناسبة جلية واضحة في وضعها هكذا.

It is also reported that Jābir ibn Zayd and Ibn 'Abbās stated regarding the order of revelation of the *sūrahs*: The *ḥā-mīm sūrahs* were revealed after al-Zumar as follows—and they were revealed one after another as in the *muṣḥaf*—: Ghāfir, al-Sajdah, al-Shūrā, al-Zukhruf, al-Dhukhān, al-Jāthiyah and then al-Aḥqāf. Nothing came in-between to disrupt this order of revelation.[388] And this concordance found in their ordering is especially exquisite.

ثم ظهر لي لطيفة أخرى، وهي: أنه في كل ربع من أرباع القرآن توالت سبع سور مفتتحة بالحروف المقطعة. فهذه [السور] السبع مصدرة بـ﴿حم﴾، وسبع في الربع الذي قبله [متوالية و] ذوات ﴿الر﴾ الست متوالية، و﴿المص﴾ الأعراف، فإنها متصلة بيونس على ما تقدمت الإشارة إليه، وافتتح أول القرآن بسورتين من ذلك، وأول النصف الثاني بسورتين.

There is also another ingenious angle apparent to me: In every quarter

387 Al-Dhukhān: 2

388 See *al-Itqān* (1/97). This was transmitted from Abī Bakr Muḥammad ibn al-Ḥārith ibn Abyaḍ in his famous work.

of the Qurʿān, there appears a group of seven *sūrahs* which start off with the same split-letters. These seven *sūrahs* commence with *ḥā-mīm*, and another seven *sūrahs* in the preceding quarter, and six *alif-lām-rā sūrahs*, and al-Aʿrāf which begins with *alif-lām-mīm-ṣād* and is connected to Yūnus as previously mentioned. The beginning of the Qur'ān starts with two [split-lettered] *sūrahs*—and the beginning of the second half of the Qur'ān starts with two such *sūrahs*.

وقال الكرماني في (العجائب): ترتيب الحواميم السبع لما بينها من التشاكل الذي خصت به، وهو: أن كل سورة منها استفتحت بالكتاب أو وصفه، مع تفاوت المقادير في الطول والقصر، وتشاكل الكلام في النظام. انتهى.

Al-Kirmānī said in his book *al-ʿAjā'ib*,[389] "The order of the *ḥā-mīm sūrahs* is such that all of them begin with mention of the Book or in giving description of it, irrespective of how long or short the description is, and the use of homophones."

قلت: وانظر إلى مناسبة ترتيبها، فإن مطلع غافر مناسب لمطلع الزمر، ومطلع فصلت التي هي ثانية الحواميم مناسب لمطلع هود، التي هي ثانية ذوات ﴿الر﴾، ومطلع الزخرف مؤاخٍ لمطلع الدخان، وكذا مطلع الجاثية لمطلع الأحقاف.

I say: When one ponders upon the appropriateness of the ordering of these *sūrahs* it makes the connection of Ghāfir even more resounding to al-Zumar as they both commence with a similar description. Then

389 This was a book of *tafsīr* which he authored entitled, *Lubāb al-Tafsīr wa Ajā'ib al-Ta'wīl*, but its manuscript has been lost.

the beginning of Fuṣṣilat—the second *ḥā-mīm sūrah*—resembles the commencement of Hūd—the second *alif-lām-rā sūrah*. Thereafter, al-Zukhruf begins in the same manner as al-Dhukhān and al-Jāthiyah in the same manner as al-Aḥqāf.

سورة القتال

Sūrah Muḥammad (Sūrah al-Qitāl)

[أقول] لا يخفى وجه ارتباط أولها بقوله في آخر الأحقاف: ﴿فَهَلْ يُهْلَكُ إِلَّا الْقَوْمُ الْفَاسِقُونَ﴾ (الأحقاف: ٣٥)، واتصاله وتلاحمه وبحيث إنه لو أسقطت البسملة منه لكان متصلًا اتصالًا واحدًا لا تنافر فيه، كالآية الواحدة، آخذًا بعضه بعنق بعض.

I say: It is evident that the commencement of this *sūrah* connects to the end of al-Aḥqāf, where He states: **{But shall any nation be destroyed except if they are rebellious?}**[390] [The beginning of Sūrah Muḥammad expands upon this subject and goes on to describe the legislations connected to warfare,][391] to the extent that had the *basmallah* been removed from between the two, they would certainly be

390 Al-Aḥqāf: 35

391 Sūrah Muḥammad has also been named Sūrah al-Qitāl or the Sūrah of Warfare and is connected to Sūrah al-Aḥqāf because al-Aḥqāf is themed at describing the rejection of those who are stubborn and arrogant to the truth. Al-Aḥqāf explains that throughout the ages, every nation has had its warner(s), calling them to having faith and rectifying their morals and deeds. The *sūrah* also presents rational proofs against their rejection, so on the back of this, if they reject then Sūrah Muḥammad gives explanation to some of the laws and principles connected to warfare.

considered to be one fluid *āyah*.

سورة الفتح

Sūrah al-Fatḥ

[أقول] لا يخفى وجه حُسن وضعها هنا، لأن الفتح بمعنى النصر، مرتَّب على القتال، وقد ورد في الحديث: أنها [نزلت] مبينة لما يفعل به وبالمؤمنين، بعد إبهامه في قول تعالى في الأحقاف: ﴿وَمَآ أَدْرِي مَا يُفْعَلُ بِي وَلَا بِكُمْ﴾ (الأحقاف: ٩)، فكانت متصلة بسورة الأحقاف من هذه الجملة.

I say: The appropriateness of Sūrah al-Fatḥ being placed here is striking, because al-Fatḥ is defined as victory and support, and victory is brought about by striving and fighting. It is reported in some narrations that this *sūrah* was revealed to clarify what would be done by the Prophet ﷺ and the believers, clearing the ambiguity in al-Aḥqāf: **{I do not know what will be done with me or with you.}**[392] [393] So it is connected to Sūrah al-Aḥqāf from this aspect.

---

392 Al-Aḥqāf: 9

393 This is a view reported from Ibn 'Abbās by 'Alī ibn Talḥah, and it was also stated by 'Ikrimah, al-Ḥasan and Qatādah that this *āyah* was later explained in Sūrah al-Fatḥ: **{We have given you (O Muhammad)…}** (al-Fatḥ: 2) and about his followers: **{That He may admit the believing men and the believing women to Gardens under which rivers flow}** (al-Fatḥ: 5). See *Tafsīr Ibn Kathīr* (7/260).

سورة الحجرات

Sūrah al-Ḥujarāt

[أقول] لا يخفى تآخي هاتين السورتين [الفتح والحجرات] مع ما قبلهما، لكونهما مدنيتين، ومشتملتين على أحكام، فتلك فيها قتال الكفار، وهذه فيها قتال البغاة، وتلك خُتمت بالذين آمنوا، وهذه افتتحت بالذين آمنوا، وتلك تضمنت تشريفًا له صلى الله عليه وسلم خصوصًا مطلعها، وهذه أيضًا في مطلعها أنواع من التشريف له صلى الله عليه وسلم.

I say: It is obvious that Sūrah al-Fatḥ and Sūrah al-Ḥujarāt share a trait with the previous *sūrah* as they are both Madanī *sūrahs* and both are themed at explaining legislative rulings. Al-Fatḥ has legislation connected to warfare with the disbelievers and al-Ḥujarāt has rulings connected to fighting oppressive rebels.[394] Sūrah al-Fatḥ ends with description of the believers[395] and al-Ḥujarāt begins with description of them,[396] and that includes honouring the Prophet ﷺ, particularly in its beginning. The beginning of this *sūrah* also includes holding the Prophet ﷺ in high esteem.[397]

---

394 Al-Ḥujarāt: 9

395 Al-Fatḥ: 29

396 Al-Ḥujarāt: 1

397 See al-Fatḥ: 2, al-Ḥujarāt: 1 and al-Ḥujarāt: 3-4

سورة الذاريات

Sūrah al-Dhāriyāt

أقول: لما ختمت (ق) بذكر البعث، واشتملت على ذكر الجزاء، والجنة، والنار، وغير ذلك من أحوال القيامة، افتتح هذه السورة بالإقسام على أن ما توعدون من ذلك لصادق، وإن الدين -وهو الجزاء- لواقع.

I say: As Sūrah Qāf—which preceded it—ended with description of the resurrection, the types of recompense, Jannah, the Fire and other matters connected to the Last Day, al-Dhāriyāt begins with a divine oath, swearing to the truth of the events that will take place on that day and that the "*dīn*"—which refers to recompense—is true.

ونظير ذلك: افتتاح المرسلات بذلك، بعد ذكر الوعد والوعيد والجزاء في سورة الإنسان.

This is similar to how al-Mursalāt starts, after mentioning the promise, threat and recompense that is found in Sūrah al-Insān.

سورة الطور

Sūrah al-Ṭūr

أقول: وجه وضعها بعد الذاريات: تشابههما في المطلع والمقطع، فإن في مطلع كل منهما صفة حال المتقين بقوله: ﴿إِنَّ الْمُتَّقِينَ فِي جَنَّاتٍ﴾ (الذاريات: ١٥، الطور: ١٧) الآيات، وفي مقطع كل منهما صفة حال الكفار، بقوله في تلك: ﴿فَوَيْلٌ لِلَّذِينَ كَفَرُوا﴾ (الذرايات: ٦٠)، وفي هذه: ﴿فَالَّذِينَ كَفَرُوا﴾ (٤٢).

I say: The reason why al-Ṭūr is placed after al-Dhāriyāt is because of them bearing similitude in their commencements and endings. Both of their commencements describe the nature of the pious and their reward: **{Surely, the pious will be in Gardens…}**[398] And the endings of both of these *sūrahs* are themed at describing the state of those who disbelieve: **{Then, woe to those who disbelieve.}**[399] And in al-Ṭūr: **{But those who disbelieve are themselves in a plot.}**[400]

398 Al-Dhāriyāt: 15 and al-Ṭūr: 17

399 Al-Dhāriyāt: 60

400 Al-Ṭūr: 42

سورة النجم

Sūrah al-Najm

أقول: وجه وضعها بعد الطور: أنها شديدة المناسبة لها، فإن الطور خُتمت بقوله: ﴿وَإِدْبَارَ النُّجُومِ﴾ (الطور: ٤٩)، وافتتحت هذه بقوله: ﴿وَالنَّجْمِ إِذَا هَوَىٰ﴾ (١).

I say: The reason why al-Najm is placed after al-Ṭūr is because it bears great resemblance and concordance to it in its theme. Al-Ṭūr finishes with His statement: {**And at the setting of the stars.**}[401] And al-Najm commences with: {**By the star when it goes down.**}[402]

ووجه آخر: [وهو] أن الطور ذكر فيها ذرية المؤمنين، وأنهم تبع لآبائهم، وهذه فيها ذكر ذرية اليهود في قوله: ﴿هُوَ أَعْلَمُ بِكُمْ إِذْ أَنْشَأَكُمْ مِنَ الْأَرْضِ [وَإِذْ أَنْتُمْ أَجِنَّةٌ فِي بُطُونِ أُمَّهَاتِكُمْ﴾ (٣٢) الآية، فقد أخرج ابن أبي حاتم، وابن المنذر، والواحدي بأسانيدهم عن ثابت بن الحارث الأنصاري، قال: كانت اليهود تقول: إذا هلك صبي صغير هو: صديق، فبلغ ذلك النبي صلى الله عليه وسلم فقال: ((كذبت يهود، ما من نسمة يخلقها الله في

401 Al-Ṭūr: 49

402 Al-Najm: 1

بطن أمه إلا أنه شقي أو سعيد))، وأنزل الله عند ذلك ﴿هُوَ أَعْلَمُ بِكُمْ إِذْ أَنْشَأَكُمْ مِنَ الْأَرْضِ﴾ الآية].

From another aspect, Sūrah al-Ṭūr [is also themed at mentioning the reward in the hereafter,] so it makes mention of the children of the believers and that they will be with their parents in the hereafter.[403] It also mentions the children of the Jews and their place in the hereafter,[404] as in His statement in al-Najm: **{He knows of you very well when He created you from the earth (Ādam), and when you were foetuses in your mothers' wombs...}**[405] It is reported by Ibn Abī Ḥātim, Ibn al-Munthir and al-Wāḥidī on the authority of Thābit ibn al-Ḥārith al-Anṣārī, "[Some of] the Jews used to say, 'If one of our children passes away [at an early age] then he is a truthful believer.' This reached the Prophet ﷺ so he said, 'They have lied; there is not a foetus that Allah has created in the womb of its mother except their faith is written—either being wicked [and destined to the Fire] or happy [and being destined to Jannah].' Then Allah revealed the *āyah* [in al-Najm] because of this: **{He knows of you very well when He created you from the earth (Ādam), and when you were foetuses in your mothers' wombs.}**"[406]

ولما قال هناك في المؤمنين: ﴿أَلْحَقْنَا بِهِمْ ذُرِّيَّتَهُمْ وَمَا أَلَتْنَاهُمْ مِنْ عَمَلِهِمْ مِنْ شَيْءٍ﴾ (الطور: ٢١) أي: ما نقصنا الآباء بما أعطينا البنين، مع نفعهم بما

403 See al-Tur: 21

404 This is the case for all disbelievers and not the Jews alone. Since the creation of Ādam all of mankind are in one of two parties: a party in Jannah and a party in the flames. See *Tafsir Ibn Kathīr* (7/437).

405 Al-Najm: 32

406 See *al-Durr al-Manthūr* of al-Suyūṭī (6/128), where he said it was reported by al-Ṭabarānī.

عمل آباؤهم، قال هنا في صفة الكفار أو بني الكفار: ﴿وَأَنْ لَيْسَ لِلْإِنْسَانِ إِلَّا مَا سَعَىٰ﴾ (٣٩) خلاف ما ذكر في المؤمنين الصغار.

Then in al-Ṭūr, Allah describes for the believers in the hereafter: **{Whose offspring follow them in faith, to them shall We join their offspring, and We shall not decrease the reward of their deeds in anything.}**[407] Meaning, children will join their parents in the higher station in Jannah without any of the parents' reward being taken away from them in the slightest. Rather, they will join their parents by the virtue of the good deeds their parents performed. In al-Najm, on the other hand, it says about the disbelievers or their children: **{And that man can have nothing except that which he strives for.}**[408] The very opposite of the virtue given to the believers.

وهذا وجه بيِّن بديع في المناسبة، من وادي التضاد.

This displays the eloquent reasoning behind their order, they clarify each other through clarifying contrasting situations.

407 Al-Ṭūr: 21

408 Al-Najm: 39

سورة القمر

Sūrah al-Qamar

أقول: لا يخفى ما في توالي هاتين السورتين من حُسْن التناسق [والتناسب] في التسمية، لما بين النجم والقمر من الملابسة، ونظيره توالي الشمس والليل والضحى، وقبلها سورة الفجر.

I say: It is extremely fitting that these two *sūrahs* are mentioned alongside one another—simply by looking at their names—as there is a strong correlation between the stars (al-Najm) and the moon (al-Qamar). This is similar to the sun (Sūrah al-Shams), the night (Sūrah al-Layl) and the morning day (Sūrah al-Ḍuḥa) being placed together, with all of them following the dawn (Sūrah al-Fajr).

ووجه آخر وهو: أن هذه السورة بعد النجم كالأعراف بعد الأنعام [وكالشعراء بعد الفرقان]، وكالصافات بعد يس، في أنها تفصيل لأحوال الأمم المشار إلى إهلاكهم في قوله هناك: ﴿وَأَنَّهُ أَهْلَكَ عَادًا الْأُولَىٰ۝وَثَمُودَ فَمَآ أَبْقَىٰ۝وَقَوْمَ نُوحٍ مِن قَبْلُ إِنَّهُمْ كَانُوا هُمْ أَظْلَمَ وَأَطْغَىٰ۝وَالْمُؤْتَفِكَةَ أَهْوَىٰ﴾ (النجم: ٥٠-٥٣).

From another angle, Sūrah al-Qamar following Sūrah al-Najm is like Sūrah al-A'rāf following al-An'ām, al-Shua'rā following al-Furqān and al-Ṣāffāt following Yā-sīn; as al-Qamar provides detail regarding the destroyed nations indicated to in al-Najm:[409] {**And it is He Who destroyed the first [people of] 'Ād. And Thamūd, He spared none of them. And the people of Nūḥ before them, surely, they were more unjust and more rebellious. And He destroyed the overthrown cities [of Sodom].**}[410]

409 These are explained in detail in al-Qamar in the very same order. See al-Qamar: 9 and 42.

410 Al-Najm: 50-53

سورة الرحمن

Sūrah al-Raḥmān

أقول: لما قال سبحانه وتعالى في آخر القمر: ﴿بَلِ السَّاعَةُ مَوْعِدُهُمْ وَالسَّاعَةُ أَدْهَى وَأَمَرُّ﴾ (القمر: ٤٦)، ثم وصف حال المجرمين في سقر، وحال المتقين في جنات ونهر، فصَّل هذا الإجمال في هذه السورة أتم تفصيل، على الترتيب الوارد في الإجمال.

I say: Allah ﷻ ended al-Qamar with: **{Rather, the Hour is their appointed time, and the Hour will be more grievous and more bitter.}**[411] It then gives a general description to the recompense for the people destined to the Fire and the state of the pious in Jannah and their rivers. Sūrah al-Raḥmān provides detail regarding these matters which are mentioned broadly in al-Qamar, and in the same order.

فبدأ بوصف مرارة الساعة، والإشارة إلى إذهابها، ثم وصف النار وأهلها، والجنة وأهلها، ولذا قال [﴿يُعْرَفُ الْمُجْرِمُونَ بِسِيمَاهُمْ﴾ (٤١)، فلم يقل: الكافرون أو نحوه لاتصاله بقوله هناك: ﴿إِنَّ الْمُجْرِمِينَ﴾ (القمر: ٤٧)، ثم وصف الجنة وأهلها، وكذا قال] فيهم: ﴿وَلِمَنْ خَافَ مَقَامَ رَبِّهِ جَنَّتَانِ﴾ (٤٦)، وذلك هو عين التقوى، ولم يقل: [و] لمن آمن وأطاع، أو نحوه،

411 Al-Qamar: 46

لتتوافق الألفاظ في التفصيل والمفصل.

Sūrah al-Raḥmān begins with a description of the commencement of the Hour. It then describes what happens after it; a description of the Fire[412] and its people, and Jannah and its people.[413] For example: **{The criminals will be known by their marks, and they will be seized by their forelocks and their feet.}**[414] This *āyah* does not mention the word "disbelievers" or something similar, rather it uses the same wording which came in al-Qamar before it: **{The criminals are in error.}**[415] Then al-Raḥmān mentions Jannah and its people, saying about them: **{But for him who fears the standing before his Lord, he will have gardens.}**[416] This is the true meaning of *taqwā*.[417] The wording here [is "fears the standing before..."] and not something like "for the one who believes and obeys", and this is so the wordings complement and define one another.[418]

وعرف بذلك أن هذه السورة بأسرها شرح لآخر السورة التي قبلها، فلله الحمد على ما ألهم وفهَّم.

From this we know that this *sūrah*—and I praise Allah alone for the understanding and inspiration He bestowed—explains the end of the previous *sūrah*, and all praises are to the One who inspires and gave us this understanding.

412 Al-Raḥmān: 31-44
413 Al-Raḥmān: 46-78
414 Al-Raḥmān: 41
415 Al-Qamar: 47
416 Al-Raḥmān: 46
417 See Sūrah al-Qamar: 54
418 *Taqwā* is to fear standing in front of Allah, so al-Qamar mentions *taqwā* in the *āyah* **{Indeed the righteous will be amongst gardens and rivers}** (al-Qamar: 54) and then its exact definition in wording comes in Sūrah al-Raḥmān.

سورة الواقعة

Sūrah al-Wāqi'ah

أقول: هذه السورة متآخية مع سورة الرحمن في أن كلًّا منهما في وصف القيامة، والجنة والنار، وانظر إلى اتصال قوله هنا: ﴿إِذَا وَقَعَتِ الْوَاقِعَةُ﴾ (١)بقوله هناك: ﴿فَإِذَا انْشَقَّتِ السَّمَآءُ﴾ (الرحمن: ٣٧)، ولهذا اقتصر في الرحمن على ذكر انشقاق السماء، وفي الواقعة على ذكر رجّ الأرض، فكأن السورتين لتلازمهما واتحادهما سورة واحدة.

I say: The theme of both Sūrah al-Raḥmān and Sūrah al-Wāqi'ah is to describe the Day of Judgement, and the Fire and Jannah. One should see the connection between the statement in al-Wāqi'ah: **{When the Event befalls}**[419] with that in al-Raḥmān: **{Then when the heaven is rent asunder.}**[420] For this reason, al-Raḥmān briefly describes the events of the Day of Judgement with this one line, whereas al-Wāqi'ah describes the shaking of the earth.[421] As they share in this theme, it is as if both of these *sūrahs* are conjoined.

ولهذا عكس في الترتيب، فذكر في أول هذه السورة ما ذكره في آخر تلك، وفي آخر هذه ما في أول تلك، كما أشرت إليه في سورة آل عمران

419 Al-Wāqi'ah: 1
420 Al-Raḥmān: 37
421 Al-Wāqi'ah: 4

مع سورة البقرة.

For this reason, despite the themes in both remaining the same, the order has differed. So that which al-Raḥmān begins with, al-Waqi'ah ends with and vice versa. This is similar to what we mentioned when discussing the relationship between al-Baqarah and Āli 'Imrān.

فافتتح [في سورة] الرحمن بذكر القرآن، ثم ذكر الشمس والقمر، ثم ذكر النبات، ثم خلق الإنسان، والجان من مارج من نار، ثم صفة [يوم] القيامة، ثم صفة النار، ثم صفة الجنة.

So Sūrah al-Raḥman begins with mention of the Qur'ān, then the sun and the moon, the plants, the creation of man, and then the creation of jinn from smokeless fire, and then it moves onto describing the Last Day and then the Fire and Jannah.

وابتدأ هذه بذكر القيامة ثم صفة الجنة، ثم صفة النار، ثم خلق الإنسان، ثم النبات، ثم الماء، ثم النار، ثم [ذكر] النجوم، ولم يذكرها في الرحمن، كما لم يذكر هنا الشمس والقمر، ثم ذكر القرآن.

Whereas al-Wāqi'ah commences with description of the Day of Judgement, then Jannah, then the Fire, the creation of man, plants, water, fire, the stars—which were not mentioned in al-Raḥmān, just as the sun and moon were not mentioned here—and then it gives mention of the Qur'ān.

فكانت هذه السورة كالمقابلة لتلك، وكردِّ العَجُز على الصَّدْر.

So this *sūrah* complements al-Raḥmān i.e. its beginning addressed topics similar to the topic addressed at the end of al-Raḥmān, and vice versa.

سورة الحديد

Sūrah al-Ḥadīd

قال بعضهم: وجه اتصالها بالواقعة: أنها بدأت بذكر التسبيح، وتلك خُتمت بالأمر به.

Some scholars stated that the connection of al-Ḥadīd with al-Wāqiʿah is that it commences with the mention of *tasbīḥ*, while al-Wāqiʿah ends with the order to perform it.

قلت: وتمامه: أن أول الحديد واقع موقع العلة للأمر به، وكأنه قيل: ﴿فَسَبِّحْ بِاسْمِ رَبِّكَ الْعَظِيمِ﴾ (الواقعة: ٩٦)؛ لأنه ﴿سَبَّحَ لِلَّهِ مَا فِي السَّمَاوَاتِ وَالْأَرْضِ﴾ (١).

I say: The reason why al-Ḥadīd starts with glorification is due to the description given of Him at the end of al-Wāqiʿah which commands glorification of Him, so it is as if He said: {**So glorify with praises the Name of your Lord, the Most Great.**}[422] And this is because: {**Whatsoever is in the heavens and the earth glorifies Allah, and He is the All-Mighty, All-Wise.**}[423]

---

422 Al-Wāqiʿah: 96

423 Al-Ḥadīd: 1

سورة المجادلة

Sūrah al-Mujādilah

أقول: لما كان في مطلع الحديد ذكر صفاته الجليلة، ومنها: الظاهر والباطن، وقال: ﴿يَعْلَمُ مَا يَلِجُ فِي الْأَرْضِ وَمَا يَخْرُجُ مِنْهَا وَمَا يَنْزِلُ مِنَ السَّمَآءِ وَمَا يَعْرُجُ فِيهَا وَهُوَ مَعَكُمْ أَيْنَ مَا كُنْتُمْ﴾ (الحديد: ٤) افتتح هذه بذكر أنه سمع قول المجادِلة التي شكت إليه صلى الله عليه وسلم؛ ولهذا قالت عائشة رضي الله عنها حين نزلت: ((سبحان الذي وسع سمعه الأصوات، إني لفي ناحية البيت لا أعرف ما تقول)).

I say: The beginning of Sūrah al-Ḥadīd is based upon giving glorification of Allah and His Noble Attributes. It describes that Allah has full knowledge of the apparent and the hidden, so He said: {**He knows what goes into the earth and what comes out of it, what descends from the heaven and what ascends to it, and He is with you [by His Knowledge] wherever you may be.**}[424] Sūrah al-Mujādilah gives an example of this where Allah heard the disputing woman who complained to the Prophet ﷺ. For this reason, 'Āishah ؓ said that when this *āyah* was revealed, "{**Glorified is the One whose Hearing extends across all voices**} I was [sitting] in a corner of the house, [and she complained about her husband,] but I did not hear what she said."[425]

---

424 Al-Ḥadīd: 4

425 Collected by Ibn Mājah (1/67), Imām Aḥmad in *al-Musnad* (6/46) and al-

وذكر بعد ذلك قوله: ﴿أَلَمْ تَرَ أَنَّ اللَّهَ يَعْلَمُ مَا فِي السَّمَاوَاتِ وَمَا فِي الْأَرْضِ مَا يَكُونُ مِنْ نَجْوَى ثَلَاثَةٍ إِلَّا هُوَ رَابِعُهُمْ﴾ (٧)، وهو تفصيل لإجمال قوله: ﴿وَهُوَ مَعَكُمْ أَيْنَ مَا كُنْتُمْ [وَاللَّهُ بِمَا تَعْمَلُونَ بَصِيرٌ]﴾ (الحديد: ٤).

After this, He said: {**Have you not seen that Allah knows everything that is in the heavens and is on the earth? There is no gathering of three except He is their fourth [with His Knowledge.]**}[426] This is an explanation of what was mentioned broadly in al-Ḥadīd: {**And He is with you wherever you may be. And Allah, of what you do, is seeing.**}[427]

وبذلك تعرف الحكمة في الفصل بها بين الحديد والحشر، مع تآخيهما في الافتتاح بـ﴿سَبَّحَ﴾.

With this, one comes to see the wisdom of placing this *sūrah* here to serve as a separator between al-Ḥadīd and al-Ḥashr, despite both of these *sūrahs* opening with {**Sabbaḥa**}.

Bukhārī (9/144) in a *mu'allaq* report.

426 Al-Mujādilah: 7

427 Al-Ḥadīd: 4

سورة الحشر

Sūrah al-Ḥashr

[أقول:] آخر سورة المجادلة نزل فيمن قتل أقرباؤه من الصحابة يوم بدر، وأول الحشر نازل في غزوة بني النضير، وهي عقبها، وذلك نوع من المناسبة والربط.

I say: Sūrah al-Mujādilah ends with reference to the Companions whose relatives were killed during the Battle of Badr,[428] and al-Ḥashr begins with reference to the Battle of Banī al-Naḍīr,[429] which took place after it. This illustrates their concordance and connection.

وفي آخر تلك: ﴿كَتَبَ اللَّهُ لَأَغْلِبَنَّ أَنَا وَرُسُلِي﴾ (المجادلة: ٢١)، وفي أول هذه: ﴿فَأَتَاهُمُ اللَّهُ مِنْ حَيْثُ لَمْ يَحْتَسِبُوا وَقَذَفَ فِي قُلُوبِهِمُ الرُّعْبَ﴾ (٢).

And at the end of al-Mujādilah: Allah has decreed, {**Verily! It is I and**

428 This refers to the *āyah*: {**Those—He has decreed within their hearts faith and supported them with spirit from Him.**} It has been said that "they" in this *āyah* refers to Abū 'Ubaydah—who killed his father at the Battle of Badr, Abū Bakr who wanted to fight his son 'Abdul Raḥmān, Muṣ'ab ibn 'Umayr who killed his brother, 'Umar who killed a relative and Ḥamzah, 'Alī and 'Ubaydah ibn al-Ḥārith who killed 'Utbah, Shaybah and al-Walīd ibn 'Utbah. See *Ṭabaqāt Ibn Sa'd* (1/300). [T:] I.e. during the midst of the battle.

429 See al-Ḥashr: 2. Also see al-Bukhārī (6/183) in the Chapter of *Tafsīr* and Muslim (8/245) in the Chapter of *Tafsīr* on the authority of Ibn 'Abbās.

My Messengers who shall be the victorious.}[430] And at the beginning of al-Ḥashr: {**But Allah's [retribution] reached them from a place where they did not expect it, and He cast panic into their hearts.}**[431]

وفي آخر تلك ذكر من حاد الله ورسوله، وفي أول هذه ذكر من شاق الله ورسوله.

At the end of al-Mujādilah Allah mentions those who oppose (*ḥāda*) Him and His Messenger,[432] and Sūrah al-Ḥashr begins with mentioning those who opposed (*shāqa*) Allah and His Messenger.[433]

430 Al-Mujādilah: 21
431 Al-Ḥashr: 2
432 Al-Mujādilah: 22
433 Al-Ḥashr: 4

سورة الممتحنة

Sūrah al-Mumtaḥinah

أقول: لما كانت سورة الحشر في المعاهَدين من أهل الكتاب، عقبت بهذه، لاشتمالها على ذكر المعاهَدين من المشركين، لأنها نزلت في صلح الحديبية.

I say: As Sūrah al-Ḥashr is themed at events that happened with some of the People of the Book they had treaties with, it is followed by al-Mumtaḥinah which is themed at explaining rulings connected to treaties the Muslims had with the polytheists, as it was revealed due to the Treaty of al-Ḥudaybiyyah.[434]

ولما ذكر في الحشر موالاة المؤمنين بعضهم بعضًا ثم موالاة الذين [نافقوا الكفار] من أهل الكتاب، افتتح هذه السورة بنهي المؤمنين عن اتخاذ الكفار أولياء، لئلا يشابهوا المنافقين في ذلك، وكرر ذلك وبسطه، إلى أن ختم به، فكانت في غاية الاتصال، ولذلك فصل بها بين الحشر

---

434 It was revealed because of Ḥāṭib ibn Abī Balt'ah who gave the polytheists of Makkah information of the Prophet's oncoming plan to conquer Makkah after the polytheists proved treacherous to the Treaty of al-Ḥudaybiyyah. See al-Bukhārī (6/185-186) in the Chapter of *Tafsīr*.

والصف، مع تآخيهما في الافتتاح بـ﴿سَبَّحَ﴾.

As Sūrah al-Ḥashr mentions the support and loyalty of the believers to each other, and then mentions the support of the hypocrites to disbelievers from the People of the Book, this *sūrah* begins with instruction to the believers in not taking the disbelievers as close protectors, lest they end up resembling the hypocrites mentioned in al-Ḥashr. Al-Mumtaḥinah repeats this message and explains it in detail, and it closes with it. This shows the connection of themes between the two *sūrahs*. This is why al-Mumtaḥinah is placed after al-Ḥashr but before al-Ṣaff; despite al-Ḥashr and al-Ṣaff both beginning with {**Sabbaḥa**}.

سورة الصف

Sūrah al-Ṣaff

أقول: في سورة الممتحنة ذكر الجهاد في سبيل الله، وبسطه في هذه السورة أبلغ بسط.

I say: Sūrah al-Mumtaḥina makes mention of *jihād* in the path of Allah [and rulings connected to it,] and this is explained further in Sūrah al-Ṣaff.

سورة الجمعة

Sūrah al-Jumuʿah

أقول: ظهر لي في وجه اتصالها بما قبلها: أنه تعالى لما ذكر في سورة الصف حال موسى مع قومه، وأذاهم له، ناعيًا عليهم ذلك، وذكر في هذه السورة حال الرسول صلى الله عليه وسلم، وفضل أمته؛ تشريفًا لهم، ليظهر فضل ما بين الأمتين، ولذا لم يعرض فيها لذكر اليهود.

I say: What appears to me to be the case—in terms of its connection to the previous *sūrah*—is that Allah ﷻ describes in al-Ṣaff the story of Mūsā with his people, the harm he received from them, and this is met with heavy reproach towards them for their behaviour.[435] Sūrah al-Jumuʿah gives description to the Messenger of Allah ﷺ, the virtue of his Ummah and the nobility given to them. This is in order to display the honour of his nation over the Jews, which therefore explains the reason why the Jews were not mentioned.

وأيضًا لما ذكر هناك قول عيسى: ﴿وَمُبَشِّرًا بِرَسُولٍ يَأْتِي مِنْ بَعْدِي اسْمُهُ أَحْمَدُ﴾ (الصف: ٦)، قال هنا: ﴿هُوَ الَّذِي بَعَثَ فِي الْأُمِّيِّينَ رَسُولًا مِنْهُمْ﴾ (٢) إشارة

435 See Sūrah al-Ṣaff: 5. This *āyah* and those after it describe those who disbelieved in their Prophets Mūsā and ʿĪsā, and thus disbelieved in Allah. Āyāt 5-8 of al-Jumuʿah then refute the reasoning behind their rejection and their claim that they are the chosen of Allah.

إلى أنه الذي بشر به عيسى، وهذا وجه حسن في الربط.

Sūrah al-Ṣaff also quotes the statement of 'Īsā: {**I am the Messenger of Allah unto you confirming the Torah before me, and giving glad tidings of a Messenger to come after me, whose name shall be Ahmed.**}[436] Sūrah al-Jumu'ah begins with the glad tidings of this messenger prophesied by 'Īsā: {**He it is who sent amongst the unlettered ones a Messenger from among themselves, reciting to them His *āyāt*, purifying them.**}[437] This shows that there is a strong relation between the two *sūrahs*.

وأيضًا لما ختم تلك السورة بالأمر بالجهاد وسماه تجارة، ختم هذه بالأمر بالجمعة، وأخبر أنها خير من التجارة الدنيوية.

Also, al-Ṣaff ends with encouragement to perform *jihād* for the sake of Allah, and it was referred to as a "trade". Al-Jumu'ah ends [with reference to trade] in the order to the Friday prayer; informing us that it is better than trade in the worldly sense.

وأيضًا فتلك سورة الصف، والصفوف تشرع في موضعين: القتال، والصلاة، فناسب تعقيب سورة صف القتال بسورة صلاة تستلزم الصف ضرورة، وهي الجمعة، لأن الجماعة شرط فيها دون سائر الصلوات.

Also, al-Ṣaff is named as it is (i.e. the rows), and the commandment to make rows is legislated during the prayer and during battle. So it is fitting that a *sūrah* which mentions the rows of fighting, is followed by a *sūrah* which mentions a prayer in which the making of rows is essential, namely the Jumu'ah prayer. More so, the presence of a con-

436 Al-Ṣaff: 6

437 Al-Jumu'ah: 2

gregation is a prerequisite for the Friday prayer to be valid, unlike for all the other prayers (i.e. congregation is not a prerequisite for them).

فهذه وجوه أربعة فتح الله بها.

These are four aspects—which Allah has facilitated me to perceive—in which al-Ṣaff is connected to al-Jumuʿah.

سورة المنافقون

Sūrah al-Munāfiqūn

أقول: وجه اتصالها بما قبلها: أن سورة الجمعة ذكر فيها المؤمنون، وهذه ذكر فيها أضدادهم، وهم المنافقون، ولهذا أخرج الطبراني في الأوسط عن أبي هريرة: أن رسول الله صلى الله عليه وسلم كان يقرأ في صلاة الجمعة بسورة الجمعة يحرض بها المؤمنين، وبسورة المنافقين يفزع بها المنافقين.

I say: Sūrah al-Munāfiqūn is connected to al-Jumu'ah because al-Jumu'ah gives description to the believers, whereas al-Munāfiqūn describes the opposite of belief: hypocrisy. For this reason, it is reported by al-Ṭabarānī in *al-Awsaṭ* on the authority of Abu Hurayrah that the Messenger of Allah used to recite in the Jumu'ah prayers Sūrah al-Jumu'ah, to motivate the believers, and al-Munāfiqūn, to warn against hypocrisy.[438]

وتمام المناسبة: أن السورة التي بعدها فيها ذكر المشركين، والسورة التي قبل الجمعة فيها ذكر أهل الكتاب من اليهود والنصارى، والتي قبلها وهي

---

438 Collected by al-Haythamī in *Majma' al-Zawā'id* (2/191) on the authority of Abī Hurayrah, and al-Haythamī attributed it to al-Ṭabarānī in *al-Awṣat* who classed it as *ḥasan*.

الممتحنة فيها ذكر المعاهَدين من المشركين، والتي قبلها وهي الحشر فيها المعاهدين من أهل الكتاب، فإنها نزلت في بني النضير حين نبذوا العهد وقوتلوا.

What completes the connection between the two is that Sūrah al-Munāfiqūn addresses the polytheists of Quraysh whereas the *sūrah* before al-Jumuʿah (i.e. al-Ṣaff) addresses the People of the Book, from the Jews and the Christians. Likewise, al-Mumtaḥinah discusses policies in dealing with treachery from polytheists living under the rule of Muslims, whereas al-Ḥashr before it discusses policies in dealing with treachery from the People of the Book, living under the rule of Muslims, as it was revealed in relation to Banī al-Naḍīr when they broke their treaty and the Muslims fought them.

وبذلك اتضحت المناسبة في ترتيب هذه السور الست هكذا، لاشتمالها على أصناف الأمم، وفي الفصل بين المسبحات بغيرها، لأن إيلاء سورة المعاهدين من أهل الكتاب بسورة المعاهدين من المشركين أنسب من ترك ذلك، وإيلاء سورة المؤمنين بسورة المنافقين أنسب من غيره.

For this reason, it is clear that the order of these six *sūrahs* (from al-Ḥashr to al-Taghābun) is arranged so for the deeper reason of addressing the various nations; and the separation between the Musabiḥḥāt with other *sūrahs* is because placing the *sūrah* that talks about polytheists under Muslim rule and the *sūrah* that talks about the People of the Book who are under Muslim rule next to each other is more appropriate than not doing so, and as such, placing the *sūrah* in which it mentions the believers with the *sūrah* in which it mentions the hypocrites is more appropriate than not doing so.

فظهر بذلك أن الفصل بين المسبحات التي هي نظائر لحكمة دقيقة من لدن حكيم خبير، فلله الحمد على ما فهم وألهم.

This also explains why the *sūrahs* that begin with glorification of Allah amongst this order are split; separated for a precise and intricate reason from the All-Wise, the All-Knower. So all praise is to Allah for giving us this knowledge and intuition.

هذا وقد ورد عن ابن عباس في ترتيب النزول: أن سورة التغابن نزلت عقب الجمعة، وتقدم نزول سورة المنافقون فما فصل بينهما إلا لحكمة، والله أعلم.

It is also reported from Ibn 'Abbās regarding the order of revelation: Al-Taghābūn was revealed after al-Jumu'ah, while al-Munāfiqūn was revealed earlier.[439] However, the placement of al-Munāfiqūn between al-Jumu'ah and al-Taghābūn was certainly due to a greater wisdom. And Allah knows best.

---

439 See *al-Itqān* (1/97). This was reported by Jābir ibn Zayd, and he was one of the scholars of the Qur'ān amongst the Tābi'īn.

سورة التغابن

Sūrah al-Taghābun

أقول: لما وقع في آخر سورة المنافقون: ﴿وَأَنْفِقُوا مِنْ مَا رَزَقْنَاكُمْ مِنْ قَبْلِ أَنْ يَأْتِيَ أَحَدَكُمُ الْمَوْتُ﴾ (المنافقون: ١٠) الآية، عقب بسورة التغابن، لأنه قيل في معناه: إن الإنسان يأتي يوم القيامة، وقد جمع مالًا، ولم يعمل فيه خيرًا، فأخذه وارثه بسهولة، من غير مشقة في جمعه، فأنفقه في وجوه الخير، فالجامع محاسَب معذَّب مع تعبه في جمعه، والوارث منعَّم مثاب، مع سهولة وصوله إليه، وذلك هو التغابن.

I say: As Sūrah al-Munāfiqūn ends with His statement: {**And spend from which We have provided you, before death comes to one of you.**}[440] Sūrah al-Taghābun is located after it in order to explain this *āyah*; it is as if the meaning is, "The Day of Judgement is drawing close for mankind, and they have amassed wealth but have not amassed good deeds. Material wealth which will pass on to the heirs with great ease and without the difficulty endured in procuring it. So spend before you pass away in goodly causes because without this, the one who passes away has spent a lifetime saving but will be punished by it, whereas the ones who will enjoy his material wealth will be the heirs—due to the ease with which it reached them." This is the defini-

440 Al-Munāfiqūn: 10

tion of al-Taghābun [translated to mean, "mutual loss".][441]

فارتباطه بآخر السورة المذكورة في غاية الوضوح، ولهذا قال هنا: ﴿وَأَنْفِقُوا خَيْرًا لِأَنْفُسِكُمْ وَمَنْ يُوقَ شُحَّ نَفْسِهِ فَأُولَئِكَ هُمُ الْمُفْلِحُونَ﴾ (١٦).

So al-Taghābun's connection to the end of the previous *sūrah* is due to them sharing this clear objective. Thus it says here: {**And spend in charity, that is better for yourselves, and whoever is protected from his own greed, then they are the successful ones.**}[442]

وأيضًا ففي آخر تلك: ﴿لا تُلْهِكُمْ أَمْوَالُكُمْ وَلا أَوْلادُكُمْ عَنْ ذِكْرِ اللَّهِ﴾ (المنافقون: ٩)، وفي هذه: ﴿إِنَّمَا أَمْوَالُكُمْ وَأَوْلادُكُمْ فِتْنَةٌ﴾ (١٥)، وهذه الجملة كالتعليل لتلك الجملة، ولذا ذكرت على ترتيبها.

From another viewpoint, Sūrah al-Munāfiqūn is concluded with: {**Do not let your wealth or your children divert you from the remembrance of Allah.**}[443] Likewise, it states in al-Taghābun: {**Surely it is your wealth and your children which are a test.**}[444] So it is as if the latter sentence provides the reason for the former sentence, and it is for this reason that the two things are mentioned in the same order in both *āyahs*.

وقال بعضهم: لما كانت سورة المنافقون رأس ثلاث وستين سورة، أشير فيها إلى وفاة النبي صلى الله عليه وسلم بقوله: ﴿وَلَنْ يُؤَخِّرَ اللَّهُ نَفْسًا إِذَا جَاءَ

441 See *Tafsīr al-Kuwāsh* (4/112).
442 Al-Taghābun: 16
443 Al-Munāfiqūn: 9
444 Al-Taghābun: 15

أَجَلُهَا﴾ (المنافقون: ١١)، وأنه مات على رأس ثلاث وستين سنة، وعقبها بالتغابن، ليظهر التغابن في فقده صلى الله عليه وسلم.

Some scholars have stated that Sūrah al-Munāfiqūn is the sixty third *sūrah* in the Qur'ān which also indicates towards the death of the Prophet with His statement: {**And Allah grants respite to no one when his appointed time (death) comes.**}[445] He passed away at sixty three and so Sūrah al-Taghābun follows this *āyah*, as if to say that the passing of the Prophet ﷺ is not comparable in terms of its gravity to any loss one could face.[446]

445 Al-Munāfiqūn: 11

446 See *al-Itqān* (4/30).

سورة الطلاق

Sūrah al-Ṭalāq

أقول: لما وقع في [آخر] سورة التغابن: ﴿إِنَّ مِنْ أَزْوَاجِكُمْ وَأَوْلَادِكُمْ عَدُوًّا لَكُمْ﴾ (التغابن: ١٤)، وكانت عداوة الأزواج تفضي إلى الطلاق، وعداوة الأولاد قد تفضي إلى القسوة، وترك الإنفاق عليهم، فعقبت ذلك بسورة فيها ذكر أحكام الطلاق، والإنفاق على الأولاد والمطلقات بسببهم.

I say: As it states at the end of Sūrah al-Taghābun: {**Surely some of your wives and your children are enemies for you.**}[447] This enmity towards wives often leads to divorce. Enmity towards children often leads to foul manners and a lack of expenditure towards them. So after al-Taghābun, al-Ṭalāq explains ruling pertaining to divorce, family-maintenance and causes for divorce.

447 Al-Taghābun: 14

سورة التحريم

Sūrah al-Taḥrīm

أقول: هذه السورة متآخية مع التي قبلها في الافتتاح بخطاب النبي صلى الله عليه وسلم وتلك مشتملة على طلاق النساء، وهذه على تحريم الإيلاء، وبينهما من المناسبة ما لا يخفى.

I say: This *sūrah* begins in the same manner that al-Ṭalāq does; addressing the Prophet ﷺ. Sūrah al-Ṭalāq is themed at discussing divorce but al-Taḥrīm is themed at forbidding the vow of continence, so both of these *sūrahs* are heavily linked.

ولما كانت تلك في خصام نساء الأمة، ذكر في هذه خصومة نساء النبي صلى الله عليه وسلم إعظامًا لمنصبهن أن يذكرن مع سائر النسوة، فأفردن بسورة خاصة، ولهذا ختمت بذكر امرأتين في الجنة: آسية امرأة فرعون، ومريم بنة عمران.

As the preceding *sūrah* talked about the marital disputes of Muslim women, the marital disputes that occurred in the Prophet's ﷺ house are mentioned in this *sūrah*. [This actually gives virtue to the wives of the Prophet,] as they possess a level of rank above that of all other women, [given that they are the Mothers of the Believers;] so they were mentioned in a separate *sūrah* solely for them, which is concluded by giving mention to two woman of Jannah: Āsiya, the wife of Fir'awn, and Maryam bint 'Imrān.[448]

448 Al-Taḥrīm:11-12.

سورة تبارك

Sūrah al-Tabārak (i.e. al-Mulk)

أقول: ظهر لي بعد الْجُهْد: أنه لما ذكر آخر التحريم امرأتي نوح ولوط الكافرتين، وامرأة فرعون المؤمنة، افتتحت هذه السورة بقوله: ﴿الَّذِي خَلَقَ الْمَوْتَ وَالْحَيَاةَ﴾ (٢) مرادًا بهما الكفر والإيمان في أحد الأقوال، للإشارة إلى أن الجميع بخلقه وقدرته، ولهذا كفرت امرأتا نوح ولوط، ولم ينفعهما اتصالهما بهذين النبيين الكريمين، وآمنت امرأة فرعون، ولم يضرها اتصالها بهذا الجبار العنيد، لما سبق في كل من القضاء والقدر.

I say: What appears to me [that connects al-Tabārak with al-Taḥrīm]—after I exerted effort in analysis—is how al-Taḥrīm is concluded with mention of the wives of Nūḥ and Lūṭ, who were both disbelievers. It compares their situation to the believing wife of Fir'awn, so al-Tabārak begins with His statement: **{Who has created death and life.}**[449] This means disbelief and *īmān* (belief), according to one of the views of the exegetes.[450] To indicate that all created beings are subject to the will and power of Allah. This is why the disbelieving wives of Nūḥ and Lūṭ did not profit from their marriage to two noble prophets. Likewise, the wife of Fir'awn believed and was not harmed by the oppressive stubbornness of her husband. Therefore, the *āyah* in al-Mulk

---

449 Al-Mulk: 2

450 Referring to al-Sulamī in *Ḥaqā'iq al-Tafsīr* (p. 201).

is explained from the perspective of divine pre-decree.

[ثم ظهر لي] وجه آخر: وهو أن [أول] تبارك متصل بقوله في آخر الطلاق: ﴿اللَّهُ الَّذِي خَلَقَ سَبْعَ سَمَاوَاتٍ وَمِنَ الْأَرْضِ مِثْلَهُنَّ﴾ (الطلاق: ١٢)، فزاد ذلك بسطًا في هذه الآية: ﴿الَّذِي خَلَقَ سَبْعَ سَمَاوَاتٍ طِبَاقًا مَا تَرَى فِي خَلْقِ الرَّحْمَٰنِ مِنْ تَفَاوُتٍ فَارْجِعِ الْبَصَرَ هَلْ تَرَى مِنْ فُطُورٍ﴾ إلى قوله: ﴿وَلَقَدْ زَيَّنَّا السَّمَاءَ الدُّنْيَا بِمَصَابِيحَ﴾ (٣-٥)، وإنما فصلت بسورة التحريم؛ لأنها كالتتمة لسورة الطلاق.

It also appears to me that there is a connection from another direction, Sūrah al-Mulk's commencement is connected to that which al-Ṭalāq finishes with: **{It is Allah Who has created seven heavens and of the earth the like thereof (i.e. seven).}**[451] So this is expanded upon in the *āyah*: **{Who has created the seven heavens one above another, you can see no fault in the creations of the Most Beneficent. Then look again: Do you see any breaks?}** Until His statement: **{And indeed We have adorned the nearest heaven with lamps.}**[452] And the reason that these two *sūrahs* are separated is because al-Taḥrīm (the *sūrah* between them) serves as somewhat of a completion of Sūrah al-Ṭalāq.

451 Al-Ṭalāq: 12
452 Al-Mulk: 3-5

سورة ن

Sūrah Nūn (al-Qalam)

أقول: لما ذكر سبحانه في آخر [سورة] تبارك التهديد بتغوير الماء، استظهر عليه في هذه السورة بإذهاب ثمر أصحاب البستان في ليلة بطائف طاف عليه وهم نائمون، فأصبحوا لم يجدوا له أثرًا، حتى ظنوا أنهم ضلوا الطريق، وإذا كان هذا في الثمار وهي أجرام كثيفة، فالماء الذي هو لطيف رقيق أقرب إلى الإذهاب؛ ولهذا قال: ﴿وَهُمْ نَائِمُونَ ۝ فَأَصْبَحَتْ كَالصَّرِيمِ﴾ (١٩، ٢٠)، وقال هناك: ﴿إِنْ أَصْبَحَ مَاؤُكُمْ غَوْرًا﴾ (الملك: ٣٠) إشارة إلى أنه يسري عليه في ليلة كما أسري على الثمرة في ليلة.

I say: At the end of Sūrah al-Mulk, the Glorified challenges the readers on how they would bring about water if it was to be taken away from them.[453] This connects itself to Sūrah Nūn which has within it the story of the companions of the garden—who lost their fruits when it was struck by a disaster overnight whilst they were sleeping.[454] When they awoke they found their garden was destroyed, to the extent that they thought they had taken the wrong route and confused somebody else's garden for their own (despite knowing the route to their garden very well). So if this occurred to solid objects in the shape of fruits,

---

453 Al-Mulk: 30

454 Al-Qalam: 17-31

then it is easier to occur to water, a soft liquid which can easily evaporate or be absorbed. For this reason, Sūrah Nūn has the *āyahs*: {**While they were asleep. So it became as though it was reaped by the morning.**}[455] And before this, He said in al-Mulk: {**If your water was to become sunken.**}[456] This indicates that water can be taken away during the night, just like those fruits were taken away from them overnight.

455 Al-Qalam: 19-20

456 Al-Mulk: 30

سورة الحاقة

Sūrah al-Ḥāqqah

أقول: لما وقع في (ن) ذكر يوم القيامة مجملًا في قوله: ﴿يَوْمَ يُكْشَفُ عَنْ سَاقٍ﴾ (القلم: ٤٢) الآية، شرح ذلك في هذه السورة نبأ هذا اليوم، وشأنه العظيم.

I say: Sūrah Nūn, in general terms, explains the Day of Judgement. This appears in His statement: {**The day when the shin shall be laid bare (i.e. the Day of Resurrection).**}[457] This *sūrah* provides description of the Last Day, giving greater details to its events,[458] and highlighting its magnificence.

457 Al-Qalam: 42

458 Al-Ḥāqqah: 1-37

سورة سأل

Sūrah Sa'ala (al-Ma'ārij)

أقول: هذه السورة كالتتمة لسورة الحاقة في بقية وصف يوم القيامة والنار.

I say: This *sūrah* is like a complement to Sūrah al-Ḥāqqah, as it provides further description to the events of the Last Day, and the Fire.[459]

و[قد] قال ابن عباس: إنها نزلت عقب سورة الحاقة، وذلك أيضًا من وجوه المناسبة في الوضع.

Ibn 'Abbās said that Sūrah al-Ma'ārij was revealed after al-Ḥāqqah,[460] and this further is another aspect of the appropriateness of its location.

459 Al-Ma'ārij: 1-18
460 See *al-Itqān* (1/97).

سورة نوح

Sūrah Nūḥ

أقول: أكثر ما ظهر [لي] في وجه اتصالها بما قبلها بعد طول الفكر: أنه سبحانه لما قال في (سأل): ﴿إِنَّا لَقَادِرُونَ۝عَلَىٰ أَنْ نُبَدِّلَ خَيْرًا مِنْهُمْ﴾ (المعارج: ٤٠، ٤١) عقبه بقصة قوم نوح، المشتملة على إغراقهم عن آخرهم، بحيث لم يبقَ منهم ديار وبدل خيرًا منهم، [فوقعت موقع الاستدلال والاستظهار لتلك الدعوى، كما وقعت قصة أصحاب الجنة في سورة (ن) موقع الاستدلال والاستظهار] لما ختم به تبارك.

I say: After long and hard consideration, I feel that this *sūrah* is connected to the previous one because the Glorified said at the beginning of al-Maʿārij: **{Surely We are able. To replace them by [others] better than them.}**[461] This is followed [in the next *sūrah*] by the story of the People of Nūḥ which gives description on how they belied and He was able over them and drowned them all, leaving none behind, and so the earth was later inherited by the pious. Thus it serves as a demonstration of Allah's ability that is mentioned in al-Maʿārij, just like how the story of the people of the garden in Sūrah Nūn reflects the end of Tabārak.

هذا مع تآخي مطلع السورتين في ذكر العذاب الموعد به الكافرين.

461 Al-Maʿārij: 40-41

Further to this, there is a strong correlation between the commencement of both *sūrahs* as both are themed at warning the disbelievers of a terrible end.

سورة الجن

Sūrah al-Jinn

أقول: قد فكرت مدة في وجه اتصالها بما قبلها، فلم يظهر لي سوى أنه [سبحانه] قال في سورة نوح: ﴿اسْتَغْفِرُوا رَبَّكُمْ إِنَّهُ كَانَ غَفَّارًا ۝ يُرْسِلِ السَّمَاءَ عَلَيْكُم مِّدْرَارًا﴾ (نوح: ١٠، ١١)، وقال في هذه السورة [لكفار مكة]: ﴿وَأَلَّوِ اسْتَقَامُوا عَلَى الطَّرِيقَةِ لَأَسْقَيْنَاهُم مَّاءً غَدَقًا﴾ (١٦)، وهذا وجه بيِّن في الارتباط.

I say: After careful thought, what appears to me to be the only aspect connecting it to the preceding *sūrah* is the statement of the Glorified in Nūḥ: **{Ask forgiveness from your Lord; verily, He is Ever-Forgiving; He will send rain to you in abundance.}**[462] In al-Jinn, the polytheists of Makkah are given a similar message: **{If they had believed in Allah, and went on the right way, We surely would have bestowed upon them water (rain) in abundance.}**[463] This shows that there is a connection between the two *sūrahs*.[464]

---

462 Nūḥ: 10-11

463 Al-Jinn: 16

464 There is another way in which the two *sūrahs* explain one another. In Sūrah Nūḥ (21), Nūḥ talked about the disbelief and deviation of his people, and then he made *du'ā* against them. As for the beginning of Sūrah al-Jinn (4-11), it explains that the jinn are like humans, there are believers and disbelievers among them, and that the disbelievers among the jinn are in contact with the disbe-

سورة المزمل

Sūrah al-Muzzamil

أقول: لا يخفى وجه اتصال أولها: ﴿قُمِ اللَّيْلَ﴾ (٢) بقوله في آخر تلك: ﴿وَأَنَّهُ لَمَّا قَامَ عَبْدُ اللهِ يَدْعُوهُ﴾ (الجن: ١٩)، وبقوله: ﴿وَأَنَّ الْمَسَاجِدَ لِلَّهِ﴾ (الجن: ١٨).

I say: It is evident that there is a connection between the statement at the start of this *sūrah*: **{Stand the night}**[465] with that found at the end of al-Jinn: **{When the slave of Allah stood up invoking in prayer to Him}**[466] and **{And the *masājid* are for Allah [alone.]}**[467]

---

lieving humans. So Sūrah Nūh is themed at the rejection and misguidance of his people whereas al-Jinn explains the relationship between man and jinn, and makes a comparison between them.

465 Al-Muzzamil: 2

466 Al-Jinn: 19

467 There is also another way in which the two *sūrahs* are connected. At the end of Sūrah al-Jinn, the *āyah* frees any knowledge of the unseen from the jinn and affirms it only for Allah, to which He reveals to His chosen messenger (al-Jinn: 26-27), so it is appropriate that Sūrah al-Muzzamil begins with Muḥammad being bestowed as a messenger ﷺ and mentions the obligations he is assigned to; rituals, acts of worship and calling people to Islam. This is because the Prophet was sent in a time that is close to the Hour as established in the Sunnah. And, Allah said in al-Jinn **{Say: I do not know when the Hour will be established}** (al-Jinn: 25). This was as if He said: The coming of this *muzzamil* (shrouded one) is an indication that the Hour has drawn close, and he is the one that Allah

سورة المدثر

Sūrah al-Mudathir

أقول: هذه متآخية مع السورة التي قبلها في الافتتاح بخطاب النبي صلى الله عليه وسلم وصدر كليهما نازل في قصة واحدة.

I say: This *sūrah* is in concordance with the *sūrah* before it, as both of them commence by addressing the Prophet ﷺ and the beginning parts of both *sūrahs* were revealed regarding the same incident.

وقد ذكر عن ابن عباس في ترتيب نزول السور: أن المدثر نزلت عقب المزمل [كذا] أخرجه ابن الضريس، وأخرجه غيره عن جابر بن زيد.

Ibn ʿAbbas mentioned that this *sūrah* was revealed after al-Muzzamil, as was reported by Ibn al-Ḍarīs and other than him, on the authority of Jābir ibn Zayd.[468]

---

selected to let him know matters from the unseen.

468 Likewise, Sūrah al-Mudathir concludes with knowledge of the signs of the Hour and some of its description, which then connects to the theme of the *sūrah* after it.

سورة القيامة

Sūrah al-Qiyāmah

أقول: لما قال سبحانه في آخر المدثر: ﴿كَلَّا بَلْ لا يَخَافُونَ الْآخِرَةَ﴾ (المدثر: ٥٣) بعد ذكر الجنة والنار، وكان عدم خوفهم إياها لإنكارهم البعث، ذكر في هذه السورة الدليل على البعث [من أوجه]، ووصف يوم القيامة، وأهواله، وأحواله، ثم ذكر من قبل ذلك [من خروج الروح من البدن ثم ما قبل ذلك] من مبدأ الخلق، فذكرت الأحوال [الثلاثة] في هذه السورة على عكس ما هي في الواقع.

I say: The Glorified concluded Sūrah al-Mudathir with: **{Truly! But they fear not the Hereafter.}**[469] This *āyah* comes after mentioning the Jannah and Fire, yet despite this, the disbelievers are not in any fear of retribution for their denial of the resurrection. So in al-Qiyāmah, there is extensive proof and affirmation of the resurrection and also from another angle, al-Qiyāmah provides description regarding the Day of Judgement in greater detail; its people, its scenarios etc. Then it describes what comes before that, detailing the process of death, and then it describes what comes before that, shifting attention to how life was created—mentioning these three states of life in reverse order of how they occur.

469 Al-Mudathir: 53

سورة الإنسان

Sūrah al-Insān

أقول: وجه اتصالها بسورة القيامة في غاية الوضوح، فإنه تعالى ذكر في آخر تلك مبدأ خلق الإنسان من نطفة، ثم ذكر مثل ذلك في مطلع هذه السورة، مفتتحًا بخلق آدم أبي البشر.

I say: Sūrah al-Insān connects to the previous *sūrah* from the aspect of clarifying it, for Allah ﷻ concluded al-Qiyāmah with description of the creation of man from semen. Sūrah al-Insān opens with something similar, describing the creation of Ādam, the father of man.

ولما ذكر هناك خلقه [من نطفة] منهما، قال هنا: ﴿فَجَعَلَ مِنْهُ الزَّوْجَيْنِ الذَّكَرَ وَالْأُنْثَىٰ﴾ (القيامة: ٣٩)، ولما ذكر هناك خلقه منهما، قال هنا: ﴿فَجَعَلْنَاهُ سَمِيعًا بَصِيرًا﴾ (٢)، فعلق به غير ما علق بالأول، ثم رتب عليه هداية السبيل، وتقسيمه إلى شاكر وكفور، ثم أخذ في جزاء كل.

Furthermore both *sūrahs* have reference to creation from a mixed liquid, however al-Qiyāmah follows it with the creation of both genders from it: **{And made him in two sexes, male and female.}**[470] Sūrah al-Insān, on the other hand, does not mention this; rather it adds the detail: **{[We created man from a sperm-drop mixture that we may try**

470 Al-Qiyāmah: 39

him;] and We made him hearing and seeing.}[471] So this *sūrah* adds detail not given in the previous one, and then further adds to it the guidance to the path, classifying people into the thankful and the ingrate, and then the recompense for both parties.

ووجه آخر هو: أنه لما وصف حال يوم القيامة في تلك السورة، ولم يصف فيها حال النار والجنة، بل ذكرهما على سبيل الإجمال، فصلهما في هذه السورة، وأطنب في وصف الجنة، وذلك كله شرح لقوله تعالى هناك: ﴿وُجُوهٌ يَوْمَئِذٍ نَاضِرَةٌ﴾ (القيامة: ٢٢)، وقوله هنا: ﴿إِنَّآ أَعْتَدْنَا لِلْكَافِرِينَ سَلَاسِلَا وَأَغْلَالًا وَسَعِيرًا﴾ (١٤)، شرح لقوله هناك: ﴿تَظُنُّ أَنْ يُفْعَلَ بِهَا فَاقِرَةٌ﴾ (القيامة: ٢٥).

From another angle, al-Qiyāmah details the Day of Judgement but does not describe the Fire and Jannah except with brevity, rather this is detailed here in al-Insān. Al-Insān provides heavy detail regarding Jannah,[472] so it is as if all of this is in explanation of the *āyah* in al-Qiyāmah: **{Some faces that Day shall be radiant.}**[473] And His statement in al-Insān: **{Verily, We have prepared for the disbelievers iron chains, iron collars, and a blazing fire}**[474] explains the *āyah* in al-Qiyāmah: **{Thinking that some calamity was about to fall on them.}**[475]

وقد ذكر هناك: ﴿كَلَّا بَلْ تُحِبُّونَ الْعَاجِلَةَ ۝ وَتَذَرُونَ الْآخِرَةَ﴾ (القيامة: ٢٠، ٢١)، وذكر هنا في هذه السورة: ﴿إِنَّ هَؤُلَاءِ يُحِبُّونَ الْعَاجِلَةَ وَيَذَرُونَ وَرَآءَهُمْ

471 Al-Insān: 2
472 Al-Insān: 5-22
473 Al-Qiyāmah: 22
474 Al-Insān: 4
475 Al-Qiyāmah: 25

يَوْمًا ثَقِيلًا﴾ (٢٧)، وهذا من وجوه المناسبة.

And al-Qiyāmah states: **{But you love the present life of this world. And neglect the Hereafter.}**[476] In al-Insān, further description is given: **{Verily! They love the present life of this world, and put behind them a heavy day.}**[477] So from these aspects there exists a strong connection between the two *sūrahs*.[478]

476 Al-Qiyāmah: 20-21

477 Al-Insān: 27

478 From another viewpoint, both *sūrahs* also give detail as to the state of man at the time of death approaching. In al-Qiyāmah (26-35) there is a description to those who disbelieve, whereas in al-Insān (7-11) there is description of the traits of the believer in this life and the delight promised for them.

سورة المرسلات

Sūrah al-Mursalāt

أقول: وجه اتصالها بما قبلها: أنه تعالى لما أخبر في خاتمتها أنه ﴿يُدْخِلُ مَنْ يَشَآءُ فِي رَحْمَتِهِ وَالظَّالِمِينَ أَعَدَّ لَهُمْ عَذَابًا أَلِيمًا﴾ (الإنسان: ٣١)، افتتح هذه بالقسم على أن ما يوعدون واقع، فكان ذلك تحقيقًا لما وعد به هناك المؤمنين، وأوعد الظالمين.

I say: The connection between al-Mursalāt and the preceding *sūrah* can be seen from His statement at the end of al-Insān: {**He admits into His Mercy whomever He Wills and for the wrong-doers He has prepared a painful torment.**}[479] Sūrah al-Mursalāt commences with a divine oath affirming that what they are promised will occur; so it affirms that disbelievers will certainly receive their promised punishment and believers will certainly receive their promised reward.

ثم ذكر وقته وأشراطه بقوله: ﴿فَإِذَا النُّجُومُ طُمِسَتْ﴾ (٨) إلى آخره.

He then goes on to describe time and signs of this recompense: {**When the stars lose their lights...**}[480] until the end of the *sūrah*.[481]

---

479 Al-Insān: 31

480 Al-Mursalāt: 8

481 There is also another aspect indicating the appropriateness of these three *sūrahs* being placed together: In al-Qiyāmah it mentions the end of creation (al-Qiyāmah: 37-39), then in al-Insān the beginning of creation is mentioned:

ويحتمل أن تكون الإشارة بما توعدون إلى جميع ما تضمنته السورة من وعيد للكافرين، ووعد للأبرار.

It is possible that the part "what you are promised" refers to all the promises contained within the *sūrah*, the promise of punishment for the disbelievers and the promise of reward for the believers.

{We have created them and strengthened their forms} (al-Insān: 28) and then, to avert man from feeling pride in this strength, Allah mentions in al-Mursalāt: **{Did We not create you from a liquid disdained?}** (al-Mursalāt: 20).

سورة عم

Sūrah ‘Amma (al-Naba’)

أقول: وجه اتصالها بما قبلها: تناسبها معها في الجمل، ففي المرسلات: ﴿أَلَمْ نُهْلِكِ الْأَوَّلِينَ ۝ ثُمَّ نُتْبِعُهُمُ الْآخِرِينَ﴾ (المرسلات: ١٦، ١٧)، ﴿أَلَمْ نَخْلُقكُّم مِّن مَّاءٍ مَّهِينٍ﴾ (المرسلات: ٢٠)، ﴿أَلَمْ نَجْعَلِ الْأَرْضَ كِفَاتًا﴾ (المرسلات: ٢٥) إلى آخره، وفي عم: ﴿أَلَمْ نَجْعَلِ الْأَرْضَ مِهَادًا﴾ (٦) إلى آخره، فذلك نظير تناسب جمل: ألم نشرح، والضحى، بقوله في الضحى: ﴿أَلَمْ يَجِدْكَ يَتِيمًا فَآوَىٰ﴾ (الضحى: ٦) إلى آخره، وقوله: ﴿أَلَمْ نَشْرَحْ لَكَ صَدْرَكَ﴾ (الشرح: ١) مع اشتراك هذه السورة والأربع قبلها في الاشتمال على وصف الجنة والنار، ما عدا المدثر في الاشتمال على وصف يوم القيامة وأهواله، وعلى ذكر بدء الخلق، وإقامة الدليل على البعث.

I say: The manner in which Sūrah al-Naba’ connects to al-Mursalāt is that certain linguistic forms of words and styles in al-Mursalāt are repeated in a similar manner in al-Nabā. Examples of this within the *āyāt* of al-Mursalāt are: **{Did not We destroy the previous generations? Then We made the later generations follow them.}**[482] And: **{Did We not create you from a liquid disdained?}**[483] And: **{Have We not made**

---

482 Al-Mursalāt: 16-17

483 Al-Mursalāt: 20

the earth a receptacle?}[484] until the end of the *sūrah*. And in al-Naba': **{Have We not made the earth a resting place?}** etc. In fact, this use of similar linguistics forms is also found in al-Ḍuhā and al-Sharḥ, with His statement: **{Did He not find you an orphan and give you a refuge?}**[485] And: **{Have We not opened your breast for you?}**[486] Aside from this linguistic aspect, al-Naba' also shares the same theme as the previous four *sūrahs*: Description of the Fire and Jannah and—with the exception of al-Mudathir—the Day of Judgement and its graveness, the beginning of creation and the affirmation of a resurrection.

وأيضًا في سورة المرسلات: ﴿لِأَيِّ يَوْمٍ أُجِّلَتْ۝لِيَوْمِ الْفَصْلِ۝وَمَآ أَدْرَاكَ مَا يَوْمُ الْفَصْلِ﴾ (المرسلات: ١٢-١٤)، وفي هذه السورة: ﴿إِنَّ يَوْمَ الْفَصْلِ كَانَ مِيقَاتًا۝يَوْمَ يُنْفَخُ فِي الصُّورِ فَتَأْتُونَ أَفْوَاجًا﴾ (١٧، ١٨) إلى آخره، فكأن هذه السورة شرح يوم الفصل المجمل ذكره في السورة التي قبلها.

Also, in al-Mursalāt there is His statement: **{For what Day are these signs postponed? For the day of decision. And what do you know about the day of decision?}**[487] In al-Naba' this question is answered: **{Verily, the day of decision is on a fixed day. The day when the trumpet will be blown, and you shall come forth in groups...}**[488] So it is as if this *sūrah* explains what was not covered within the brief mention of the day of decision in al-Mursalāt.

---

484 Al-Mursalāt: 25

485 Al-Ḍuhā: 6

486 Al-Sharḥ: 1

487 Al-Mursalāt: 12-14

488 Al-Naba' 17-18

[سورة النازعات

Sūrah al-Nāzi'āt

ورد عن ابن عباس رضي الله عنهما: أنها عقب سورة عم، وأولها يشبه أن يكون قسمًا لتحقيق ما في آخر عم، أو ما تضمنته كلها على حد ما تقدم في ﴿وَالْمُرْسَلاتِ﴾ مع ﴿هَلْ أَتَى﴾، ﴿وَالذَّارِيَاتِ﴾ مع ﴿ق﴾].

I say: It is reported that Ibn 'Abbās ﵄ placed al-Nāzi'āt after al-Naba' as the beginning of al-Nāzi'āt seems to serve as an affirmation to the end of al-Naba', or due to it connecting in its overall content, similar to how al-Mursalāt is connected to al-Insān, and al-Dhāriyāt to Qāf.[489]

---

489 The author did not mention the connection of al-Naba' with al-Nāzi'āt, and what appears to be the case, and Allah knows best, is that al-Nāzi'āt is themed at refuting doubts of those who think the topic of the previous *sūrahs* will not be established, i.e. the Day of Judgement. For this reason, al-Nāzi'āt begins with describing their doubts (see: al-Nāzi'āt: 10-11) and then goes on to refute them (see: al-Nāzi'āt: 12 onwards). Therefore, al-Nāzi'āt establishes the proof upon those who deny what the previous *sūrahs* established.

سورة عبس

Sūrah ʿAbasa

أقول: وجه وضعها عقب النازعات مع تآخيهما في المقطع، لقوله هناك: ﴿فَإِذَا جَآءَتِ الطَّآمَّةُ﴾ (النازعات: ٣٤)، وقوله هنا: ﴿فَإِذَا جَآءَتِ الصَّآخَّةُ﴾ (٣٣)، وهما من أسماء يوم القيامة.

I say: ʿAbasa connects itself to al-Nāziʿāt as they share similitude in their endings. In al-Nāziʿāt there is His statement: **{But when the greatest catastrophe comes.}**[490] And in ʿAbasa there is His statement: **{But when the second blowing is established.}**[491] Both of these contain names for the Day of Judgement.[492]

490 Al-Nāziʿāt: 34

491 ʿAbasa: 33

492 The author does not give a detailed explanation as to what connects the "catastrophe" in al-Nāziʿāt and the "second blowing" of ʿAbasa. We say that the catastrophe is a name for the Day of Judgement because everything will suffer. As for the second blowing, then this is also another term for the Day of Judgement but refers to a very large cry or scream. The reason why al-Nāziʿāt mentions the catastrophe before the blowing is because the suffering will come before the loud cry, so it is as if the senses mentioned in al-Nāziʿāt come before those mentioned in ʿAbasa. See *Asrār al-Takrār fī al-Qurʾān* (p. 201).

سورة التكوير

Sūrah al-Takwīr

أقول: لما ذكر في [آخر] عبس: ﴿فَإِذَا جَآءَتِ الصَّآخَّةُ۝يَوْمَ يَفِرُّ الْمَرْءُ مِنْ أَخِيهِ﴾ (عبس: ٣٣، ٣٤) الآيات، ذكر يوم القيامة كأنه رأي عين [شرح حاله في هذه السورة والتي بعدها، ولهذا ورد] في لحديث: ((من سره أن ينظر إلى يوم القيامة كأنه رأي عين، فليقرأ: ﴿إِذَا الشَّمْسُ كُوِّرَتْ﴾ [١] و﴿إِذَا السَّمَآءُ انْفَطَرَتْ﴾ [الانفطار: ١] و﴿إِذَا السَّمَاءُ انْشَقَّتْ﴾)) (الانشقاق: ٥)

I say: 'Abasa ends with: **{But when the second blowing is established. That day a man will run away from his brother...}**[493] This describes the Day of Judgement in a way as if a person can see it with his own eyes and this graphic description continues in the next *sūrah*. This is why it was mentioned in the ḥadīth, "Whoever wants to see the Day of Judgement in front of him then recite: **{When the sun will be wound round}**,[494] **{When the heaven is cleft asunder}**[495] and **{When the heaven is split asunder}**."[496] [497]

---

493 'Abasa: 33-34

494 Al-Takwīr: 1

495 Al-Infiṭār: 1

496 Al-Inshiqāq: 1

497 Collected by Aḥmad in *al-Musnad* (2/72) and al-Tirmidhī in the Chapter of *Tafsīr* (9/252—with *Tuḥfat al-Aḥwadhī*).

سورة الانفطار

Sūrah al-Infiṭār

أقول: قد عرف مما ذكرت وجه وضعها هنا، مع زيادة تآخيهما في المقطع.

I say: Its connection to the previous *sūrah* has been explained above, and it can be added that they also bear similitude in their endings.

سورة المطففين

Sūrah al-Muṭaffifīn

أقول: الفصل بهذه السورة بين الانفطار والانشقاق التي هي نظيرتها من خمسة أوجه: الافتتاح بـ﴿إِذَا السَّمَاءُ﴾ (الانفطار، الانشقاق)، والتخلص بـ﴿يَا أَيُّهَا الْإِنْسَانُ﴾ (الانفطار، الانشقاق: ٦)، وشرح حال يوم القيامة، ولهذا ضمت بالحديث السابق، والتناسب في المقدار، وكونها مكية.

I say: This *sūrah* is placed between al-Infiṭār and al-Inshiqāq due to it being similar to them from five different aspects. Both al-Infiṭār and al-Inshiqāq commence with: **{When the heaven is.}** And they have *takhalluṣ* (i.e. transition of passages from one topic to another while keeping a link between the different topics) with: **{O man!}**[498] And both go on to give details of the Day of Judgement; and that is why the *sūrahs* are referred to in the same ḥadīth (i.e. because they are similar in nature), they are alike in their length and all of them were revealed in Makkah.

وهذه السورة مدنية [وأطول منهما]، ومفتتحها ومخلَصها غير ما لهما لنكتة [لطيفة] ألهمنيها الله، وذلك أن السور الأربع لما كانت في صفة حال يوم القيامة، ذكرت على ترتيب ما يقع فيه.

---

498 Al-Infiṭār: 6 and al-Inshiqāq: 6

As for al-Muṭaffifīn, it is longer than the two other *sūrahs* and it was revealed in al-Madīnah. It opens and closes in a manner not like the other *sūrahs*, however it connects itself to them—and this is what Allah has given me understanding of—because it too describes the Day of Judgement, being part of a group of four *sūrahs* that do so. In fact, al-Muṭaffifīn gives details in the same order found in the other *sūrahs*.

فغالب ما وقع في التكوير، وجميع ما وقع في الانفطار، يقع في صدر يوم القيامة، ثم بعد ذلك يكون الموقف الطويل، ومقاساة العرق والأهوال، فذكره في هذه السورة بقوله: ﴿يَوْمَ يَقُومُ النَّاسُ لِرَبِّ الْعَالَمِينَ﴾ (٦)، ولهذا ورد في الحديث: ((يقوم أحدهم في رشحه إلى أنصاف أذنيه)).

So most of what is mentioned in al-Takwīr, and everything mentioned in al-Infiṭār, is about description of the events that will occur in the beginning of the Day of Judgement, and then it follows with the long standing for account, and the endurance of sweating and terrors;. Sūrah al-Muṭaffifīn also has an account of what will happen on that day also: **{The Day when mankind will stand before the Lord of all creation.}**[499] For this reason, it is reported in a ḥadīth, "On that day, a person will stand in his sweat [according to his sin] up to the middle of his ears."[500]

ثم بعد ذلك تحصل الشفاعة العظمى، فتنشر الكتب، فأَخْذٌ باليمين، وأَخْذٌ بالشمال، وأخذ من وراء الظهر، ثم بعد ذلك يقع الحساب.

After this comes the great intercession, the giving of the books, those taking their books in the right hand, those taking with the left hand

499 Al-Muṭaffifīn: 6

500 Collected by al-Bukhārī (6/207) in the Chapter of *Tafsīr*, on the authority of Ibn 'Umar.

and those taking from behind their backs and then the account of deeds.

هكذا وردت بهذا الترتيب الأحاديث، فناسب تأخير سورة الانشقاق التي فيها إتيان الكتب والحساب، عن السورة التي قبلها، والتي فيها ذكر الموقف عن التي فيها مبادئ يوم القيامة.

This is the order within which these events have been mentioned in the ḥadīth, so it is appropriate that Sūrah al-Inshiqāq follows the *sūrah* which mentions the beginning stages of the Day of Judgement, as it mentions the receiving of books and reckoning.

ووجه آخر وهو: أنه جل جلاله لما قال في الانفطار: ﴿وَإِنَّ عَلَيْكُمْ لَحَافِظِينَ ۝ كِرَامًا كَاتِبِينَ﴾ (الانفطار: ١٠، ١١)، وذلك في الدنيا، ذكر في هذه السورة حال ما يكتبه الحافظان، وهو: كتاب مرقوم جعل في عليين، أو في سجين، وذلك أيضًا في الدنيا، لكنه عقَّب بالكتابة، إما في يومه، أو بعد الموت في البرزخ كما في الآثار، فهذه حالة ثانية للكتاب ذكرت في السورة الثانية.

Also from another perspective, He ﷻ stated in al-Infiṭār: **{Surely, there are two that watch over you, [they are] honoured and recording.}**[501] This *āyah* refers to the *dunyā*; and [it is mentioned in this *sūrah*] that all of one's deeds are recorded by two preservers; and their names are either recorded in the book of the successful (*'iliyīn*) or the losers (*sijīn*), and this also occurs whilst he is in the *dunyā* (before starting the life in the grave). However, it follows with the recording, which hap-

501 Al-Infiṭār: 10-11

pens either during his lifetime, or after he dies during his life in the grave, as stated in *athār* (narrations). The latter refers to another state for the book, mentioned in the other *sūrah*.

وله حالة ثالثة متأخرة عنها، وهي أخذ صاحبه باليمين أو غيرها، وذلك يوم القيامة، فناسب تأخير السورة التي فيها ذلك، عن السورة التي فيها الحالة الثانية، وهي الانشقاق، فلله الحمد على ما مَنَّ بالفهم لأسرار كتابه.

Sūrah al-Inshiqāq explains that a person will be in one of three categories—and this occurs after the aforementioned events—: Either gaining his book in his right hand, his left hand or behind his back. This will happen on the Day of Judgement, [after ones deeds are recorded and scribing has been completed.] Therefore, we can see why al-Inshiqāq follows on from al-Mutafifīn, as it creates a fluency of episodes between the *sūrahs*. And all praise is to Allah for giving us this insight into the secrets of His Book.

ثم رأيت الإمام فخر الدين قال في سورة المطففين أيضًا: اتصال أولها بآخر ما قبلها ظاهر، لأنه تعالى بيَّن هناك أن يوم القيامة من صفته [أنه] ﴿لَا تَمْلِكُ نَفْسٌ لِنَفْسٍ شَيْئًا وَالْأَمْرُ يَوْمَئِذٍ لِلَّهِ﴾ (الانفطار: ١٩) وذلك يقتضي تهديدًا عظيمًا للعصاة، فلهذا أتبعه بقوله: ﴿وَيْلٌ لِلْمُطَفِّفِينَ﴾ (١) الآيات.

I have also seen Imām Fahkr al-Dīn say regarding Sūrah al-Mutafifīn, "The connection of its beginning to the ending of al-Infiṭār is clear. This is because the Most High clarifies in al-Infiṭār that from the attributes of the Day of Judgment is: **{The day when no person shall have power [to do] anything for another, and the decision, that day, will be [wholly] with Allah.}**[502] This serves as a great threat and admo-

502 Al-Infiṭār: 19

nition for those who sin. So He follows this with His statement: {**Woe to those who give less [than due...]**}"[503] [504]

503 Al-Muṭaffifīn: 1

504 See *Mafātiḥ al-Ghayb* of al-Rāzī (8/396).

سورة الانشقاق

Sūrah al-Inshiqāq

قد استوفى الكلام فيها في سورة المطففين.

Explanation regarding its placement has been given in the section of Sūrah al-Muṭaffifīn.

سورة البروج والطارق

Sūrah al-Burūj and al-Ṭāriq

أقول: هما متآخيتان فقرنتا، وقدمت الأولى لطولها، وذكرا بعد الانشقاق للمؤاخاة في الافتتاح بذكر السماء، ولهذا ورد في الحديث ذكر السماوات مرادًا بها السور الأربع، كما قيل: المسبحات.

I say: These two *sūrahs* are in unison and conjoined, and they have been split with the lengthier one placed before the shorter. [Both of them carry the same theme] and they are appropriately placed after al-Inshiqāq as all three begin with mention of the "heavens". For this reason, there is a narration which mentions the four "heavenly" *sūrahs*,[505] just as the term "the glorified ones" has been coined for those that begin with glorification of Him.

505 Collected by Aḥmad in *al-Musnad* (2/327) on the authority of Abu Hurayrah that the Prophet ﷺ commanded us to recite the "heavenly" *sūrahs* in our *'ishā* prayers (i.e. the four *sūrahs* that begin with "the heavens").

سورة الأعلى

Sūrah al-A'lā

أقول: في سورة الطارق ذكر خلق [النبات] والإنسان في قوله: ﴿وَالْأَرْضِ ذَاتِ الصَّدْعِ﴾ (الطارق: ١٢)، [وقوله: ﴿فَلْيَنْظُرِ الْإِنْسَانُ مِمَّ خُلِقَ﴾ إلى ﴿إِنَّهُ عَلَىٰ رَجْعِهِ لَقَادِرٌ﴾ (الطارق: ٥-٨)، وذكره في هذه السورة في قوله: ﴿خَلَقَ فَسَوَّىٰ﴾ (٢)، وقوله في النبات: ﴿وَالَّذِي أَخْرَجَ الْمَرْعَىٰ ۝ فَجَعَلَهُ غُثَاءً أَحْوَىٰ﴾ (٤، ٥)، وقصة النبات في هذه السورة أبسط، كما أن قصة الإنسان هناك أبسط، نعم، ما في هذه السورة أعم، من جهة شموله للإنسان وسائر المخلوقات.

I say: Sūrah al-Ṭāriq mentions the growth of plantation and mankind in His statement: {**And the earth which splits.**}[506] And about humans: {**So man should observe how he was created! He is created from a water gushing forth. Emerging from between the backbone and the ribs. Indeed, Allah, to return him [to life], is Able.**}[507] And in Sūrah al-A'lā He states: {**Who has created [everything], and then proportioned it.**}[508] And about plantation He states: {**And Who brings out**

---

506 Al-Ṭāriq: 12
507 Al-Ṭāriq: 5-8
508 Al-'Alā: 2

the pasture. And then makes it dark stubble.}[509] The description of plantation is given a greater description in al-A'la whereas the description of man in al-Ṭāriq is given greater detail. However it is true that this *sūrah* is more general, in terms of it containing discussion of both human life and the wider creation.

509 Al-'Alā: 4-5

سورة الغاشية

Sūrah al-Ghāshiyah

أقول: لما أشار سبحانه في سورة الأعلى بقوله: ﴿سَيَذَّكَّرُ مَنْ يَخْشَى ۝ وَيَتَجَنَّبُهَا الْأَشْقَى ۝ الَّذِي يَصْلَى النَّارَ الْكُبْرَى﴾ إلى قوله: ﴿وَالْآخِرَةُ خَيْرٌ وَأَبْقَى﴾ (الأعلى: ١٠-١٧) إلى المؤمن والكافر، والنار والجنة إجمالًا، فصل ذلك في هذه السورة، فبسط صفة النار والجنة مستندة إلى أهل كل منهما، على نمط ما هنالك، ولذا قال [هنا] : ﴿عَامِلَةٌ نَاصِبَةٌ﴾ (٣) في مقابل: ﴿الْأَشْقَى﴾ (الأعلى: ١١) [هناك] ، وقال [هنا] : ﴿تَصْلَى نَارًا حَامِيَةً﴾ (٤) إلى ﴿لا يُسْمِنُ وَلا يُغْنِي مِنْ جُوعٍ﴾ (٧) في مقابلة ﴿يَصْلَى النَّارَ الْكُبْرَى﴾ (الأعلى: ١٢) [هناك] ، ولما قال [هناك] في الآخرة: ﴿خَيْرٌ وَأَبْقَى﴾ (الأعلى: ١٧) بسط [هنا] صفة أكثر من صفة النار، تحقيقًا لمعنى الخيرية.

I say: The Glorified in Sūrah al-Aʿlā stated: {**The reminder will be received by him who fears [Allah]. But it will be avoided by the wretched. Who will enter the great fire and be made to taste its burning.**} Until His statement: {**Although the Hereafter is better and more lasting.**}[510] This refers to the believer and the disbeliever, the Fire and Jannah—and this was mentioned with brevity. This is explained in greater detail in al-Ghāshiyah, expanding upon the details of the Fire and

510 Al-ʿAlā: 10-17

Jannah and attaching them to their respective dwellers according to the style and pattern used therein when addressing them. For this reason, He said: **{Working [hard] and exhausted.}**[511] Which explains the statement in al-Aʿlā: **{The wretched.}**[512] Again in al-Ghāshiyah: **{They will enter in the hot blazing Fire.}**[513] Until He states, **{[Food] which will neither nourish nor avail hunger.}**[514] Which explains the statement in al-Aʿlā: **{Who will enter the great fire and be made to taste its burning.}**[515] In al-Aʿlā a broad description of the hereafter is given: **{While the hereafter is better and more lasting.}**[516] In al-Ghāshiyah, further detail is given and the description of Jannah is greater in proportion to that of the Fire. This serves to establish the meaning of "better" which was referred to in the previous *sūrah*.

511 Al-Ghāshiyah: 3

512 Al-Aʿlā: 11

513 Al-Ghāshiyah: 4

514 Al-Ghāshiyah: 7

515 Al-Aʿlā: 12

516 Al-Aʿlā: 17

سورة الفجر

Sūrah al-Fajr

أقول: لم يظهر لي في وجه ارتباطها سوى أن أولها كالإقسام على صحة ما ختم به السورة التي قبلها، من قوله جل جلاله: ﴿إِنَّ إِلَيْنَآ إِيَابَهُمْ۝ثُمَّ إِنَّ عَلَيْنَا حِسَابَهُمْ﴾ (الغاشية: ٢٥، ٢٦)، وعلى ما تضمنه من الوعد والوعيد، كما أن أول الذاريات قسم على تحقيق ما في (ق)، وأول المرسلات قسم على تحقيق ما في [﴿هَلْ أَتَىٰ﴾ وأول ﴿وَالنَّازِعَاتِ﴾ قسم على تحقيق ما في] (عم).

I say: Nothing apparent appears to me to connect al-Ghāshiyah with al-Fajr except that Sūrah al-Fajr begins with a divine oath taken from Allah, as if to confirm what al-Ghāshiyah ends with: **{Verily, to Us they will return. Then verily, upon Us will be their account.}**[517] This contains a strong level of promise [for good] and threat [for bad]. And this is just as al-Dhāriyāt begins with a divine oath to confirm what was in Qāf, likewise how al-Mursalat began with an oath to confirm what was in al-Insān and how al-Nāzi'āt begins with an oath to confirm what was in al-Naba'; [all of these *sūrahs* are connected with a promise and a threat which is affirmed by a divine oath in the following *sūrah*.]

---

517 Al-Ghāshiyah: 25-26

هذا مع أن جملة: ﴿أَلَمْ تَرَ كَيْفَ فَعَلَ رَبُّكَ﴾ (٦) هنا، مشابهة لجملة ﴿أَفَلا يَنْظُرُونَ﴾ (الغاشية: ١٧) هناك.

From another angle, [both al-Ghāshiyah and al-Fajr are themed at provoking thought in the reader.] So in al-Fajr: **{Did you not see how your Lord…?}**[518] And this resembles what came in al-Ghāshiyah: **{Do they not look…?}**[519]

518 Al-Fajr: 6

519 There are other aspects which connect the two *sūrahs* also, perhaps some which are clearer than what the author has mentioned. Al-Ghāshiyah gives description to the Fire and the Jannah in detail—in the same order as it was mentioned in Sūrah al-A'la—but Sūrah al-Fajr gives reasons as to why such people end up in the Fire. So the Most High gives a number of examples in al-Fajr as to what happened to 'Ād, Fir'awn etc. (al-Fajr: 6-14). After mentioning their stubbornness and cause for rejection, Allah, the Most High, gives examples of how the polytheists of Makkah displayed stubbornness, rejection (al-Fajr: 17) and both of these establish the proof against them. In the end, both *sūrahs* explain that their remorse on the Day of Judgement will not avail them from any punishment. (See al-A'la: 21-22 and al-Fajr: 23-24)

سورة البلد

Sūrah al-Balad

أقول: وجه اتصالها بما قبلها: أنه لما ذم فيها من أحب المال، وأكل التراث، ولم يحض على طعام المسكين، ذكر في هذه السورة الخصال التي تطلب من صاحب المال، من فك الرقبة، والإطعام في يوم ذي مسغبة.

I say: Sūrah al-Balad is connected to that which comes before it as al-Fajr rebukes excessive love for wealth and money, consuming the inheritance of others unjustly and not giving any consideration for the needy. Sūrah al-Balad focuses upon a few characteristics which are sought from the person possessing wealth, i.e. using their wealth pro-actively by freeing slaves and feeding people on a day of severe hunger.[520]

---

520 There are other ways in which the two are connected; Allah, the Most High, informs us that people are tested in their wealth when they do not feed the poor or look after orphans, and He condemned them for loving money, He mentioned in this one that he will regret in the hereafter due to the love of wealth and withholding his wealth. See al-Fajr: 24.

سورة الشمس والليل والضحى

Sūrah al-Shams, al-Layl and al-Ḍuhā

أقول: هذه الثلاثة حسنة التناسق جدًّا، لما في مطالعها من المناسبة، لما بين الشمس والليل والضحى من الملابسة، ومنها سورة الفجر، لكن فصلت بسورة البلد لنكتة أهم، كما فصل بين الانفطار والانشقاق، وبين المسبحات، لأن مراعاة التناسب بالأسماء والفواتح وترتيب النزول، إنما يكون حيث لا يعارضها ما هو أقوى وآكد في المناسبة.

I say: These three *sūrahs* are arranged in the most perfect of ways, due to the connection and relevance between the beginning of the three *sūrahs*; the sun (*al-shams*), the night (*al-layl*) and the morning day (*al-ḍuḥā*). Sūrah al-Fajr is similar to them but their direct succession to it is prevented by Sūrah al-Balad due to the strength of connection between al-Fajr and al-Balad. This is similar to how al-Infiṭār and al-Inshiqāq were separated and how the *sūrahs* which begin with *tasbīḥ* were split. This is because consideration of the connection in terms of names, beginnings [of *sūrahs*,] and their arrangements is given precedence when there is no other stronger and more established factor to consider in this regard.

ثم إن سورة الشمس ظاهرة الاتصال بسورة البلد، فإنه سبحانه لما ختمها بذكر أصحاب الميمنة، وأصحاب المشأمة، أراد الفريقين في سورة

الشمس على سبيل الفَذْلَكَة، فقوله: [في الشمس] ﴿قَدْ أَفْلَحَ مَنْ زَكَّاهَا﴾ (٩) هم أصحاب الميمنة في سورة البلد، وقوله: ﴿وَقَدْ خَابَ مَنْ دَسَّاهَا﴾ (١٠) [في الشمس] ، هم أصحاب المشأمة في سورة البلد، فكانت هذه السورة فَذْلَكَة تفصيل تلك السورة، ولهذا قال الإمام: المقصود من هذه السورة: الترغيب في الطاعات، والتحذير من المعاصي.

Furthermore, Sūrah al-Shams carries on the theme that was set down in al-Balad. Allah ﷻ ends Sūrah al-Balad by mentioning those who will receive their book in the right hand and those who will receive them in the left hand, and both of these parties were indicated to in al-Shams in His statement: **{Indeed he succeeds who purifies his own self.}**[521] These are the people who receive the book in their right hand as mentioned in al-Balad. And His statement: **{And he has failed who instils it [with corruption].}**[522] These are the people who receive the book in their left hand as mentioned in al-Balad. Thus this *sūrah* serves as the detail for the other, and it is for this reason that the *imām* [al-Rāzī] said, "The objective of al-Shams is to motivate goodness and warn against disobedience."

ونزيد في سورة الليل: أنها تفصيل إجمال سورة الشمس، فقوله: ﴿فَأَمَّا مَنْ أَعْطَى وَاتَّقَى﴾ (الليل: ٥) وما بعدها، تفصيل ﴿قَدْ أَفْلَحَ مَنْ زَكَّاهَا﴾ (الشمس: ٩)، وقوله: ﴿وَأَمَّا مَنْ بَخِلَ وَاسْتَغْنَى﴾ (الليل: ٨) الآيات، تفصيل قوله: ﴿وَقَدْ خَابَ مَنْ دَسَّاهَا﴾ (الشمس: ١٠).

Sūrah al-Layl gives even further description, expanding upon the

521 Al-Shams: 9

522 Al-Shams: 10

generalities found in Sūrah al-Shams. His statement: {**As for those who give [in charity] and fear Him**}[523] and that which follows it explains the *āyah* in al-Shams: {**Indeed he succeeds who purifies his own self.**}[524] His statement in al-Layl: {**But he who is a greedy miser and thinks himself self-sufficient**}[525] explains the *āyah* in al-Shams: {**And indeed he fails who corrupts his own self.**}[526]

ونزيد في سورة الضحى: أنها متصلة بسورة الليل من وجهين، فإن فيها: ﴿وإن لنا للآخرة والأولى﴾ (الليل: ١٣)، وفي الضحى: ﴿وَلَلْآخِرَةُ خَيْرٌ لَكَ مِنَ الْأُولَى﴾ (٤)، وفي الليل: ﴿وَلَسَوْفَ يَرْضَى﴾ (الليل: ٢١)، وفي الضحى: ﴿وَلَسَوْفَ يُعْطِيكَ رَبُّكَ فَتَرْضَى﴾ (٥).

Sūrah al-Ḍuḥā gives description to the above also, and it is connected to Sūrah al-Layl from two viewpoints: Al-Layl has His statement: {**And truly, unto Us [belong] the last (hereafter) and the first (this world).**}[527] Sūrah al-Ḍuḥā explains: {**And indeed the hereafter is better for you than the present [life of this world.]**}[528] Al-Layl also has His statement: {**He surely will be pleased [when he will enter Paradise.]**}[529] Al-Ḍuḥā explains: {**And verily, your Lord will give you so that you shall be well-pleased.**}[530]

ولما كانت سورة الضحى نازلة في شأنه صلى الله عليه وسلم افتتحت

523 Al-Layl: 5
524 Al-Shams: 9
525 Al-Layl: 8
526 Al-Shams: 10
527 Al-Layl: 13
528 Al-Ḍuḥā: 4
529 Al-Layl: 21
530 Al-Ḍuḥā: 5

بالضحى، الذي هو نور، ولما كانت سورة الليل [نازلة في بخيل في قصة طويلة، افتتحت بالليل الذي هو ظلمة.

The reason for the revelation of Sūrah al-Ḍuḥā was in regards to the Prophet ﷺ, and it begins with mention of the morning day, which is synonymous with light. And as Sūrah al-Layl was revealed to lengthily address the stingy and those who prevent themselves from goodness, it has been named after a synonym of darkness, i.e. night.

قال الإمام: سورة الليل] سورة أبي بكر، يعني: ما عدا قصة البخيل، وكانت سورة الضحى سورة محمد، عقب بها، ولم يجعل بينهما واسطة ليعلم ألا واسطة بين محمد وأبي بكر.

The *imām* said, "Sūrah al-Layl is also known as Sūrah Abī Bakr,[531] i.e. except for what is mentioned about the stingy ones, and Sūrah al-Ḍuḥā is also known as Sūrah Muḥammad. One follows the other without an intermediary, displaying through this that there was likewise no intermediary to separate between Muḥammad and Abū Bakr."

---

531 The part of this *sūrah* which was revealed in relation to Abū Bakr is {**As for he who gives and fears Allah and believes in the best [reward], We will ease him toward ease**} (al-Layl: 5-7). It is reported by Ibn Jarīr that he used to free slaves and assist the poor that accepted Islam in Makkah, especially women who were disowned by their families. For this reason these *āyāt* were revealed. See *Tafsīr al-Ṭabarī* (3/142).

سورة أَلَمْ نَشْرَحْ

Sūrah al-Sharḥ

أقول: هي شديدة الاتصال بسورة الضحى، لتناسبهما في الجمل، ولهذا ذهب بعض السلف إلى أنهما سورة واحدة بلا بسملة بينهما. قال الإمام: والذي دعاهم إلى ذلك هو: أن قوله: ﴿أَلَمْ نَشْرَحْ﴾ كالعطف على ﴿أَلَمْ يَجِدْكَ يَتِيمًا فَآوَى﴾ (الضحى: ٦) [في الضحى].

I say: Sūrah al-Sharḥ is strongly interlinked with Sūrah ad-Duḥā that came before it, as both *sūrahs* compliment each other in wording and theme. For this reason, many of the Salaf opined that they were one *sūrah* and there is no *basmallah* between them. The *imām* said, "That which they base their opinion upon is the statement of the Most High: **{Have We not opened your breast for you?}** As if it is conjoined to, **{Did He not find you an orphan and gave you a refuge?}**"[532]

532 From another viewpoint, Sūrah al-Ḍuḥā mentions the hardships that the Prophet faced in his early life and this was met with ease afterwards, which explains why Sūrah al-Sharḥ (i.e. the relief) follows it directly. This *sūrah* explains the preceding *sūrah*, because it explains the elements leading to such relief; he was an orphan so He gave him refuge, unaware of guidance so He guided him, and poor so He made him self-sufficient. All of these are factors leading the heart to feel open and relieved for *īmān*, particularly so because all of them come after the promise [in al-Ḍuḥā] that Allah is going to give him, and that he will be satisfied.

قلت: وفي حديث الإسراء أن الله تعالى قال: ((يا محمد، ألم أجدك يتيمًا فأويت، وضالًّا فهديت، وعائلًا فأغنيت، وشرحت لك صدرك، وحططت عنك وزرك، ورفعت لك ذكرك، فلا أذكر إلا ذكرت)) الحديث، أخرجه ابن أبي حاتم، وفي هذا أَوْفَى دليل على اتصال السورتين معنى.

I say: In the ḥadīth of the ascension, Allah ﷻ stated: "O Muḥammad! Did I not find you as an orphan and give you refuge? Were you not astray and I guided you? Were you not poor and I gave you sustenance? Did I not open your breast? Removed from you sin? Raised your mention—so that I am not mentioned except that you are mentioned alongside me?" This was reported by Ibn Abī Ḥātim.[533] This is the greatest piece of evidence which connects the two *sūrahs* and their meanings.

533 Reported in *Tafsīr al-Qur'ān al-Aẓīm* of Ibn Abī Ḥātim (10/3443), also Ibn Kathīr (8/452) and al-Suyūṭī in *al-Durr al-Manthūr* (8/545-546).

سورة التين

Sūrah al-Tīn

أقول: لما تقدم في سورة الشمس: ﴿وَنَفْسٍ وَمَا سَوَّاهَا﴾ (الشمس: ٧) فصل في هذه السورة بقوله: ﴿لَقَدْ خَلَقْنَا الْإِنْسَانَ فِي أَحْسَنِ تَقْوِيمٍ۝ثُمَّ رَدَدْنَاهُ أَسْفَلَ سَافِلِينَ﴾ (٤، ٥) إلى آخره.

I say: Sūrah al-Shams has the *āyah*: **{And [by] the soul and He who proportioned it.}**[534] Sūrah al-Tīn provides further detail upon this: **{Verily, We created man with the best stature. Then We reduced him to the lowest of the low}**[535] until its end.

وأخرت هذه السورة لتقدم ما هو أنسب بالتقديم من السور الثلاث واتصالها بسورة البلد لقوله: ﴿وَهَذَا الْبَلَدِ الْأَمِينِ﴾ (٣)، وأخرت لتقدم ما هو أولى بالمناسبة مع سورة الفجر.

However, Sūrah al-Tīn has been delayed from preceding due to the three *sūrahs* that come before it having a stronger connection to it. Sūrah al-Tīn also connects itself to Sūrah al-Balad, in the statement: **{And by this city of security (Makkah).}**[536] But again, al-Tīn is not connected to al-Balad because of the stronger connection al-Balad

534 Al-Shams: 7

535 Al-Tīn: 4-5

536 Al-Tīn: 3

has with al-Fajr.

لطيفة:

Benefit:

نقل الشيخ تاج الدين بن عطاء الله السكندري في (لطائف المنن) عن الشيخ أبي العباس المرسي، قال: قرأت مرة: ﴿وَالتِّينِ وَالزَّيْتُونِ﴾ إلى أن انتهيت إلى قوله: ﴿لَقَدْ خَلَقْنَا الْإِنْسَانَ فِي أَحْسَنِ تَقْوِيمٍ۝ثُمَّ رَدَدْنَاهُ أَسْفَلَ سَافِلِينَ﴾ (٤، ٥) ففكرت في معنى هذه الآية، فألهمني الله أن معناها: لقد خلقنا الإنسان في أحسن تقويم، رُوحًا وعقلًا ثم رددناه أسفل سافلين نفسًا وهوًى.

It is reported by Shaykh Tāj al-Dīn ibn 'Aṭā Allah al-Askandarī in his book *Laṭā'if al-Minan* that Shaykh Abū al-'Abbās al-Mursī said, "I once read {**By the fig and the olive**} until I reached, {**Verily, We created man with the best stature. Then We reduced him to the lowest of the low**}, so I thought and pondered upon the meaning of this *āyah*, and then Allah gave me the understanding of it: We have created humans in the best of forms, in their intellect and the soul they have been given, and then We return them to the lowest of the low, through their desires and whims."[537]

قلت: فظهر من هذه المناسبة وضعها بعد ﴿أَلَمْ نَشْرَحْ﴾ ، فإن تلك أخبر فيها عن شرح صدر النبي صلى الله عليه وسلم وذلك يستدعي كمال عقله ورُوحِه، فكلاهما في القلب الذي محله الصدر، وعن تبرئته من

537 See *Laṭā'if al-Minan* (p. 118).

الوِزْر الذي ينشأ عن النفس والهوى، وهو معصوم منهما، وعن رفع الذكر، حيث نزه مقامه عن كل وصم.

I say: This makes it clearer that the beginning of al-Sharḥ: {**Have We not opened your breast for you?**} is appropriate in its preceding of al-Tīn, because Allah has opened the heart of the Prophet and preserved him; completing his intellect and soul and placing both of these in his heart—which is located in the breast. It also frees him from having any fault or any sin which could be a result of him following his desires. For he is infallible from them both, and his name is raised in mention to the extent that his entire life is free from all forms of stigmatisation.

فلما كانت هذه السورة في هذا العلَم الفرد من الإنسان، أعقبها بسورة مشتملة على بقية الأناسي، وذكر ما خامرهم من متابعة النفس والهوى.

Thus, as this *sūrah* (i.e. al-Sharḥ) describes an individual being, it is followed by a *sūrah* that is themed at describing the rest of human beings and mention that they gravitate towards whatever fulfils their desires.

سورة العلق

Sūrah al-ʿAlaq

أقول: لما تقدم في سورة التين بيان خلق الإنسان في أحسن تقويم، بيَّن هنا أنه تعالى: ﴿خَلَقَ الْإِنْسَانَ مِنْ عَلَقٍ﴾ (٢) وذلك ظاهر الاتصال، فالأول بيان العلة الصورية، وهذا بيان العلة المادية.

I say: As Sūrah al-Tīn describes that man was created in the best of fashions, Sūrah al-ʿAlaq explains this further: **{He has created man from a clot.}**[538] From this the connection between the two is clear: Al-Tīn highlights the form and al-ʿAlaq highlights the substance they (i.e. the progeny of Ādam) are created from.[539]

---

538 Al-ʿAlaq: 2

539 There are other ways which connect the two *sūrahs* also. For instance, (i) al-Tīn ends with declaration that Allah is the best of those who judge (al-Tīn: 8) and al-ʿAlaq begins with the description of knowledge and wisdom for Him—and that He is the source of knowledge of his slaves, through His wisdom (al-ʿAlaq: 4-5). Allah has used the verb "read" to begin the *sūrah* and stated that it is He who taught man what he never knew, so as people can seek and perfect their knowledge by the help of the wisdom of the All-Wise.

Also (ii) Sūrah al-Tīn talks about the best of statures in which man was created in but that they debase themselves with sin (al-Tīn: 6-7). Sūrah al-ʿAlaq gives description as to how this happens; that man is self-oppressive and sees himself as self-sufficient (al-ʿAlaq: 6-14).

سورة القدر

Sūrah al-Qadr

قال الخطابي: لما اجتمع أصحاب النبي صلى الله عليه وسلم على القرآن، ووضعوا سورة القدر عقب العلق، استدلوا بذلك على أن المراد بهاء الكناية في قوله: ﴿إِنَّا أَنْزَلْنَاهُ فِي لَيْلَةِ الْقَدْرِ﴾ (١) الإشارة إلى قوله: ﴿اقْرَأْ﴾ (العلق: ١).

Al-Khaṭṭabī[540] said, "When the Companions of the Prophet ﷺ compiled the Qur'ān they placed Sūrah al-Qadr behind al-'Alaq. Their reasoning was that the deeper meaning of the *āyah*: **{Surely, We have sent it down in the Night of Power}**[541] was an indication to His statement: **{Read! In the Name of your Lord.}**"[542]

قال القاضي أبو بكر بن العربي: وهذا بديع جدًّا.

Al-Qāḍī Abū Bakr ibn al-'Arabī said, "This is an ingenious explanation."[543]

---

540 He is Aḥmad ibn Muḥammad ibn Ibrāhīm, known as Abū Sulaymān and nicknamed as al-Khaṭṭābī. From his works is the commentary on *Sunan Abī Dāwūd*. He passed away in 388h. See *Wafayāt al-'Ayān* (1/166).

541 Al-Qadr: 1

542 Al-'Alaq: 1

543 There is also a hidden connection between them; Sūrah al-'Alaq ends with the command to make *sujūd* and get closer to Him. The slave will receive close-

سورة لم يكن

Sūrah al-Bayyinah

أقول: هذه السورة واقعة موقع العلة لما قبلها، كأنه لما قال سبحانه: ﴿إِنَّا أَنْزَلْنَاهُ﴾ (القدر: ١) قيل: لِمَ أنزل؟ فقيل: لأنه لم يكن الذين كفروا منفكين عن كفرهم، حتى تأتيهم البينة، وهو رسول من الله يتلو صحفًا مطهرة، وذلك هو المنزَّل.

I say: This *sūrah* in reality is utilised as the reasoning for that which preceded it, as if it was asked after the statement of the Glorified: **{Surely, We have sent it}**,[544] what was the purpose of it being sent? Then it was answered: In order for it be a proof against those who disbelieve and stubbornly continue to do so when a clear proof had come to them. The clear proof refers to the Messenger of Allah and the Qur'ān he recites to them, and that is the matter which was sent.

وقد ثبتت الأحاديث بأنه كان في هذه السورة قرآن نُسخ رسمه وهو: (إنا أنزلنا المال لإقامة الصلاة وإيتاء الزكاة، ولو أن لابن آدم واديًا لابتغى إليه الثاني، ولو أن له الثاني لابتغى إليه الثالث، ولا يملأ جوف ابن آدم إلا

ness and His Mercy and Favour. This occurs especially in the *ṣalāt* and there is no *ṣalāt* without the Qur'ān, and the Qur'ān was revealed during the Night of al-Qadr as a method of gaining peace for the entire world.

544 Al-Qadr: 1

التراب، ويتوب الله على من تاب).

It is also established in traditions that al-Bayyinah had the following content within it, which was later abrogated: "I have sent down wealth so that the *ṣalāt* can be established and *zakāt* can be paid. If one from the children of Ādam possessed a valley of wealth, he would seek another valley. If he possessed two, he would have sought a third—yet the child of Ādam is never satisfied except with earth (i.e. death), and Allah accepts the repentance of all those who repent to Him."[545]

وبذلك تشتد المناسبة بين هذه السورة وبين ما قبلها، حيث ذكر هناك إنزال القرآن، وهنا إنزال المال، وتكون السورتان تعليلًا لما تضمنته سورة اقرأ، لأن [في] أولها ذكر العلم، وفي أثنائها ذكر المال، فكأنه قيل: إنا لم ننزل المال للطغيان والاستطالة والفخر، بل ليُستعان به على تقوانا، وإقامة الصلاة، وإيتاء الزكاة.

With this report, the connection between al-Bayyinah and al-Qadr becomes even stronger as al-Qadr mentions the descent of the Qurʿān while al-Bayyinah [initially] mentioned the descent of wealth. So these two *sūrahs* provide reasons for that which was mentioned in al-ʿAlaq, [al-ʿAlaq has two profound messages:] the incentive to seek knowledge[546]—during its beginning—and to use ones wealth carefully—in its middle.[547] Based upon this, it is as if it is being said: "We

545 Collected by Aḥmād (5/218) in *al-Musnad*, al-Ṭabarānī in *al-Muʿjam al-Kabīr* (3/247-248), al-Dāraquṭnī in *al-ʿIlal* (6/298) and it was strengthened by al-Haythamī in *Majmaʿ al-Zawāʿid* (7/140), who said that the men in the chain of Aḥmad are *ṣaḥīḥ*.

546 Al-ʿAlaq: 5

547 Al-ʿAlaq: 6-7

have not revealed wealth for it to be abused with oppression, colonisation and arrogance, rather we have given it to you to fear Us, to establish the *ṣalāt* and pay the *zakāt*."

سورة الزلزلة

Sūrah al-Zalzalah

أقول: لما ذكر في آخر (لم يكن) أن جزاء الكافرين جهنم، وجزاء المؤمنين جنات، فكأنه قيل: متى يكون ذلك؟ فقيل: ﴿إِذَا زُلْزِلَتِ الْأَرْضُ زِلْزَالَهَا﴾ (١) أي: [حين] تكون زلزلة الأرض، إلى آخره.

I say: As al-Bayyinah concludes with description of the recompense for the disbelievers (i.e. Jahannam) and the reward for the believers (i.e. Jannah), it is as if the description of its time also needs to be explained. So it is said **{When the earth is shaken with its [final] earthquake.}**[548] Meaning, the recompense will be ordered when the earth has its final earthquake.

هكذا ظهر لي، ثم لما راجعت تفسير الإمام الرازي، ورأيته ذكر نحوه فحمدت الله كثيرًا، وعبارته: ذكروا في مناسبة هذه السورة لما قبلها وجوهًا منها: أنه تعالى لما قال: ﴿جَزَاؤُهُمْ عِنْدَ رَبِّهِمْ جَنَّاتُ عَدْنٍ﴾ (البينة: ٨)، فكأن المكلف قال: ومتى يكون ذلك يا رب؟ فقال: ﴿إِذَا زُلْزِلَتِ الْأَرْضُ﴾ (١).

This is what appeared to me to be the case, and when I referred back

548 Al-Zalzalah: 1

to the *tafsīr* of Imām al-Rāzī I saw that he mentioned something similar, so I thanked Allah abundantly for this. His wording is, "It has been mentioned that this *sūrah* is appropriate to be connected to that which precedes it due to a number of reasons, and from them is the statement of the Most High in al-Bayyinah: {**Their reward with their Lord will be gardens of perpetual residence.**}[549] So it might be that a *mukallaf* (i.e. an accountable person who is pubescent, sane, and has received the message of Islam) asks, "How do we know when this will take place?" So He ﷻ stated: {**When the earth is shaken with its [final] earthquake.**}[550]

ومنها: أنه لما ذكر فيها وعيد الكافرين، ووعد المؤمنين، أراد أن يزيد في وعيد الكافرين فقال: ﴿إِذَا زُلْزِلَتِ الْأَرْضُ﴾ ونظيره: ﴿يَوْمَ تَبْيَضُّ وُجُوهٌ وَتَسْوَدُّ وُجُوهٌ﴾ ثم ذكر ما للطائفتين فقال: ﴿يَوْمَ تَبْيَضُّ وُجُوهٌ وَتَسْوَدُّ وُجُوهٌ فَأَمَّا الَّذِينَ اسْوَدَّتْ وُجُوهُهُمْ﴾ إلى آخره، ثم جمع بينهما هنا في آخر السورة بذكر الذرة من الخير والشر. انتهى.

Also, al-Bayyinah carries a serious warning for disbelief and a fulfilling promise to the believers, Sūrah al-Zalzalah seeks to extend the warning against those who disbelieve: {**When the earth is shaken.**} This is similar to where a warning was issued elsewhere: {**On the Day when some faces will become white and some faces will become black.**}[551] Then, He mentioned the recompense for both parties: {**And for those whose faces will become white, they will be in Allah's Mercy (Paradise), they will dwell there forever. As for those whose faces will turn black...**}[552] All of these points are then concluded at the end

549 Al-Bayyinah: 8
550 Al-Bayyinah: 1
551 Āli 'Imrān: 106
552 Āli 'Imrān: 106

of al-Zalzalah by mentioning the atom of good and atom of evil."[553]

553 See *Mafātīḥ al-Ghayb of al-Rāzī* (8/658).

سورة العاديات

Sūrah al-ʿĀdiyāt

أقول: لا يخفى ما بين قوله في الزلزلة: ﴿وَأَخْرَجَتِ الْأَرْضُ أَثْقَالَهَا﴾ (الزلزلة: ٢)، وقوله في هذه السورة: ﴿إِذَا بُعْثِرَ مَا فِي الْقُبُورِ﴾ (٩) من المناسبة والعَلاقة.

I say: The connection is clear between His statement in al-Zalzalah: **{And when the earth throws out its burdens}**[554] and His statement in this *sūrah*: **{Knows he not that when the contents of the graves are brought out.}**[555] This shows that both *sūrahs* have a firm relationship with one another.[556]

---

554 Al-Zalzalah: 2

555 Al-ʿĀdiyāt: 9

556 There is also another aspect which connects the two, in that both *sūrahs* are generally themed at explaining the guidance of man or their misguidance. So Sūrah al-Zalzalah ends with both good and bad being promised to be recompensed, and al-ʿĀdiyāt explains that the inclination of man is to desire good for himself—and this can be either good in the worldly life alone or good in the hereafter. The latter is the true form of goodness and this is what motivates him to act, this will then be recompensed and Sūrah al-ʿĀdiyat then mentions that a day will come where man will be raised from the grave and the hidden intentions of the heart will be revealed and disclosed (al-ʿĀdiyāt: 9-10).

سورة القارعة

Sūrah al-Qāri‘ah

قال الإمام: لما ختم الله سبحانه السورة السابقة بقوله: ﴿إِنَّ رَبَّهُم بِهِمْ يَوْمَئِذٍ لَّخَبِيرٌ﴾ (١١) فكأنه قيل: وما ذاك؟ فقال: هي القارعة، قال: وتقديره: ستأتيك القارعة على ما أخبرت عنه في قولي: ﴿إِذَا بُعْثِرَ مَا فِي الْقُبُورِ﴾ (٩).

The *imām* said, "As Allah ﷻ completed the previous *sūrah* with His statement: {**Surely, that Day their Lord will be well-acquainted with them.**}[557] It is as if the next statement must explain what it is, and so He replied that, 'It is *al-qāri'ah* (the striking calamity). The meaning of this is that there is going to come to you a striking hour and this is what I have previously informed you about: {**But does he not know that when the contents of the graves are scattered.**}'"[558]

557 Al-Qāri'ah: 11

558 Al-'Ādiyāt: 9

سورة التكاثر

Sūrah al-Takāthur

أقول: هذه السورة واقعة موقع العلة لخاتمة ما قبلها، كأنه لما قال هناك: ﴿فَأُمُّهُ هَاوِيَةٌ﴾ (القارعة: ٩) قيل: لِمَ ذلك؟ فقال: لأنكم ﴿أَلْهَاكُمُ التَّكَاثُرُ﴾ (١) فاشتغلتم بدنياكم [عن دينكم]، وملأتم موازينكم بالحطام، فخفت موازينكم بالآثام، ولهذا عقَّبها بسورة والعصر، المشتملة على أن الإنسان في خسر، بيان لخسارة تجارة الدنيا، وربح تجارة الآخرة، ولهذا عقَّبها بسورة الهمزة، المتوعَّد فيها مَن ﴿جَمَعَ مَالًا وَعَدَّدَهُ۝يَحْسَبُ أَنَّ مَالَهُ أَخْلَدَهُ﴾ (الهمزة: ٢، ٣)، فانظر إلى تلاحم هذه السور الأربع، وحسن اتساقها.

I say: This entire *sūrah* explains the very reason as to why people fall into what has been described at the end of al-Qāriʿah: {**His refuge will be an abyss.**}[559] So an explanation as to why they are going to be placed in the fire is relevant here, so He said: {**Competition in [worldly] increase diverts you.**}[560] [So it is clear]—they became distracted by the *dunyā* in exchange for their religion, they polluted their scales, their deeds were light due to their sins; so for this reason al-Takāthur is followed by al-ʿAsr. Sūrah al-ʿAsr states that mankind is in loss, detailing that the trade of the *dunyā* brings loss and that the trade of

559 Al-Qāriʿah: 9

560 Al-Takāthur: 1

the hereafter brings profit. And it is due to this that it is followed by al-Humazah, which includes a threat to a type of person: **{Who has gathered wealth and counted it. He thinks that his wealth will make him last forever!}**[561] Look closely at how these four *sūrahs* complement one another and have been coordinated together in the best of ways.

561 Al-Humazah: 2-3

سورة الفيل

Sūrah al-Fīl

[أقول:] ظهر لي في وجه اتصالها بعد الفكرة: أنه تعالى لما ذكر حال الهمزة اللمزة، الذي جمع مالًا وعدَّده، وتعزز بماله وتقوَّى، عقَّب ذلك بذكر قصة أصحاب الفيل، الذين كانوا أشد منهم قوة وأكثر أموالًا وعتوًّا، وقد جعل كيدهم في تضليل، وأهلكهم بأصغر الطير وأضعفه، وجعلهم كعصف مأكول، ولم يغنِ عنهم مالُهم ولا عددُهم ولا شوكتُهم، ولا فِيلُهُمْ شيئًا.

I say: What appears to me to be the case—after careful consideration—is that Allah ﷻ mentions those who engage in back-biting and slander, gather wealth and sacrifice obedience for the sake of money, and then the story of the People of the Elephants is mentioned. [They resemble those in al-Humazah] because they are formidable in their strength, strong physically and militarily, they had more wealth but despite all of this their plots were left in ruin and were destroyed by the smallest and weakest of birds. Their corpses were then like eaten straw; so their money, strength and numbers did not avail them in the slightest, and their elephants did not come to their rescue either.

فمن كان قصارى تعززه وتقويه بالمال، وهمز الناس بلسانه، أقرب إلى

الهلاك، وأدنى إلى الذلة والمهانة.

So whoever takes pride in his wealth alone and also slanders people with his tongue, he is bordering ruin and facing humiliation.

سورة قريش

Sūrah Quraysh

هي شديدة الاتصال بما قبلها، لتعلق الجار والمجرور في أولها بالفعل في آخر تلك، ولهذا كانتا في مصحف أبي سورة واحدة.

This *sūrah* is directly connected to al-Fīl because the *al-jār wal-majrūr* compound[562] in the beginning of Quraysh is connected to the action which al-Fīl ended with. For this reason, Ubayy ibn Ka'b placed these two *sūrahs* together in his *muṣḥaf* as one *sūrah* [without a *basmallah* in between.][563]

---

562 [T] An Arabic grammar term which refers to a structure comprised of a preposition that causes the genitive state in the word that follows it, and the subsequent genitive word.

563 Al-Suyūṭī quotes al-Sakhāwī in his book *Jamāl al-Qurrā'* that the Prophet said, "Allah gave honour to the Quraysh with seven things: a *sūrah* was revealed to them in which no one else was addressed, they were protected against the people of the elephants, the elephants stood still for them, they were given ease in their trade journeys in winter and summer whilst Abraha was trying to plot an end to the Quraysh's robust trade industry." This was reported by al-Ḥākim and al-Ṭabarānī from the ḥadīth of Umm Hānī.

سورة الماعون

Sūrah al-Maʿūn

أقول: لما ذكر [الله] تعالى في سورة قريش: ﴿الَّذِي أَطْعَمَهُمْ مِنْ جُوعٍ﴾ (قريش: ٤)، ذكر هنا ذم من لم يحض على طعام المسكين.

I say: After Allah ﷻ mentioned at the end of Sūrah Quraysh: **{Who has fed them, [saving them] from hunger}**[564] He then mentions a censure towards those who do not want to feed the poor and needy.

ولما قال هناك: ﴿فَلْيَعْبُدُوا رَبَّ هَذَا الْبَيْتِ﴾ (قريش: ٣) ذكر هنا من سَهَا عن صلاته.

Also, as He stated in Quraysh: **{So worship the Lord of this House.}**[565] In al-Maʿūn He mentions those who are heedless in establishing the *ṣalāt*.

564 Quraysh: 4
565 Quraysh: 3

سورة الكوثر

Sūrah al-Kawthar

قال الإمام فخر الدين: هي كالمقابلة للتي قبلها؛ لأن السابقة وصف الله سبحانه فيها المنافقين بأربعة أمور: البخل، وترك الصلاة، والرياء فيها، ومنع الزكاة، وذكر في هذه السورة في مقابلة البخل: ﴿إِنَّآ أَعْطَيْنَاكَ الْكَوْثَرَ﴾ (١) أي: الخير الكثير، وفي مقابلة ترك الصلاة ﴿فَصَلِّ﴾ (٢) أي: دُم عليها، وفي مقابلة الرياء: ﴿لِرَبِّكَ﴾ (٢) أي: لرضاه، لا للناس، وفي مقابلة منع الماعون: ﴿وَانْحَرْ﴾ (٢) وأراد به: التصدق بلحوم الأضاحي، قال: فاعتبر هذه المناسبة العجيبة.

Imām Fakhr al-Dīn al-Rāzī said, "It is as if this *sūrah* provides the inverse of that which is mentioned in the previous *sūrah*. In al-Mā'ūn Allah ﷻ describes the hypocrites and gives them four characteristics: stinginess, abandonment of the *ṣalāt*, having ostentation in it and preventing *zakāt*. In al-Kawthar, the opposite of stinginess is mentioned: **{Surely, We have granted you *al-Kawthar*}**,[566] i.e. a great deal of good. It mentions the opposite of abandoning the *ṣalāt*: **{So pray}**,[567] meaning maintain it and do not abandon it. It mentions the opposite

566 Al-Kawthar: 1

567 Al-Kawthar: 2

of ostentation: **{To your Lord}**,[568] i.e. do so sincerely for His pleasure and not for the sake of people. It mentions the opposite of preventing small kindness: **{And sacrifice}**,[569] meaning, give away the meat from the *uḍḥiyah* in charity. So ponder upon the intricacies found herein between them."[570]

568 Al-Kawthar: 2

569 Al-Kawthar: 2

570 See *Mafātiḥ al-Ghayb* of al-Rāzī (8/700-701).

سورة الكافرون

Sūrah al-Kāfirūn

أقول: وجه اتصالها بما قبلها: أنه تعالى لما قال: ﴿فَصَلِّ لِرَبِّكَ﴾ (الكوثر: ٢) أمره أن يخاطب الكافرين بأنه لا يعبد إلا ربه، ولا يعبد ما يعبدون، وبالغ في ذلك فكرر، وانفصل منهم على أن لهم دينهم وله دينه.

I say: al-Kāfirūn is connected to al-Kawthar due to His statement: **{So pray to your Lord.}**[571] The command [to the Prophet] in this *āyah* is to address the disbelievers and tell them that he worships no one except his Lord, and that he does not worship what they worship. This message is repeated in al-Kāfirūn to show reinforcement and concludes by expressing religious disassociation from them, as they have their religion and the Prophet ﷺ has his.

571 Al-Kawthar: 2

سورة النصر

Sūrah al-Naṣr

أقول: وجه اتصالها بما قبلها: أنه [لما] قال في آخر ما قبلها: ﴿وَلِيَ دِينِ﴾ (الكافرون: ٦) فكان فيه إشعار بأنه خلص له دينه، وسلم من شوائب الكدر والمخالفين، فعقَّب ببيان وقت ذلك، وهو مجيء الفتح والنصر، فإن الناس حين دخلوا في دين الله أفواجًا، فقد تم الأمر وذهب الكفر، وخلص دين الإسلام ممن كان يناوئه، ولذلك كانت السورة إشارة إلى وفاته صلى الله عليه وسلم.

I say: Al-Naṣr is connected to the preceding *sūrah* due to it ending with: {**And to me is my religion.**}[572] This is to indicate that his religion will prevail and be safe from the defects and debasement of disbelievers, and so He added right after it the time wherein which this will occur; that is when the victory and conquest take place. This is because when the victory and conquest took place, droves of people entered into Islam, and so this promise was completed; disbelief was eradicated [from Makkah] and the religion of Islam became liberated from its opposition. For this reason, al-Naṣr was an indication [that the message had been delivered] and that the passing away of the Prophet ﷺ was close.[573]

---

572 Al-Kāfirūn: 6

573 Reported by al-Bukhārī (6/220-221) in the Chapter of *Tafsīr* on the authori-

وقال الإمام فخر الدين: كأنه تعالى يقول: لما أمرتك في السورة المتقدمة بمجاهدة جميع الكفار، بالتبري منهم، وإبطال دينهم، جزيتك على ذلك بالنصر والفتح، وتكثير الأتباع.

Imām Fakhr al-Dīn said, "It is as if the Most High is saying that in the previous *sūrah* He commanded the Prophet ﷺ to strive against the disbelievers, shun their [false] ways and explain their error; all of this is rewarded with a divine victory, conquest and [the pleasure of] droves accepting Islam."[574]

قال: ووجه آخر، وهو: أنه لما أعطاه [الله] الكوثر، وهو: الخير الكثير، ناسب تحميله مشقاته وتكاليفه، فعقَّبها بمجاهدة الكفار، والتبري منهم، فلما امتثل ذلك أعقبه بالبشارة بالنصر والفتح، وإقبال الناس أفواجًا إلى دينه، وأشار إلى دنو أجله، فإنه ليس بعد الكمال إلا الزوال.

And he said, "From another angle: As Allah has promised an immense reward for the Prophet ﷺ in al-Kawthar, He placed upon him a difficult challenge and a series of tests; so this was followed by a command to strive against the disbelievers and abandon them. And when the Prophet complied with this, it was followed by the good news of victory, conquest and the satisfaction that people will accept his message, entering into Islam in large numbers. This was an indication that his time was close, as after completion there is only demise.

توقع زوالًا إذا قيل تم

ty of Ibn ʿAbbās, Imām Aḥmad in *al-Musnad* (1/217, 344 and 356) and Ibn Jarīr in his *tafsīr* (30/215).

574 See *Mafātiḥ al-Ghayb* of al-Rāzī (8/729).

Expect the end once it is said that it is completed."[575]

575 See *Mafātiḥ al-Ghayb* of al-Rāzī (8/743).

سورة تبت

Sūrah al-Masad

قال الإمام: وجه اتصالها بما قبلها: أنه لما قال: ﴿لَكُمْ دِينُكُمْ وَلِيَ دِينِ﴾ (الكافرون: ٦)، فكأنه قيل: إلهي، وما جزائي؟ فقال الله له: النصر والفتح، فقال: وما جزاء عمي الذي دعاني إلى عبادة الأصنام؟ فقال: ﴿تَبَّتْ يَدَآ أَبِي لَهَبٍ﴾ (١) الآيات.

The *imām* said, "The manner in which it connects to that which precedes it arises from His statement: **{To you is your religion, and to me is my religion.}**[576] So it is as if the Prophet ﷺ was asking, 'What is the reward for me?' Then Allah states that it is victory and the conquest of Makkah. Then it is as if he asked, 'What is the recompense of my uncle who invited me to the worship of idols?' Thus Allah states: **{May the hands of Abu Lahab be ruined! May he be ruined too!}**[577]

وقدم الوعد على الوعيد ليكون النصر معللًا بقوله: ﴿وَلِيَ دِينِ﴾، ويكون الوعيد راجعًا إلى قوله: ﴿لَكُمْ دِينُكُمْ﴾ على حد قوله: ﴿يَوْمَ تَبْيَضُّ وُجُوهٌ وَتَسْوَدُّ وُجُوهٌ فَأَمَّا الَّذِينَ اسْوَدَّتْ وُجُوهُهُمْ﴾ (آل عمران: ١٠٦).

[By placing al-Naṣr before al-Masad,] the promise of success is placed

576 Al-Kāfirūn: 6
577 Al-Lahab: 1

before the threat of punishment, so that *al-naṣr* (the divine support and conquest) is directly connected to its cause and reason: **{And to me is my religion.}**[578] Therefore, the threat of punishment refers to His statement: **{To you is your religion.}**[579] This is the same manner in which Allah gives the greetings of good news and the warning of punishment elsewhere: **{On the Day when some faces will become white [illuminated with cheer] and some faces will become black [darkened with humiliation]. As for those whose faces turn black...}**"[580]

قال: فتأمل في هذه المجانسة الحافلة بين هذه السور، مع أن سورة النصر من أواخر ما نزل بالمدينة، والكافرون وتبت من أوائل ما نزل بمكة، ليعلم أن ترتيب هذه السور من الله، وبأمره.

He continued, "So ponder carefully regarding the caravan of subjects that are being carried amongst these *sūrahs*. This is the case despite al-Naṣr being from the very last *sūrahs* to be revealed in Madīnah,[581] whilst al-Kāfirūn and al-Masad are from the very first Makkan *sūrahs*. This will make you come to understand that the order of these *sūrahs* is divinely set by Allah and from His command."

قال: ووجه آخر: وهو: أنه لما قال: ﴿لَكُمْ دِينُكُمْ وَلِيَ دِينِ﴾ (الكافرون: ٦) كأنه قيل: يا إلهي، ما جزاء المطيع؟ قال: حصول النصر والفتح، فقيل: وما ثواب العاصي؟ قال: الخسارة في الدنيا، والعقاب في العقبى، كما دلت عليه سورة تبت.

578 Al-Kāfirūn: 6

579 Al-Kāfirūn: 6

580 Āli 'Imrān: 106

581 Reported by Muslim (8/242, 243) on the authority of Ibn 'Abbās.

He continued, "Another angle arises from the statement of Allah: {**To you is your religion, and to me is my religion.**}[582] It is as if the Prophet asked, 'O Allah, what is the reward of the dutiful?' He replied, 'The one who obeys will have the reward of victory and the conquest.' Then it is as if he asked, 'And what is the recompense for the wayward?' He replied, 'The recompense for the wayward is that he faces loss in this world and torment in the hereafter.' This is the description given in Sūrah al-Masad."[583]

582 Al-Kāfirūn: 6

583 See *Mafātiḥ al-Ghayb* of al-Rāzī (8/744).

سورة الإخلاص

Sūrah al-Ikhlāṣ

قال بعضهم: وضعت هاهنا للوزان في اللفظ بين فواصلها ومقطع سورة تبت.

Some scholars were of the view that Sūrah al-Ikhlāṣ has been placed after Sūrah al-Masad because the metre and rhyme in al-Ikhlāṣ correspond with that of al-Masad.

وأقول: ظهر لي هنا غير الوزان في اللفظ: أن هذه السورة متصلة بـ﴿قُلْ يَا أَيُّهَا الْكَافِرُونَ﴾ في المعنى، ولهذا قيل: من أسمائها أيضًا: الإخلاص، وقد قالوا: إنها اشتملت على التوحيد، وهذه أيضًا مشتملة عليه، ولهذا قرن بينهما في القراءة في الفجر، والطواف، والضحى، وسنة المغرب، وصبح المسافر، ومغرب ليلة الجمعة.

I say: What appears to me to be the case is that it is not just placed here for that reason, rather it is connected to al-Kāfirūn in meaning and theme. For this reason, some of the scholars are of the view that from al-Kāfirūn's names is "al-Ikhlāṣ". And some of the scholars said that both *sūrahs* share the trait of defining *tawḥid*, and so the Prophet used to recite them both [in prayers] such as the two *sunnan* of *al-fajr*, the two units of *ṭawāf*, *al-ḍuḥā*, the *sunan* of *al-maghrib*, the two obligatory prayers of *al-fajr* when travelling, and in the *maghrib* prayers on the eve of al-Jumu'ah.[584]

وذلك أنه لما نفى عبادة ما يعبدون، صرح هنا بلازم ذلك، وهو أن معبوده أحد، وأقام الدليل عليه بأنه صمد، لم يلد ولم يولد ولم يكن له كفوًا أحد، ولا يستحق العبادة إلا من كان كذلك، وليس في معبوداتهم ما هو كذلك.

This is because in [al-Kāfirūn] there is the negation of worshipping that which the disbelievers do, and al-Ikhlāṣ is explicit in terms of worthiness of worship only belonging to Allah, as the deity worthy of being worshipped can only be one. Al-Ikhlāṣ gives evidence to this and describes Him as being al-Ṣamad, the one who was not born and does not give birth and that He is completely unique. If this is His description then this is the description of the only object that can be duly worshipped. As nothing can be compared to Him, nothing else is then deserved of worship. Their deities cannot match the attributes and criteria which al-Ikhlāṣ stipulates for objectification of worship.

وإنما فصل بين النظيرتين بالسورتين لما تقدم من الحكمة، وكأن إيلاءها سورة تبت ورد عليه بخصوصه.

The reason why al-Kāfirūn and al-Ikhlas are separated [by al-Naṣr and al-Masad,] although they are considered counterparts and complement one another, is for the previously mentioned wisdom. It is as

584 It is collected by al-Haythamī in *Majma' al-Zawā'id* (2/120) on the authority of Ibn 'Umar that the Prophet ﷺ used to recite al-Kāfirūn and al-Ikhlās in the obligatory *fajr* prayers when travelling. It is also collected by Ibn Ḥajar in *al-Maṭālib al-'Āliyah* (399/3) that the Prophet used to recite these two in the two units of the *ṣalāh*; he did it over twenty different times.

if placing al-Ikhlāṣ after al-Masad was specifically to address it.

سورة الفلق والناس

Sūrah al-Falaq and al-Nās

قال: أقول: هاتان السورتان نزلتا معًا، كما في الدلائل للبيهقي، فلذلك قُرنتا، مع ما اشتركتا فيه من التسمية بالمعوذتين، ومن الافتتاح بـ﴿قُلْ أَعُوذُ﴾، وعقب بهما سورة الإخلاص؛ لأن الثلاثة سميت في الحديث بالمعوذات وبالقواقل.

[The *imām*] said that these two *sūrahs* were revealed together, as al-Bayhaqī reported in his book *al-Dalā'il*. They have been placed together for this reason and have been named as al-Mu'awwidhatayn (the two [*sūrahs*] for seeking refuge) as they both start with seeking refuge in Allah. They are both placed after Sūrah al-Ikhlas because all three have been termed in a ḥadīth as Mu'awwidhāt or the Qawāqil (i.e. commencing with "*qul*").[585]

وقدمت الفلق على الناس -وإن كانت أقصر منها- لمناسبة مقطعها في الوزان لفواصل الإخلاص مع مقطع تبت.

Al-Falaq comes before al-Nās, despite al-Falaq being shorter, because its metre and rhyme corresponds with the end of al-Ikhlāṣ and al-Masad.

---

585 See Aḥmad in *al-Musnad* (5/312), Abū Dāwūd in *al-Adab* (2/176), al-Nasā'ī in *al-Isti'ādha* (8/250) and al-Tirmidhī in *al-Da'wāt* (9/347).

وهذا آخر ما مَنَّ الله به عليَّ من استخراج مناسبات ترتيب السور، وكله من مستنبطاتي، ولم أعثر فيه على شيء لغيري إلا النزر اليسير الذي صرحت بعزوي له، فلله الحمد على ما ألهم، والشكر على ما مَنَّ به وأنعم، سبحانك لا أحصي ثناء عليك، أنت كما أثنيت على نفسك.

This concludes what Allah has made apparent for me in identifying the appropriateness of the order of the *sūrahs*. All of this has been from my own judgement and capability in understanding, except for the few places where I have benefited and borrowed from others—and this has all been cited clearly in the book. So all praise and thanks are due to Allah for giving us this understanding, and full appreciation is shown to Him for favouring us and blessing us with His generosity. How perfect and glorified He is, we cannot praise and thank You enough, the best of praises are the praises You have praised Yourself with.

ثم رأيت الإمام فخر الدين ذكر في تفسيره كلامًا لطيفًا في مناسبات هذه السور، فقال في سورة الكوثر:

Before completion, I wanted to add something excellent I saw mentioned by Imām Fakhr al-Dīn al-Rāzī in his *tafsīr* regarding the order of these final *sūrahs*, starting from al-Kawthar:

اعلم أن هذه السورة كالمتممة لما قبلها من السور، وكالأصل لما بعدها.

You should know that Sūrah al-Kawthar acts as if it concludes the *sūrahs* that came before it and forms a basis for the *sūrahs* that come after it.

أما الأول، فلأنه تعالى جعل سورة (الضحى) في مدح النبي صلى الله عليه وسلم وتفصيل أحواله، فذكر في أولها ثلاثة أشياء تتعلق بنبوته: ﴿مَا وَدَّعَكَ رَبُّكَ وَمَا قَلَىٰ ۝ وَلَلْآخِرَةُ خَيْرٌ لَّكَ مِنَ الْأُولَىٰ ۝ وَلَسَوْفَ يُعْطِيكَ رَبُّكَ فَتَرْضَىٰ﴾ (الضحى: ٣-٥)، ثم ختمها بثلاثة أحوال من أحواله فيما يتعلق بالدنيا، ﴿أَلَمْ يَجِدْكَ يَتِيمًا فَآوَىٰ ۝ وَوَجَدَكَ ضَالًّا فَهَدَىٰ ۝ وَوَجَدَكَ عَائِلًا فَأَغْنَىٰ﴾ (الضحى: ٦-٨).

As for it being a conclusion, Allah made the theme of al-Ḍuhā in praise of the Prophet ﷺ, describing his affairs and mentioning three aspects of his prophethood: **{Your Lord has neither forsaken you nor does He hate you. And indeed the Hereafter is better for you than the present. And verily, your Lord will give you so that you shall be well-pleased.}**[586] Then these aspects of prophethood are closely followed by three aspects of his worldly life: **{Did He not find you as an orphan and gave you refuge? And He found you unaware and guided you? And He found you poor, and made you rich.}**[587]

ثم ذكر في سورة ﴿ألم نشرح﴾ أنه شرفه بثلاثة أشياء: شرح الصدر، ووضع الوزر، ورفع الذكر.

Then in Sūrah al-Sharḥ the Prophet's virtues are explained and he is honoured with having three qualities: having his breast opened, having his sins removed and having his mention raised.

ثم شرفه في سورة التين بثلاثة أنواع [من التشريف]: أقسم ببلده، وأخبر

586 Al-Ḍuḥā: 3-5
587 Al-Ḍuḥā: 6-8

بخلاص أمته من الناس بقوله: ﴿إِلَّا الَّذِينَ آمَنُوا﴾ ووصولهم إلي الثواب بقوله: ﴿فَلَهُمْ أَجْرٌ غَيْرُ مَمْنُونٍ﴾ (التين: ٦).

Then in Sūrah al-Ṭīn there are three areas of special virtue mentioned for him also: Allah swore by his city, He informed him that his Ummah will be the saved one amongst mankind in the statement {**Except those who believe and do righteous deeds**} and that they will be granted their reward in full, {**Then they shall have a reward without end.**}[588]

وشرَّفه في سورة اقرأ بثلاثة أنواع: ﴿اقْرَأْ بِاسْمِ رَبِّكَ﴾ (العلق)، وقهر خصمه بقوله: ﴿فَلْيَدْعُ نَادِيَهُ۝سَنَدْعُ الزَّبَانِيَةَ﴾ (العلق: ١٧، ١٨)، وتخصيصه بالقرب في قوله: ﴿وَاسْجُدْ وَاقْتَرِبْ﴾ (العلق: ١٩).

The Prophet is then praised further in Sūrah al-'Alaq from three different aspects: [knowledge, as in] {**Read! In the Name of your Lord**}, promise of victory over his enemies: {**Then, let him call upon his council. We will call the guards of Hell [to deal with him]**}[589], and a special honour of closeness he is described to have with Allah in His statement {**But prostrate and draw near to Allah.**}[590]

وشرفه في سورة (القدر) بليلة القدر، وفيها ثلاثة أنواع من الفضيلة: كونها خيرًا من ألف شهر، وتنزل الملائكة والروح فيها، وكونها سلامًا حتى مطلع الفجر.

---

588 Al-Tīn: 6
589 Al-'Alaq: 17-18
590 Al-'Alaq: 19

Thereafter in Sūrah al-Qadr, the Prophet is honoured with another set of three specialities—related to the Night of Power: it is a night which is better than a thousand months, the angels and the Rūḥ (i.e. Jibrīl) descend on that night, and that it is a night filled with tranquillity until the break of dawn.

وشرَّفه في (لم يكن) بثلاثة أشياء: أنهم خير البرية، وجزاؤهم جنات، ورضي عنهم.

Then in Sūrah al-Bayyinah the Prophet is described with three more virtues: he is described as being the best of creation, his Ummah's reward is Jannah and that Allah is pleased with them.

وشرَّفه في (الزلزلة) بثلاثة أنواع: إخبار الأرض بطاعة أمته، ورؤيتهم أعمالهم، ووصولهم إلى ثوابها حتى وزن الذرة.

Sūrah al-Zalzalah provides three more of his virtues: The earth will bear witness for his nation's acts of obedience,[591] that his Ummah will see their good deeds [and achievement] on the day of judgement, and that not even an atom's weight of deeds will be left unrewarded.

وشرَّفه في (العاديات) بإقسامه بخيل الغزاة من أمته، ووصفها بثلاث صفات.

Sūrah al-ʿĀdiyāt also displays elements of prestige for the Prophet; it begins by swearing a divine oath using the chariots and steeds of the fighters from amongst his Ummah, and the oath is connected to three positive attributes of their expeditions.

591 Al-Zalzalah: 4

وشرَّفه في (القارعة) بثقل موازين أمته، وكونهم في عيشة راضية، ورؤيتهم أعداءهم في نار حامية.

Sūrah al-Qāri'ah praises the Prophet also; that his Ummah will have their deeds made heavy on the scales, they will be given an eternal life of bliss and that they will see justice afflict their enemies when they are placed in a blazing fire.

وفي (ألهاكم التكاثر) هدد المعرضين عن دينه بثلاثة: يرون الجحيم، ثم يرونها عين اليقين، ويسألون عن النعيم.

Sūrah al-Takāthur also has a mention of three things, that those who reject him will have three forms of punishment cast upon them; they will see the fire, they will see it with certainty and that they will be asked regarding each and every luxury they had in this world.

وشرَّفه في (العصر) بمدح أمته بثلاثة: الإيمان، والعمل الصالح، وإرشاد الخلق إليه، وهو: التواصي بالحق والصبر.

Sūrah al-'Asr also displays the prestige of the Prophet through praise of his Ummah in three things: they are the ones who have *īmān* and righteous deeds, that they are a source of guidance for the rest of mankind and that they help one another to pursue truth and endure it with patience.

وشرَّفه في سورة (الهمزة) بوعيد عدوه بثلاثة أنواع من العذاب: ألا ينتفع بدنياه، وينبذ في الحطمة، ويغلق عليه.

Sūrah al-Humazah displays his prestige by giving three forms of warning against those who deny him: they will not benefit from their worldly matters [in the hereafter], they will be cast in a blazing fire and that Hellfire will be closed down upon them.

وشرَّفه في سورة (الفيل) أن رد كيد عدوه بثلاث: بأن جعله في تضليل، وأرسل عليهم طيرًا أبابيل، وجعلهم كعصف مأكول.

Sūrah al-Fīl gives nobility to the Prophet also, in that the plot of his foes was deterred in three ways: Allah made their plot fail and go in vain, they were destroyed by the simplest of opponents and their corpses were made to look like empty stalks of vegetation [out of humiliation and signalling their insignificance.]

وشرَّفه في سورة (قريش) [بأن راعى مصلحة أسلافه من ثلاثة أوجه]: تآلف قومه، وإطعامهم، وأمنهم.

Sūrah al-Quraysh honours the Prophet by detailing how He considered the interests of his ancestors in three ways: He protected his tribe, He fed them and He gave them all security.

وشرَّفه في (الماعون) بذم عدوه بثلاث: الدناءة، واللؤم في قوله: ﴿فَذَٰلِكَ الَّذِي يَدُعُّ الْيَتِيمَ ۝ وَلَا يَحُضُّ عَلَىٰ طَعَامِ الْمِسْكِينِ﴾ (الماعون: ٢، ٣)، وترك تعظيم الخالق في قوله: ﴿فَوَيْلٌ لِّلْمُصَلِّينَ ۝ الَّذِينَ هُمْ عَن صَلَاتِهِمْ سَاهُونَ ۝ الَّذِينَ هُمْ يُرَاءُونَ﴾ (الماعون: ٤-٦)، وترك انتفاع الخلق في قوله: ﴿وَيَمْنَعُونَ الْمَاعُونَ﴾ (الماعون: ٧).

He is honoured in al-Mā'ūn as it rebukes his enemies in three ways: Describing their level of meanness in His statement: **{He repulses the**

orphan. And does not urge feeding the poor.}[592] It also blames them for not venerating their Creator, in His statement: {**So woe to those who pray. Those who are neglectful of their prayers. Those who pray only to be seen by others.**}[593] And also for when they avoid benefiting others from the creation of Allah, in His statement: {**And refuse acts of [even small amounts of] kindness.**}[594]

فلما شرَّفه في هذه السور بهذه الوجوه العظيمة قال: ﴿إِنَّآ أَعْطَيْنَاكَ الْكَوْثَرَ﴾ أي: هذه الفضائل المتكاثرة المذكورة في هذه السور، التي كل واحدة منها أعظم من ملك الدنيا بحذافيرها، فاشتغل أنت بعبادة ربك، إما بالنفس، وهو قوله: ﴿فَصَلِّ لِرَبِّكَ﴾ (الكوثر: ٢)، وإما بالمال وهو قوله: ﴿وَانْحَرْ﴾ وإما بإرشاد العباد إلى الأصلح، وهو قوله: ﴿قُلْ يَا أَيُّهَا الْكَافِرُونَ ۝ لا أَعْبُدُ مَا تَعْبُدُونَ﴾ (الكافرون: ١، ٢) الآيات، فثبت أن هذه السورة كالتتمّة لما قبلها.

So after He praised the nobility of the Prophet ﷺ and extolled his honour in the above *sūrahs*, Allah then stated: {**Surely, We have granted you al-Kawthar**}, meaning We have granted you all of these virtues that have been mentioned in the various *sūrahs*, each of which is greater than the worldly virtues, as a result: focus on worshipping your Lord, either in your actions, {**Therefore turn in prayer to your Lord**}[595] or in your wealth, {**... and sacrifice**} or in advising people towards what is good for them [in the next *sūrah*, al-Kāfirūn,] {**Say,**

---

592 Al-Mā'ūn: 2-3
593 Al-Mā'ūn: 4-6
594 Al-Mā'ūn: 7
595 Al-Kawthar: 2

"O Kāfirūn, 'I worship not that which you worship.'"}[596] So al-Kawthar is a conclusion for what came before it.

وأما كونها كالأصل لما بعدها فهو: أنه تعالى يأمره بعد هذه أن يكف عن أهل الدنيا جميعًا بقوله: ﴿قُلْ يَا أَيُّهَا الْكَافِرُونَ﴾ إلى آخر السورة، ويبطل أديانهم، وذلك يقتضي نصرهم على أعدائهم؛ لأن الطعن على الإنسان في دينه أشد عليه من الطعن في نفسه وزوجه، وذلك مما يجبن عنه كل أحد من الخلق؛ فإن موسى وهارون أرسلا إلى فرعون واحد فقالا: ﴿إِنَّنَا نَخَافُ أَنْ يَفْرُطَ عَلَيْنَآ أَوْ أَنْ يَطْغَى﴾ (طه: ٤٥) ومحمد صلى الله عليه وسلم مرسَل إلى الخلق جميعًا، فكأن كل واحد من الخلق كفرعون بالنسبة إليه، فدبر الله في إزالة الخوف الشديد تدبيرًا لطيفًا، بأن قدم هذه السورة، وأخبر فيها بإعطائه الخير الكثير، ومن جملته أيضًا: الرئاسة، ومفاتيح الدنيا، فلا يلتفت إلى ما بأيديهم من زهرة الدنيا، وذلك أدعى إلى مجاهرتهم بالعداوة، والصدع بالحق؛ لعدم تطلعه إلى ما بأيديهم.

As for how it serves as the basis for the *sūrahs* that come after it, Allah ﷻ—after al-Kawthar—commands the Prophet to abstain from the *dunyā* and its people, in His statement: **{Say: "O al-Kāfirūn… [to the end of the *sūrah*}**, meaning, their religions are false [so advise them] and you will be supported and victorious over your enemies. This is because insulting a person on account of his religion is the worst form of abuse. It is even worse than insulting one's honour or the honour of his wife. However, at the same time, it is the honour of one's religion which can cause the person to become timid. Allah said about Mūsā

596 Al-Kāfirūn: 1-2

and Hārūn after they were commanded to proclaim the message to Fir'awn, that one of them said: {**They said, "Our Lord! Surely, we fear that he will punish us or oppress us in some way.**}[597] Muḥammad ﷺ was given an even more daunting task, which was to proclaim the message to the entire creation [and not to one man alone]. [Mūsā and Hārūn had to face one person, namely Fir'awn] and it is as if the Prophet had to face numerous Fir'awns since he was sent to call everyone. So Allah removed from the Prophet ﷺ the element of extreme fear as He placed this *sūrah* here, [and He gave him greetings of a successful end in the coming *sūrahs*.] He told the Prophet ﷺ that He will give him a great deal of goodness in return for his efforts, and from what He has promised to give him: Control and leadership in the land and that He will open the *dunyā* for him; so that he would not be disheartened by their statements and the favours they had been given from the pomp of the *dunyā*. This made it all the more reason for him to be averse to them publicly, and proclaim the truth out loud, for he had no interest in whatever worldly possessions they had.

ثم ذكر بعد سورة (الكافرين) سورة (النصر) فكأنه تعالى يقول: وعدتك بالخير الكثير، وإتمام أمرك، وأمرتك بإبطال أديانهم، والبراءة من معبوداتهم، فلما امتثلت أمري أنجزت لك الوعد بالفتح والنصر، وكثرة الأتباع، بدخول الناس في دين الله أفواجًا.

Allah then mentions al-Naṣr after Sūrah al-Kāfirūn and it is as if Allah ﷻ is saying: "I have promised you a great deal of goodness and I will complete your religion for you. I ordered you to counteract their religions and free yourself from worshipping their false deities. And when you have complied with my order, I have brought for you the promise of victory and conquest, and that made the number of your

597 Ṭa-ha: 45

followers become numerous by letting droves of people enter into the religion of Allah."

ولما تم أمر الدعوة والشريعة، شرع في بيان ما يتعلق بأحوال القلب والباطن وذلك أن الطالب إما أن يكون طلبه مقصورًا على الدنيا، فليس له إلا الذل والخسارة والهوان، والمصير إلى النار، وهو المراد من سورة (تبت) وإما أن يكون طالبًا للآخرة، فأعظم أحواله أن تصير نفسه كالمرآة التي تنتقش فيها صور الموجودات.

When the propagation to the religion and its legislation was completed, Allah ﷻ moved onto explaining matters related to the heart and the inner-self, as it is often the case that one's desires are limited to worldly affairs, and this is naught except a harbinger of loss, disgrace and the path to the fire. And this is the essential theme of al-Masad. However, if a person seeks after the hereafter, the worst that could happen to him is that whatever he sees does not last and goes away, as his heart will be like a mirror that reflects the images of the creatures only and does not contain them.

وقد ثبت أن طريق الخلق في معرفة الصانع على وجهين: منهم من قال: أعرف الصانع، ثم أتوسل بمعرفته إلى معرفة مخلوقاته، وهذا هو الطريق الأشرف، ومنهم من عكس، وهو طريق الجمهور.

It is established that the creation comes to know the Creator by one of two ways: (i) he knows his Creator and then uses the knowledge of Him to understand the creation, and this is the best of stations, or (ii) the opposite [i.e. he uses his knowledge of the creation to know the Creator or of His existence], and this is the way most people follow to know their creator.

ثم إنه سبحانه ختم كتابه المكرم بتلك الطريقة التي هي أشرف، فبدأ بذكر صفات الله، وشرح جلاله، في سورة (الإخلاص)، ثم أتبعه بذكر مراتب مخلوقاته في (الفلق)، ثم ختم بذكر مراتب النفس الإنسانية في (الناس)، وعند ذلك ختم الكتاب. فسبحان مَن أرشد العقول إلى معرفة هذه الأسرار الشريفة [المودَعة] في كتابه المكرم! هذا كلام الإمام.

And this is how the Glorified has concluded his Glorious Book, by enabling the believer to know Him in the most noble of ways. [So in the final three *sūrahs*,] He began by having a *sūrah* (al-Ikhlāṣ) which is themed at explaining His attributes, and His glory and magnificence. After it, He placed al-Falaq which discusses the different levels of His creation. He then concluded His Book with al-Nās, which details the levels of the inner-selves of mankind. So glorified is the One who gives intellect and enabled us to excavate what is hidden in His Noble Book."[598] And this is the end of the *imām's* words.

ثم قال في (الفلق): سمعت بعض العارفين يقول: لما شرح الله سبحانه أمر الإلهية في سورة (الإخلاص)، ذكر هاتين السورتين عقبها في شرح مراتب الخلق على ما قال: ﴿أَلَا لَهُ الْخَلْقُ وَالْأَمْرُ﴾.

Then he said about al-Falaq, "I have heard some of the knowledgeable ones say that Allah explains the concept of *tawḥīd* in Sūrah al-Ikhlāṣ, so He then follows it with al-Falaq and al-Nās to explain the different levels and degrees of humans stated in His statement: **{His is the Cre-**

598 See *Tafsīr al-Rāzī* (8/704).

ation and Commandment}[599]

فعالم الأمر كله خيرات محضة، بريئة عن الشرور والآفات، [و] أما عالم الخلق فهو الأجسام الكثيفة، والجثمانيات، فلا جرم قال في المطلع: ﴿قُلْ أَعُوذُ بِرَبِّ الْفَلَقِ ۝ مِنْ شَرِّ مَا خَلَقَ﴾ (الفلق: ١، ٢).

The realm of decree and predestination is free of evil and defects; for it is pure goodness whereas the realm of created beings comprises of creatures with substances, be they idle or animate. This explains the reason why Sūrah al-Falaq begins with: {**Say, I seek refuge in the Lord of Daybreak, from the evil of that which He created.**}.

ثم [من الظاهر أن] الأجسام إما أثيرية أو عنصرية، والأجسام كلها خيرات محضة، لأنها بريئة عن الاختلال والفطور، على ما قال: ﴿مَا تَرَى فِي خَلْقِ الرَّحْمَنِ مِنْ تَفَاوُتٍ فَارْجِعِ الْبَصَرَ هَلْ تَرَى مِنْ فُطُورٍ﴾ (تبارك: ٣).

It is apparent that bodies are either etheric or physical, but all the bodies per se are good and pure, as Allah states: {**Can you see any faults in the creations of the Most Beneficent. Then look again: "Can you see any rifts?"**}[600]

وإما عنصرية، فهي إما جمادات، فهي خالية عن جميع القوى النفسانية، فالظلمات فيها خالصة، والأنوار عنها زائلة، وهو المراد من قوله: ﴿وَمِنْ شَرِّ غَاسِقٍ إِذَا وَقَبَ﴾ (الفلق: ٣).

As for the creatures with physical substance, they are (i) inanimate

599 Al-Aʿrāf: 54
600 Al-Mulk: 3

creatures, lacking all spiritual powers, thus they have nothing but darkness, which is the intended purport of His statement: {**And from the evil of the darkening (night) as it settles.**}

وإما نبات، والقوة العادلة هي التي تزيد في الطول والعمق معًا، فهذه القوة النباتية كأنها تنفث في العقد.

(ii) Or plants, which resembles as if the power of flora blows into the knots, but a fair power is that which has its length and depth increase together.

وإما حيوان، وهو محل القوى التي تمنع الروح الإنسانية عن الانصباب إلى عالم الغيب، والاشتغال بقدس جلال الله، وهو المراد بقوله: ﴿وَمِن شَرِّ حَاسِدٍ إِذَا حَسَدَ﴾ (الفلق: ٥).

(iii) Or animalistic beings, which is the form that prevents the human soul from stepping into the world of the unseen, and from being fully occupied with the sacred and holy glory of Allah, which is the intended meaning of: {**And from the evil of the envier when he envies.**}

ثم إنه لم يبقَ من السفليات بعد هذه المرتبة سوى النفس الإنسانية، وهي المستعيذة، فلا يكون مستعاذًا منها فلا جرم قطع هذه السورة، وذكر بعدها في سورة (الناس) مراتب ودرجات النفس الإنسانية. انتهى.

After mentioning all of these lowly worldly creatures, mankind are the last category to be mentioned—and they are the ones seeking refuge—so refuge is not taken against them. This explains the reason the *sūrah* ends there and then humans and the levels of humans are mentioned in the following *sūrah*."[601]

ولم يبين المراتب المشار إليها، وقد بيَّنها ابن الزملكاني في أسراره فقال: إضافة (رب) إلى (الناس) تُؤْذِنُ بأن المراد بالناس: الأطفال؛ لأن الرب من ربَّه يربُّه، وهم إلى التربية أحوج، وإضافة (ملك) إلى (الناس) تؤذن بإرادة الشباب به، إذ لفظ (ملك) يؤذن بالسياسة والعزة [والقوة] ، والشبان إليها أحوج، وإضافة (إله) إلى (الناس) تؤذن بأن المراد به الشيوخ، لأن ذاته مستحقة للطاعة والعبادة، وهم أقرب، وقوله: ﴿يُوَسْوِسُ فِي صُدُورِ النَّاسِ﴾ (الناس: ٥) يؤذن بأن المراد بالناس: العلماء والعباد، لأن الوسوسة غالبًا عن الشُّبَه، وقوله: ﴿مِنَ الْجِنَّةِ وَالنَّاسِ﴾ (الناس: ٦) يؤذن بأن المراد بالناس الأشرار، وهم شياطين الإنس الذين يوسوسون لهم، والله تعالى أعلم.

Al-Rāzī did not clarify the different stages of man that he alluded to, but I found Ibn al-Zamalkānī clarify this in his *al-Asrār*.[602] He said, "The connection between the word "Lord" and "mankind" is to indicate that mankind in this context refers to children, as the [Arabic] word "lord" is derived from the verb "nurtured him (*rabbahu*: the attached pronoun *hu* here is the object of the verb)—nurtures him (*yurabbuhu*)."[603] This is because at that stage of human growth, the need for a good solid nurturing is the most important. Attaching the word "king" to the word "mankind" here is to allude to the stage of adolescence (i.e. the physical prime), because the word "king" alludes to

601 See *Mafātiḥ al-Ghayb* (8/272).

602 I.e. his book *Nihāyat al-Ta'mīl fi Asrār al-Tanzīl*.

603 [T] The word lord in Arabic (الرب) morphs itself to form the word for "upbringing" or "nurturing" (التربية).

political astuteness, might and strength, and the youth are especially in need of this. After this, the word "god" is connected to "mankind", alluding to the elderly. This is because human growth then reverses and the person becomes old and frail—and it is at this stage where man needs to worship Allah the most. The *sūrah* then finishes [with categorising mankind into two,] with the statement: **{Who whispers in the breasts of mankind.}**[604] The word "mankind" here refers to all servants of Allah; the scholars and worshippers alike, as Shaytān most often attacks their likes with the creation of doubts about their religion. The *sūrah* then concludes with: **{Of jinn and men.}**[605] [Unlike the first group,] the word "mankind" here refers to all evil and wretched forms of man. They are the ones who inspire and incite others to do evil and acts of disobedience. And Allah knows best."[606] [607]

تم بحمد الله تعالى وتوفيقه.

We have arrived at the end and all praises are due to Allah, the Most

604 Al-Nās: 5

605 Al-Nās: 6

606 See *Asrār al-Takrār fī al-Qur'ān* (p. 215).

607 Imām al-Rāzī mentions another benefit in his *tafsīr*: "In al-Falaq the one from whom refuge is taken has one attribute mentioned—that is He is the Lord of the daybreak but He goes on to mention in the *sūrah* three aspects of the day and the night that people ask refuge against: the evils within them, the sorcerer that acts within them and the envier that envies within them. Al-Nās, however, mentions three attributes of Allah: Lordship, Dominion and Divinity, but mentions one thing against which refuge is sought—the whispers of the *shaytān*. The reason it happened in this manner is because al-Falaq is themed at protecting one's body and soul whereas al-Nās is themed at seeking protection in one's religion; thus, praising should match the seriousness of what is being asked for from Allah. Of course, the safety in religion is more important and serious than the safety in body and wealth." See *Mafātīḥ al-Ghayb* (8/763-764) and something similar is mentioned in *Kashf al-Ma'ānī* of Ibn Jamā'ah (pp. 433-434).

High, for all of His assistance.

قال مؤلفه -نفعنا الله ببركاته، وأمدنا من نفحاته: فرغت من تأليفه يوم الأحد، الثالث عشر من شعبان سنة ثلاث وثمانين وثمانمائة، ولا حول ولا قوة إلا بالله العلي العظيم، وحسبنا الله ونعم الوكيل.

The author said—may Allah benefit us from his blessings and goodness, "I completed this work on Sunday, 13th Sha'bān 883, and there is no power and no strength except with Allah, the Highest and the Greatest, Allah is sufficient for us and He is the best disposer of affairs.